CONTENTS

Life's short and we're all busy. If you're a college student, you're *really* busy. There's your part-time job (which seems full time), your social life (hopefully) and church. On top of that you're expected to go to class, do some reading, take tests and write papers. Now, while you are minding your own business, you hear about something called "integration," trying to relate your major with your Christianity. Several questions may come to mind: What is integration, anyway? Is it just a fad? Why should I care about it? And even if I do care about it, I don't have a clue as to how to go about doing it. How do I do this? These are good questions, and in this introduction we're going to address them in order. We are passionate about helping you learn about and become good at integrating your Christian convictions with the issues and ideas in your college major or your career.

WHAT IS INTEGRATION?

The word *integrate* means "to form or blend into a whole," "to unite." We humans naturally seek to find the unity that is behind diversity, and in fact coherence is an important mark of rationality. There are two kinds of integration: conceptual and personal. In conceptual integration, *our theological beliefs, especially those derived from careful study of the Bible, are blended and unified with important, reasonable ideas from our profession or college major into a coherent, intellectually satisfying Christian worldview.* As Augustine wisely advised, "We must show our Scriptures not to be in conflict with whatever [our critics] can demonstrate about the nature of things from reliable sources."[1] In personal integration we seek to live a unified life, a life in which we are the same in public as we are in private, a life in which the various aspects of our personality are consistent with each other and conducive to a life of human flourishing as a disciple of Jesus.

The two kinds of integration are deeply intertwined. All things being equal, the more authentic we are, the more integrity we have, the more we should be able to do conceptual integration with fidelity to Jesus and Scripture, and with intellectual honesty. All things being equal the more conceptual integration we accomplish, the more coherent will be our set of beliefs and the more confidence we will have in the truth of our Christian worldview. In fact, conceptual integration is so important that it is worth thinking some more about why it matters.

SEVEN REASONS WHY INTEGRATION MATTERS

1. *The Bible's teachings are true.* The first justification for integration is pretty obvious, but often overlooked. *Christians hold that, when properly interpreted, the teachings of Holy Scripture are true.* This means two things. If the Bible teaches something relevant to an issue in an academic field, the Bible's view on that topic is true and thus provides an incredibly rich resource for doing work in that academic field. It would be irresponsible to set aside an important source of relevant truth in thinking through issues in our field of study or vocation. Further, if it looks like a claim on our field tends to make a biblical claim false, this tension needs to be resolved. Maybe our interpretation of Scripture is mistaken, maybe the Bible is not even talking about the issue, maybe the claim in our field is false. Whatever the case, the Christian's commitment to the truth of Scripture makes integration inevitable.

Adolfo Lopez-Otero, a Stanford engineering professor and a self-described secular humanist, offers advice to thinking Christians who want to have an impact on the world: "When a Christian professor approaches a non-believing faculty member . . . they can expect to face a polite but condescending person [with a belief that they possess] superior metaphysics who can't understand how such an intelligent person [as

---

[1]Augustine *De genesi ad litteram* 1.21, cited in Ernan McMullin, "How Should Cosmology Relate to Theology?" in *The Sciences and Theology in the Twentieth Century*, ed. Arthur R. Peacocke (Notre Dame, Ind.: University of Notre Dame Press, 1981), p. 20.

yourself] still believes in things which have been discredited eons ago."[2] He goes on to say that "[Christian professors] cannot afford to give excuses . . . if they are honest about wanting to open spiritual and truthful dialogue with their non-believing colleagues—that is the price they must pay for having declared themselves Christians."[3] While Lopez-Otero's remarks are directed to Christian professors, his point applies to all thinking Christians: If we claim that our Christian views are true, we need to back that up by interacting with the various ideas that come from different academic disciplines. In short, we must integrate Christianity and our major or vocation.

2. *Our vocation and the holistic character of discipleship demand integration.* As disciples grow, they learn to see, feel, think, desire, believe and behave the way Jesus does in a manner fitting to the kingdom of God and their own station in life. With God's help we seek to live as Jesus would if he were a philosophy professor at Biola University married to Hope and father of Ashley and Allison, or as a political philosopher at Baylor University married to Frankie.

Two important implications flow from the nature of discipleship. For one thing the lordship of Christ is holistic. The religious life is not a special compartment in an otherwise secular life. Rather, the religious life is an entire way of life. To live Christianly is to allow Jesus Christ to be the Lord of every aspect of our life. There is no room for a secular-sacred separation in the life of Jesus' followers. Jesus Christ should be every bit as much at home in our thinking and behavior when we are developing our views in our area of study or work as he is when we are in a small group fellowship.

Further, as disciples of Jesus we do not merely have a job. We have a vocation as a Christian teacher. A job is a means for supporting ourselves and those for whom we are responsible. For the Christian a vocation (from the Latin *vocare*, which means "to call") is an overall calling from God. Harry Blamires correctly draws a distinction between a general and a special vocation:

> The general vocation of all Christians—indeed of all men and women—is the
> same. We are called to live as children of God, obeying his will in all things.

---

[2]Adolfo Lopez-Otero, "Be Humble, but Daring," *The Real Issue* 16 (September-October 1997): 10.
[3]Ibid., p. 11.

But obedience to God's will must inevitably take many different forms. The wife's mode of obedience is not the same as the nun's; the farmer's is not the same as the priest's. By "special vocation," therefore, we designate God's call to a [person] to serve him in a particular sphere of activity.[4]

As Christians seek to discover and become excellent in their special vocation, they must ask: How would Jesus approach the task of being a history teacher, a chemist, an athletic director, a mathematician? It is not always easy to answer this question, but the vocational demands of discipleship require that we give it our best shot.

Whatever we do, however, it is important that we restore to our culture an image of Jesus Christ as an intelligent, competent person who spoke authoritatively on whatever subject he addressed. The disciples of Jesus agreed with Paul when he said that all the wisdom of the Greeks and Jews was ultimately wrapped up in Jesus himself (Col 2:2-3). For them, Jesus was not merely a Savior from sin; he was the wisest, most intelligent, most attractive person they had ever seen.

In the early centuries of Christianity the church presented Jesus to unbelievers precisely because he was wiser, more virtuous, more intelligent and more attractive in his character than Aristotle, Plato, Moses or anyone else. It has been a part of the church's self-understanding to locate the spiritual life in a broader quest for the good life, that is, a life of wisdom, knowledge, beauty and goodness. So understood, the spiritual life and discipleship to Jesus were seen as the very best way to achieve a life of truth, beauty and goodness. Moreover, the life of discipleship was depicted as the wisest, most reasonable form of life available so that a life of unbelief was taken to be foolish and absurd. *Our schools need to recapture and propagate this broader understanding of following Christ if they are to be thoroughly Christian in their approach to education.*

3. Biblical teaching about the role of the mind in the Christian life and the value of extrabiblical knowledge requires integration. The Scriptures are clear that God wants us to be like him in every facet of our lives, and he desires commitment from our total being, including our intellectual life. We are told that we change spiritually by having the categories of our minds renewed (Rom 12:1-2), that we are to include an intellectual love for God in our de-

---

[4]Harry Blamires, *A God Who Acts* (Ann Arbor, Mich.: Servant Books, 1957), p. 67.

votion (Mt 22:37-38), and that we are to be prepared to give others a reasonable answer to questions others ask us about why we believe what we believe (1 Pet 3:15). As the great eighteenth-century Christian thinker and spiritual master William Law put it, "Unreasonable and absurd ways of life . . . are truly an offense to God."[5] Learning and developing convictions about the teachings of Scripture are absolutely central to these mandates. However, many of Jesus' followers have failed to see that an aggressive pursuit of knowledge in areas outside the Bible is also relevant to these directives.

God has revealed himself and various truths on a number of topics outside the Bible. As Christians have known throughout our history, common sense, logic and mathematics, along with the arts, humanities, sciences and other areas of study, contain important truths relevant to life in general and to the development of a careful, life-related Christian worldview.

In 1756 John Wesley delivered an address to a gathering of clergy on how to carry out the pastoral ministry with joy and skill. In it Wesley cataloged a number of things familiar to most contemporary believers—the cultivation of a disposition to glorify God and save souls, a knowledge of Scripture, and similar notions. However, at the front of his list Wesley focused on something seldom expressly valued by most pastoral search committees: "Ought not a Minister to have, First, a good understanding, a clear apprehension, a sound judgment, and a capacity of reasoning with some closeness?"[6]

Time and again throughout the address Wesley unpacked this remark by admonishing ministers to know what would sound truly odd and almost pagan to the average congregant of today: logic, metaphysics, natural theology, geometry and the ideas of important figures in the history of philosophy. For Wesley study in these areas (especially philosophy and geometry) helped train the mind to think precisely, a habit of incredible value, he asserted, when it comes to thinking as a Christian about theological themes or scriptural texts. According to Wesley the study of extrabiblical information and the writings of unbelievers was of critical value for growth and maturity. As he put it elsewhere, "To imagine none can

---

[5]William Law, *A Serious Call to a Devout and Holy Life* (1728; reprint, Grand Rapids: Eerdmans, 1966), p. 2.
[6]John Wesley, "An Address to the Clergy," in *The Works of John Wesley*, 3rd ed. (Grand Rapids: Baker, 1979), p. 481.

teach you but those who are themselves saved from sin is a very great and dangerous mistake. Give not place to it for a moment."[7]

Wesley's remarks were not unusual in his time. A century earlier the great Reformed pastor Richard Baxter was faced with lukewarmness in the church and unbelief outside the church. In 1667 he wrote a book to meet this need, and in it he used philosophy, logic and general items of knowledge outside Scripture to argue for the existence of the soul and the life to come. The fact that Baxter turned to philosophy and extrabiblical knowledge instead of small groups or praise hymns is worth pondering. In fact, it is safe to say that throughout much of church history, Scripture and right reason directed at extrabiblical truth were used by disciples of Jesus and prized as twin allies.

In valuing extrabiblical knowledge our brothers and sisters in church history were merely following common sense and Scripture itself. Repeatedly, Scripture acknowledges the wisdom of cultures outside Israel: for example, Egypt (Acts 7:22; cf. Ex 7:11), the Edomites (Jer 49:7), the Phoenicians (Zech 9:2) and many others. The remarkable achievements produced by human wisdom are acknowledged in Job 28:1-11. The wisdom of Solomon is compared to the wisdom of the "people of the east" and Egypt in order to show that Solomon's wisdom surpassed that of people with a longstanding, well-deserved reputation for wisdom (1 Kings 4:29-34). Paul approvingly quotes pagan philosophers (Acts 17:28), and Jude does the same thing with the noncanonical book *The Assumption of Moses* (Jude 9). The book of Proverbs is filled with examples in which knowledge, even moral and spiritual knowledge, can be gained from studying things (ants, for example) in the natural world. Jesus taught that we should know we are to love our enemies, not on the basis of an Old Testament text but from careful reflection on how the sun and rain behave (Mt 5:44-45).

In valuing extrabiblical knowledge our brothers and sisters in church history were also living out scriptural teaching about the value of general revelation. We must never forget that God is the God of creation and general revelation just as he is the God of Scripture and special revelation.

Christians should do everything they can to gain and teach important and relevant knowledge in their areas of expertise. *At the level appropriate*

---

[7]John Wesley, *A Plain Account of Christian Perfection* (London: Epworth Press, 1952), p. 87.

to our station in life, Christians are called to be Christian intellectuals, at home in the world of ideas.

4. *Neglect of integration results in a costly division between secular and sacred.* While few would actually put it in these terms, faith is now understood as a blind act of will, a sort of decision to believe something that is either independent of reason or makes up for the paltry lack of evidence for what one is trying to believe. By contrast, the Bible presents faith as a power or skill to act in accordance with the nature of the kingdom of God, a trust in what we have reason to believe is true. Understood in this way, we see that faith is built on reason and knowledge. We should have good reasons for thinking that Christianity is true before we completely dedicate ourselves to it. We should have solid evidence that our understanding of a biblical passage is correct before we go on to apply it. We bring knowledge claims from Scripture and theology to the task of integration; we do not employ mere beliefs or faith postulates.

Unfortunately, our contemporary understanding of faith and reason treats them as polar opposites. A few years ago I (J. P.) went to New York to conduct a series of evangelistic messages for a church. The series was in a high school gym and several believers and unbelievers came each night. The first evening I gave arguments for the existence of God from science and philosophy. Before closing in prayer, I entertained several questions from the audience. One woman (who was a Christian) complained about my talk, charging that if I "proved" the existence of God, I would leave no room for faith. I responded by saying that if she were right, then we should pray that currently available evidence for God would evaporate and be refuted so there would be even more room for faith! Obviously, her view of faith utterly detached it from reason.

If faith and reason are deeply connected, then students and teachers need to explore their entire intellectual life in light of the Word of God. But if faith and reason are polar opposites, then the subject matter of our study or teaching is largely irrelevant to growth in discipleship. Because of this view of faith and reason, there has emerged a secular-sacred separation in our understanding of the Christian life with the result that Christian teaching and practice are privatized. The withdrawal of the corporate body of Christ from the public sphere of ideas is mirrored by our understanding of what is required to produce an individual disciple. Religion is viewed as personal, private and a matter of how we feel about things. Often, Bible classes and paracurricular Christian activities are not taken as academically serious aspects of the Christian school, nor are they integrated into the content of "secular" areas of teaching.

There is no time like the present to recapture the integrative task. Given the abandonment of monotheism, the ground is weakened for believing in the unity of truth. This is one reason why our *uni*versities are turning in to *multi*versities.[8] The fragmentation of secular education at all levels and its inability to define its purpose or gather together a coherent curriculum are symptoms of what happens when monotheism, especially Christian monotheism, is set aside. At this critical hour the Christian educator has something increasingly rare and distinctive to offer, and integration is at the heart of who we are as Christian educators.

5. *The nature of spiritual warfare necessitates integration.* Today, spiritual warfare is widely misunderstood. Briefly, spiritual warfare is a conflict among persons—disembodied malevolent persons (demons and the devil), human beings, angels and God himself. So far, so good. But what is often overlooked is that this conflict among persons in two camps crucially involves a clash of ideas. Why? The conflict is about control, and persons control others by getting them to accept certain beliefs and emotions as correct, good and proper. This is precisely how the devil primarily works to destroy human beings and thwart God's work in history; namely, by influencing the idea structures in culture. That is why Paul makes the war of ideas central to spiritual conflict:

> For though we live in the world, we do not wage war as the world does. The weapons we fight with are not the weapons of the world. On the contrary, they have divine power to demolish strongholds. We demolish arguments and every pretension that sets itself up against the knowledge of God, and we take captive every thought to make it obedient to Christ. (2 Cor 10:3-5)

Spiritual warfare is largely, though not entirely, a war of ideas, and we fight bad, false ideas with better ones. That means that truth, reason, argumentation and so forth, from both Scripture and general revelation, are

---

[8]See Julie Reuben, *The Making of the Modern University* (Chicago: University of Chicago Press, 1996).

central weapons in the fight. Since the centers of education are the centers for dealing with ideas, they become the main location for spiritual warfare. Solid, intelligent integration, then, is part of our mandate to engage in spiritual conflict.

6. *Spiritual formation calls for integration.* It is crucial that we reflect a bit on the relationship between integration and spiritual/devotional life. To begin with, there is a widespread hunger throughout our culture for genuine, life-transforming spirituality. This is as it should be. People are weary of those who claim to believe certain things when they do not see those beliefs having an impact on the lives of the heralds. Among other things, integration is a spiritual activity—we may even call it a spiritual discipline—but not merely in the sense that often comes to mind in this context. Often, Christian teachers express the spiritual aspect of integration in terms of doxology: Christian integrators hold to and teach the same beliefs about their subject matter that non-Christians accept but go on to add praise to God for the subject matter. Thus, Christian biologists simply assert the views widely accepted in the discipline but make sure that class closes with a word of praise to God for the beauty and complexity of the living world.

The doxological approach is good as far as it goes; unfortunately, it doesn't go far enough in capturing the spiritual dimension of integration. We draw closer to the core of this dimension when we think about the role of beliefs in the process of spiritual transformation. Beliefs are the rails on which our lives run. We almost always act according to what we really believe. It doesn't matter much what we say we believe or what we want others to think we believe. When the rubber meets the road, we act out our actual beliefs most of the time. That is why behavior is such a good indicator of our beliefs. The centrality of beliefs for spiritual progress is a clear implication of Old Testament teaching on wisdom and New Testament teaching about the role of a renewed mind in transformation. Thus, *integration has as its spiritual aim the intellectual goal of structuring the mind so we can see things as they really are and strengthening the belief structure that ought to inform the individual and corporate life of discipleship to Jesus.*

Integration can also help unbelievers accept certain beliefs crucial to the Christian journey and aid believers in maintaining and developing convictions about those beliefs. This aspect of integration becomes clear when we reflect on the notion of a plausibility structure. Individuals will never be able to change their lives if they cannot even entertain the beliefs needed to bring about that change. By "entertain a belief" we mean to consider the *possibility* that the belief *might* be true. If someone is hateful and mean to a fellow employee, that person will have to change what he or she believes about that coworker before treating the coworker differently. But if a person cannot even entertain the thought that the coworker is a good person worthy of kindness, the hateful person will not change.

A person's plausibility structure is the set of ideas the person either is or is not willing to entertain as possibly true. For example, few people would come to a lecture defending a flat earth, because this idea is just not part of our common plausibility structure. Most people today simply cannot even entertain the idea. Moreover, a person's plausibility structure is largely (though not exclusively) a function of beliefs already held. Applied to accepting or maintaining Christian belief, J. Gresham Machen got it right when he said:

> God usually exerts that power in connection with certain prior conditions of the human mind, and it should be ours to create, so far as we can, with the help of God, those favorable conditions for the reception of the gospel. False ideas are the greatest obstacles to the reception of the gospel. We may preach with all the fervor of a reformer and yet succeed only in winning a straggler here and there, if we permit the whole collective thought of the nation or of the world to be controlled by ideas which, by the resistless force of logic, prevent Christianity from being regarded as anything more than a harmless delusion.[9]

If a culture reaches the point where Christian claims are not even part of its plausibility structure, fewer and fewer people will be able to entertain the possibility that they might be true. Whatever stragglers do come to faith in such a context would do so on the basis of felt needs alone, and the genuineness of such conversions would be questionable, to say the least. And believers will not make much progress in the spiritual life because they will not have the depth of conviction or the integrated noetic structure necessary for such progress. This is why integration is so crucial to spirituality. It can create a plausibility structure in a person's mind, "favor-

---

[9]J. Gresham Machen, address delivered on September 20, 1912, at the opening of the 101st session of Princeton Theological Seminary, reprinted in his *What Is Christianity? and Other Addresses* (Grand Rapids: Eerdmans, 1951), p. 162.

able conditions," as Machen put it, so Christian ideas can be entertained by that person. As Christians, our goal is *to make Christian ideas relevant to our subject matter appear to be true, beautiful, good and reasonable to increase the ranking of Christian ideas in the culture's plausibility structure.*

7. Integration is crucial to the current worldview struggle and the contemporary crisis of knowledge. Luther once said that if we defend Christ at all points except those at which he is currently being attacked, then we have not really defended Christ. The Christian must keep in mind the tensions between Christian claims and competing worldviews currently dominating the culture. Such vigilance yields an integrative mandate for contemporary Christians that the Christian Worldview Integration Series (CWIS) will keep in mind. There is a very important cultural fact that each volume in the series must face: *There simply is no established, widely recognized body of ethical or religious knowledge now operative in the institutions of knowledge in our culture.* Indeed, ethical and religious claims are frequently placed into what Francis Schaeffer called the "upper story," and they are judged to have little or no epistemic authority, especially compared to the authority given to science to define the limits of knowledge and reality in those same institutions. This raises pressing questions: *Is Christianity a knowledge tradition or merely a faith tradition, a perspective which, while true, cannot be known to be true and must be embraced on the basis of some epistemic state weaker than knowledge? Is there nonempirical knowledge in my field? Is there evidence of nonphysical, immaterial reality (e.g., linguistic meanings are arguable, nonphysical, spiritual entities) in my field? Do the ideas of Christianity do any serious intellectual work in my field such that those who fail to take them into consideration simply will not be able to understand adequately the realities involved in my field?*

There are at least two reasons why these may well be the crucial questions for Christians to keep in mind as they do their work in their disciplines. For one thing, Christianity claims to be a knowledge tradition, and it places knowledge at the center of proclamation and discipleship. The Old and New Testaments, including the teachings of Jesus, claim not merely that Christianity is true but that a variety of its moral and religious assertions can be known to be true.

Second, knowledge is the basis of responsible action in society. Dentists, not lawyers, have the authority to place their hands in our mouths because they have the relevant knowledge—not merely true beliefs—on the basis of which they may act responsibly. If Christians do little to deflect the view that theological and ethical assertions are merely parts of a tradition, ways of seeing, a source for adding a "theological perspective" to an otherwise unperturbed secular topic and so forth that fall short of conveying knowledge, then they inadvertently contribute to the marginalization of Christianity precisely because they fail to rebut the contemporary tendency to rob it of the very thing that gives it the authority necessary to prevent that marginalization, namely, its legitimate claim to give us moral and religious knowledge. Both in and out of the church Jesus has been lost as an intellectual authority, and Christian intellectuals should carry out their academic vocation in light of this fact.

We agree with those who see a three-way worldview struggle in academic and popular culture among ethical monotheism (especially Christian theism), postmodernism and scientific naturalism. As Christian intellectuals seek to promote Christianity as a knowledge tradition in their academic disciplines, they should keep in mind the impact of their work on this triumvirate. Space considerations forbid us to say much about postmodernism here. We recognize it is a variegated tunic with many nuances. But to the degree that postmodernism denies the objectivity of reality, truth, value and reason (in its epistemic if not psychological sense), to the degree that it rejects dichotomous thinking about real-unreal, true-false, rational-irrational and right-wrong, to the degree that it believes intentionality creates the objects of consciousness, to that degree it should be resisted by Christian intellectuals, and the CWIS will take this stance toward postmodernism.

Scientific naturalism also comes in many varieties, but very roughly a major form of it is the view that the spatiotemporal cosmos containing physical objects studied by the hard sciences is all there is and that the hard sciences are either the only source of knowledge or else vastly superior in proffering epistemically justified beliefs compared to nonscientific fields. In connection with scientific naturalism some have argued that the rise of modern science has contributed to the loss of intellectual authority in those fields like ethics and religion that supposedly are not subject to the types of testing and experimentation employed in science.

Extreme forms of postmodernism and scientific naturalism agree that there is no nonempirical knowledge, especially no knowledge of immaterial reality, no theological or ethical knowledge. *The authors of the CWIS seek to undermine this claim and the concomitant privatization and noncognitive treatment of religious/ethical faith and belief.* Thus, there will be three integrative tasks of central importance for each volume in the series.

How Do We Engage in Integration? Three Integrative Tasks

As noted earlier, the word *integration* means "to form or blend into a whole," "to unite." One of the goals of integration is to maintain or increase both the conceptual relevance of and epistemological justification for Christian theism. To repeat Augustine's advice, "We must show our Scriptures not to be in conflict with whatever [our critics] can demonstrate about the nature of things from reliable sources."[10] We may distinguish three different aspects of the justificatory side of integration: direct defense, polemics and Christian explanation.

1. *Direct defense.* In direct defense we engage in integration with the primary intent of enhancing or maintaining directly the rational justification of Christian theism or some proposition taken to be explicit within or entailed by it, especially those aspects of a Christian worldview relevant to our own discipline. Specific attention should be given to topics that are intrinsically important to mere Christianity or currently under fire in our field. Hereafter, we will simply refer to these issues as "Christian theism." We do so for brevity's sake. Christian theism should be taken to include specific views about a particular area of study that we believe to be relevant to the integrative task, for example, that cognitive behavioral therapy is an important tool for applying the biblical mandate to be "transformed by the renewing of your minds" (Rom 12:2).

There are two basic forms of direct defense, one negative and one positive.[11] The less controversial of the two is a negative direct defense where we attempt to remove defeaters to Christian theism. If we have a justified belief regarding some proposition P, a defeater is something that weakens or removes that justification. Defeaters come in two types.[12] A rebutting defeater gives justification for believing not-P, in this case, that Christian

---

[10]Augustine *De genesi ad litteram* 1.21.
[11]See Ronald Nash, *Faith and Reason* (Grand Rapids: Zondervan, 1988), pp. 14-18.
[12]For a useful discussion of various types of defeaters, see John Pollock, *Contemporary Theories of Knowledge* (Totowa, N.J.: Rowman & Littlefield, 1986), pp. 36-39; Ralph Baergen, *Contemporary Epistemology* (Fort Worth: Harcourt Brace, 1995), pp. 119-24.

theism is false. For example, attempts to show that the biblical concept of the family is dysfunctional and false, or that homosexuality is causally necessitated by genes or brain states and that therefore it is not a proper object for moral appraisal are cases of rebutting defeaters. An undercutting defeater does not give justification for believing not-P but rather seeks to remove or weaken justification for believing P in the first place. Critiques of the arguments for God's existence are examples of undercutting defeaters. When defeaters are raised against Christian theism, a negative defense seeks either to rebut or undercut those defeaters.

By contrast, a positive direct defense is an attempt to build a positive case for Christian theism. Arguments for the existence of God, objective morality, the existence of the soul, the value and nature of virtue ethics, and the possibility and knowability of miracles are examples. This task for integration is not accepted by all Christian intellectuals. For example, various species of what may be loosely called Reformed epistemology run the gamut from seeing a modest role for a positive direct defense to an outright rejection of this type of activity in certain areas; for example, justifying belief in God and the authority of Holy Scripture. *The CWIS will seek to engage in both negative and positive direct defense.*

2. *Polemics.* In polemics we seek to criticize views that rival Christian theism in one way or another. Critiques of scientific naturalism, physicalism, pantheism, behaviorist models of educational goals, authorless approaches to texts and Marxist theories of economics are all examples of polemics.

3. *Theistic explanation.* Suppose we have a set of items that stand in need of explanation and we offer some overall explanation as an adequate or even best explanation of those items. In such a case our overall explanation explains each of the items in question, and this fact itself provides some degree of confirmation for our overall explanation. For example, if a certain intrinsic genre statement explains the various data of a biblical text, then this fact offers some confirmation for the belief that the statement is the correct interpretation of that text. Christian theists ought to be about the business of exploring the world in light of their worldview and, more specifically, of using their theistic beliefs as explanations of various desiderata in their disciplines. Put differently, we should seek to solve intellectual problems and shed light on areas of puzzlement by using the explanatory power of our worldview.

For example, for those who accept the existence of natural moral law, the irreducibly mental nature of consciousness, natural human rights or the fact that human flourishing follows from certain biblically mandated ethical and religious practices, the truth of Christian theism provides a good explanation of these phenomena. And this fact can provide some degree of confirmation for Christian theism. *The CWIS seeks to show the explanatory power of Christian ideas in various disciplines.*

WHAT MODELS ARE AVAILABLE FOR CLASSIFYING INTEGRATIVE PROBLEMS?

When problem areas surface, there is a need for Christians to think hard about the issue in light of the need for strengthening the rational authority of Christian theism and placing it squarely within the plausibility structure of contemporary culture. We will use the term *theology* to stand for any Christian idea that seems to be a part of a Christian worldview derived primarily from special revelation. When we address problems like these, there will emerge a number of different ways that theology can interact with an issue in a discipline outside theology. Here are some of the different ways that such interaction can take place. These represent different strategies for handling a particular difficulty in integration. These strategies will be employed where appropriate on a case-by-case basis by the authors in the series.

1. *The two-realms view.* Propositions, theories or methodologies in theology and another discipline may involve two distinct, nonoverlapping areas of investigation. For example, debates about angels or the extent of the atonement have little to do with organic chemistry. Similarly, it is of little interest to theology whether a methane molecule has three or four hydrogen atoms in it.

2. *The complementarity view.* Propositions, theories or methodologies in theology and another discipline may involve two different, complementary, noninteracting approaches to the same reality. Sociological aspects of church growth and certain psychological aspects of conversion may be sociological or psychological descriptions of certain phenomena that are complementary to a theological description of church growth or conversion.

3. *The direct-interaction view.* Propositions, theories or methodologies in theology and another discipline may directly interact in such a way that

either one area of study offers rational support for the other or one area of study raises rational difficulties for the other. For example, certain theological teachings about the existence of the soul raise rational problems for philosophical or scientific claims that deny the existence of the soul. The general theory of evolution raises various difficulties for certain ways of understanding the book of Genesis. Some have argued that the big bang theory tends to support the theological proposition that the universe had a beginning.

4. *The presuppositions view.* Theology may support the presuppositions of another discipline and vice versa. Some have argued that many of the presuppositions of science (for example, the existence of truth; the rational, orderly nature of reality; the adequacy of our sensory and cognitive faculties as tools suited for knowing the external world) make sense and are easy to justify given Christian theism, but are odd and without ultimate justification in a naturalistic worldview. Similarly, some have argued that philosophical critiques of epistemological skepticism and defenses of the existence of a real, theory-independent world and a correspondence theory of truth offer justification for some of the presuppositions of theology.

5. *The practical application view.* Theology may fill out and add details to general principles in another discipline and vice versa, and theology may help us practically apply principles in another discipline and vice versa. For example, theology teaches that fathers should not provoke their children to anger, and psychology can add important details about what this means by offering information about family systems, the nature and causes of anger, and so forth. Psychology can devise various tests for assessing whether a person is or is not mature, and theology can offer a normative definition to psychology as to what a mature person is.

In this volume, Wong and Rae ask the question, What are we in business for? How should we answer that from a Christian worldview? They argue that work is a significant arena of service to God and that business exists not just to make a profit but to serve the common good. Business ought to serve its various stakeholders, including customers, employees, shareholders, the community and the environment. They further sugggest that work is a critical crucible in which a person's spiritual formation occurs, that God works through our experience in the marketplace to shape our souls.

We hope you can see why we are excited about this book. Even though you're busy and the many demands on your time tug at you from different directions, we don't think you can afford not to read this book. So wrestle, ponder, pray, compare ideas with Scripture, talk about the pages to follow with others and enjoy.

A FINAL CHALLENGE

In 2001 atheist philosopher Quentin Smith published a remarkably insightful article of crucial relevance to the task of integration. For over fifty years, Smith notes, the academic community has become increasingly secularized and atheistic even though there have been a fair number of Christian teachers involved in that community. How could this be? Smith's answer amounts to the claim that Christians compartmentalized their faith, kept it tucked away in a private compartment of their lives and did not integrate their Christian ideas with their work. Said Smith:

> This is not to say that none of the scholars in their various academic fields were realist theists [theists who took their religious beliefs to be true] in their "private lives"; but realist theists, for the most part excluded their theism from their publications and teaching, in large part because theism . . . was mainly considered to have such a low epistemic status that it did not meet the standards of an "academically respectable" position to hold.[13]

Smith goes on to claim that while Christians have recaptured considerable ground in the field of philosophy, "theists in other fields tend to compartmentalize their theistic beliefs from their scholarly work; they rarely assume and never argue for theism in their scholarly work."[14]

This has got to stop. We offer this book to you with the prayer that it will help you rise to the occasion and recapture lost territory in your field of study for the cause of Christ.

Francis J. Beckwith
J. P. Moreland
Series Editors

---

[13]Quentin Smith, "The Metaphysics of Naturalism," *Philo* 4, no. 2 (2001): 1.
[14]Ibid., p. 3. The same observation about advances in philosophy has been noted by Mark A. Noll in *The Scandal of the Evangelical Mind* (Grand Rapids: Eerdmans, 1994), pp. 235-38.

ACKNOWLEDGMENTS

There are many people who deserve our gratitude for their contribution to making this book a reality. I (Kenman) wish to recognize the following people for their help in refining the central ideas over conversations or by providing helpful feedback on specific chapters. Many of the names that follow are of colleagues at Seattle Pacific University, fellow participants in the CCCU Network Scholars Grant project on Theology and Management, or business leaders: Roger Bairstow, Cheryl Broetje, Carter Crockett, Denise Daniels, Tim Dearborn, Doug Downing, Bruno Dyck, Al Erisman, Randy Franz, Gary Karns, Rick Martinez, Blaine McCormick, Mitch Neubert, Henry Petersen, Barry Rowan, Mark Russell, Kim Sawers, Ross Stewart, John Terrill and Jeff Van Duzer. Several anonymous reviewers also provided helpful comments and suggestions. My appreciation also goes to Seattle Pacific University for providing a sabbatical during the fall of 2008, during which the formative stages of the manuscript were developed. Thanks too goes to Scott Rae. I can't believe it's been nearly twenty years of enjoyable collaboration. Can we really be that old? Most important, I would like to express my deepest gratitude to my family, Marika, Callan, Elise and Maille, who bring me deep abiding joy. Thanks for your patience and forbearance during the long stretches of time I spent hidden in my study. I will make the next trip to Great Wolf Lodge! Finally, I would like to dedicate this book to my parents, Ted and Lennie Wong. Like most immigrants, they held down "jobs" and made many sacrifices so their children and all who follow will have the chance to pursue "callings."

I (Scott) wish to thank the reviewers and editors at IVP Academic for their careful attention to the book's details. They gave us much to think about and made the book a much better work as a result of their extensive input. Special thanks go to Talbot School of Theology, Biola University and my deans, Dennis Dirks and Mike Wilkins, for their support and flexibility with my spring 2010 sabbatical that gave me the necessary time away to complete this book. I'm also grateful to my Talbot philosophy faculty colleagues for their encouragement—specifically my long-time friend and colleague J. P. Moreland for his consistent encouragement over the years. I'm also grateful to the Crowell School of Business at Biola University for their support. Many of the ideas of this book were first expressed in business ethics classes there. I'm grateful to Larry Strand, dean of the School of Business, Harold Taber and Randy Kilgore for their support for the subjects we cover in this book and their desire to see it promoted in the business community at large. I'm also very grateful to my coauthor, Kenman Wong, for the chance to work together on this project. Thanks for your partnership in this and other projects—it's been a joy to work with you. Special thanks go to my family—my wife, Sally, and boys, Taylor, Cameron and Austin, for their patience with me as we worked overtime to get this finished. This book is dedicated to my late father, Walter B. Rae, who modeled many of the things we wrote about. His company was an example of business for the common good.

Introduction

A look at business headlines over the last quarter of a century can have a sobering effect. The middle part of the 1980s produced the now largely forgotten savings and loan crisis that nearly caused the collapse of the entire industry and cost taxpayers over a $100 billion in bailout money. The later part of that decade brought the junk bond and insider trading scandals that helped land names like Milken and Boesky in infamy. In the later part of the 1990s the "Asian Economic Flu" set off a global crisis and made us all acutely aware of just how vulnerable we are as part of an interdependent global financial system. After the turn of the millennium, a significant amount of wealth was destroyed due to the "dot-com" meltdown and seemingly endless accounting scandals involving the likes of Enron and WorldCom. Then, the backdating of stock options, "after hours trading" by respected mutual fund companies, and a new round of insider trading revelations dominated the news.

As we write this book (2009 and 2010), fear and pain brought about by another global economic crisis, with fallout not seen since the Great Depression, can be felt all around us. Roughly 10 percent of the working population find themselves among the officially unemployed, many for the first time in their lives, while the rest of us are nagged by fears that we may soon join them. Almost unimaginable sums in investment accounts designated for sending children to college or to be tapped for retirement have been lost. Government budgets are being cut, home values are in decline and long-standing reputable businesses have been hurt. Some organizations that were thought to be far removed from the crisis have shut down due to severely restricted supply of credit needed to manage cash flow.

While many people and institutions—including borrowers, credit agencies and government regulators—can be faulted, much of the current trouble started with an industry, banking, that once saw itself in the more noble terms of a profession engaged in helping people achieve their dreams. More recently a distortion of purpose crept through the doors. Banks, particularly, those involved in subprime mortgage lending, saw all of the money that could be made if they "relaxed" traditional guidelines and "gamed" the system. Tenuous loans were issued and then packaged and sold off to investors, presumably washing away risk and culpability. Who would have thought that what seemed at the time to be nearly insignificant acts would come back to be a key cause of an economic crisis of global proportions?

In a provocative *Harvard Business Review* article titled "What's a Business For?" leading management thinker Charles Handy considers the question, "Could capitalists actually bring down capitalism?"[1] Based on the trust and truth telling needed to nurture and sustain a productive economic system, and the lack of it displayed in corporate accounting scandals at the turn of the millennium, Handy believes the question is one that must be considered in all earnestness. Handy could have written his article at several junctures during the past several decades, and it would have had the same degree of resonance. Put in slightly different terms, what he is asking for is a "new story" of business because the current one is fracturing under the weight of its own shortcomings.

In all, it is an important time to reconsider what business, and our current or future participation in it, is all about. What purposes should our own work, business institutions and economic systems serve? Given all that seems to be wrong with it, can business be revisioned, reformed and engaged with the passion worthy of a "vocation" or "calling," that is, a means to serve God and others around us?

Seeing how business can be anything more than a means to earning profits is a challenging task. Our churches have historically been of little assistance. (Though this is changing somewhat for the better due in large part to the recent growth of the "faith at work" and "business as mission" movements.) They have largely relegated business to low level status on the hierarchy of the spiritual value of professions.[2]

---

[1]Charles Handy, "What's a Business For?" *Harvard Business Review*, December 2002, pp. 3-8.
[2]For more on the Faith at Work and Spirituality at Work movements, see David Miller, *God*

Those in other lines of employment seem to make social contributions by the very nature of the work they do. Physicians and nurses engage in the work of healing; teachers enlighten minds, serve as mentors and pass along important skills; architects create beautiful, functional spaces; counselors help heal emotional pain and bring families together; and ministers point people toward a closer relationship with God. Members of these professions are apt to say, "It's not about the pay. It's about the *work*." In contrast, many businesspeople can only give an abstract nod to "making money" when asked to characterize the aims of their work.[3] Popular books that urge the second half of life be devoted to seeking "significance" deepen these suspicions. They imply the first half has been meaningless beyond advancing personal success.

A careful look, however, reveals that there is more to the story. Long before the idea that business is only about money became popular, influential figures thought and acted as if something else were true. Business, they thought, is about service to others and to society.

Traveling back some distance in time, Adam Smith, the father of modern capitalism, did not see business as merely a way to "make money" to facilitate private individual gain. As the title for his most well-known book, *The Wealth of Nations*, attests, he thought capitalism was the way to harness enlightened self-interest to serve the common good and make *everyone* better off.[4]

Historical business figures such as J. C. Penney thought likewise. Penney, a devout Christian whose stores were originally called the Golden Rule stores, thought "business never was and never will be anything more or less than people serving other people."[5] Penney gave shares of owner-

---

at Work: The History and Promise of the Faith at Work Movement (New York: Oxford University Press, 2007); Marc Gunther, Faith and Fortune: How Compassionate Capitalism Is Transforming America (New York: Crown Business, 2004).

[3]For a rich discussion of reductionist metaphors for business, see Robert Solomon, Ethics and Excellence: Cooperation and Integrity in Business (New York: Oxford University Press, 1992), and A Better Way to Think About Business (New York: Oxford University Press, 1999).

[4]See Patricia Werhane, Adam Smith and His Legacy for Modern Capitalism (New York: Oxford University Press, 1991). Also see Amartya Sen, Development as Freedom (New York: Alfred A. Knopf, 1999). It is worth noting that Adam Smith was actually a moral philosopher rather than an economist. When his two major works (The Wealth of Nations and The Theory of Moral Sentiments) are read together, we can see these threads more clearly.

[5]J. C. Penney, Fifty Years with the Golden Rule (New York: Harper, 1950), cited in Gunther, Faith and Fortune, pp. 19-20.

ship to every store manager long before stock options became popular, and he eschewed the offering of credit because it would encourage people to buy things they couldn't afford. Purportedly, he even chastised one store manager for making too much profit (at the possible expense of service to the community).[6]

It is also true that today most businesspeople and organizations quietly work to deliver quality products or services, pay their bills on time, and treat their employees with dignity and respect. None of these activities are typically regarded as newsworthy, so what gets reported may well contribute to a distorted view of business.

There are also movements underway to make business more intentionally focused on broader purposes. For example, Gary Hamel calls for the replacement of "Management 1.0" with a qualitatively different "Management 2.0." The first hallmark of this new management is to "ensure that the work of management serves a higher purpose."[7] He says:

> Management pioneers must find ways to infuse mundane business activities with deeper, soul-stirring ideals, such as honor, truth, love, justice, and beauty. These timeless virtues have long inspired human beings to extraordinary accomplishment and can no longer be relegated to the fringes of management.[8]

Many companies, including secular, shareholder-owned ones, have mission statements and objectives that go well beyond profit maximization.[9] Others give generously to support charitable causes and encourage volunteers to serve in local communities.

Although these steps are promising, there is still much work to be done. Despite the damage done from what some have characterized as "business as usual," strong resistence to any attempt at modifying the central as-

---

[6]See Gunther, *Faith and Fortune*, p. 20.

[7]Gary Hamel, "Moon Shots for Management: What Great Challenges Must We Tackle to Reinvent Management and Make It More Relevant to a Volatile World?" *Harvard Business Review*, February 2009, pp. 91-98; quote from p. 92.

[8]Ibid., p. 97.

[9]See, for example, Jim Collins and Jerry Porras, *Built to Last: Successful Habits of Visionary Companies* (New York: Harper Business, 2002); Rajendra Sisoda, David B. Wolfe and Jagdish Sheth. *Firms of Endearment: How World Class Companies Profit from Passion and Purpose* (Upper Saddle River, N.J.: Wharton School Publishing, 2007); and Michael Strong, *Be the Solution: How Conscious Capitalists and Entrepreneurs Can Solve All of the World's Problems* (Hoboken, N.J.: John Wiley, 2009).

sumptions and goals of commerce still exists. Why should anyone care about revisioning business? After all, some remain convinced the system we have now (with the exception of a few global scale crises here and there) seems to work well, so why not carry on as we have? What's wrong with "the business of business being business" as some have put it?

Followers of Christ should care deeply about developing and living within a broader vision for business because doing so reflects intentionality and an allegiance to the worldview that lays claim on their entire lives. Sadly, instead of allowing a gospel-oriented worldview to claim rightful authority over all of life, researchers have documented a "Sunday-Monday gap" or "divided life" that often characterizes businesspeople.[10]

The recent global economic crisis has re-alerted the general (nonbusiness) public that it too has good reasons to care about these questions. Business touches almost every area of human life, including the food we eat, the clothes we wear, the air we breathe, the value of our investments, the working conditions of our global neighbors and even our cultural values. How businesspeople and organizations envision their purpose and mission affects everyone.

For business professionals, seeing business as something more than its instrumental (moneymaking) value has profound implications for how we might approach our work. For example, why we are involved with it (motivations), what we expect to get out of it, how much energy we should put into it, how worthy it is of our passion and devotion as a vocation or calling, are all issues affected by how we see business. If reduced to nothing more than a means to make money, it does not matter where we work or what products we make or services we offer as long as we collect an adequate paycheck. Yet, researchers in the emerging field of positive organizational scholarship are making connections between meaning, engagement at work and overall life satisfaction. For example, some studies show that employment that can be recrafted into a "calling" (work that is seen as contributing to the greater good) is the most satisfying form of work because it is done for its own sake rather than for the material rewards it may

---

[10]Laura Nash and Scotty McClennan, *Church on Sunday, Work on Monday: The Challenge of Fusing Christian Values with Business Life* (San Francisco: Jossey-Bass, 2001); Robert Wuthnow, *Rethinking Materialism: Perspectives on the Spiritual Dimension of Economic Activity* (Grand Rapids: Eerdmans, 1995); and *Poor Richard's Principle* (Princeton, N.J.: Princeton University Press, 1998).

bring.[11] If business can be reframed as, and reformed into, a means of participation in lasting, sacred work, it's not far-fetched to suggest that it would be approached with much more passion, and more attention would be paid to its effects.

Even those who do not claim allegiance to Christ or any religious or spiritual tradition have something to gain by engaging these issues. In fact, significant parts of the recent and well-documented spirituality at work movement is not religious at all, but is motivated by a quest for more meaningful connections between work and life purpose.[12] Many people, especially those of the Millennial Generation, place great importance on doing work that benefits the world around them. So, even if someone doesn't go as far as acknowledging the "sacred value" of business, seeing it as a venue for contributing to human betterment and society might, in the least, offer more motivation and meaning.

Employers seeking motivated employees should take note too. A recent Conference Board survey (2009) indicates that job satisfaction is at its lowest point (only 45 percent of those surveyed report being satisfied with their work) in the twenty-two years the organization has tracked the indicator.[13] Of course, this is only one study, but the results may be quite alarming since it was conducted during a time of high unemployment, which has typically served as moderating force against reported work dissatisfaction.

The consequences of a lack of connection to work are not inconsequential. A Gallup Organization survey concludes that "engaged employees" are "more productive . . . more profitable, more customer-focused, safer, and more likely to withstand temptations to leave."[14] Looking directly at the data gathered in a recent version of this survey, only 29 percent of employees reported being "truly engaged" with their work, while 55 percent

---

[11]Martin Seligman, *Authentic Happiness* (New York: Free Press, 2002), pp. 165-69. Also see Amy Wrzesniewski et al., "Jobs, Careers, and Callings: People's Relations to Their Work," *Journal of Research in Personality* 31 (1997): 21-33; and Amy Wrzesniewski, "Finding Meaning in Work," in *Positive Organizational Scholarship, Foundations of a New Discipline*, ed. Kim Cameron, Jane Dutton and Robert Quinn (San Francisco: Barrett-Kohler, 2003).

[12]See Ian Mitroff and Elizabeth Denton, *A Spiritual Audit of Corporate America: A Hard Look at Religion, Spirituality and Values in the Workplace* (San Francisco: Jossey-Bass, 1999).

[13]Linda Barrington, Lynn Franco, and John Gibbons, "I Can't Get No . . . Job Satisfaction That Is," *Conference Board Report R-1459-09-RR* (New York: Conference Board, 2010).

[14]"Employee Engagement: A Leading Indicator of Financial Performance," Gallup Organization, n.d., www.gallup.com/consulting/52/employee-engagement.aspx.

of workers reported they are "not engaged." Most alarming is the fact that another 15 percent say they are "actively disengaged," defined in part as actually "undermining what their engaged co-workers accomplish."[15]

Furthermore, broader societal expectations for business are changing. The "business is business" or "shareholder value" mantras are becoming less acceptable.[16] At a minimum the public expects that businesspeople and organizations will refrain from harming other in matters such as fair working conditions and truth telling. And, in a more positive direction, society seems to increasingly expect that business will be an active partner in matters such as community development and environmental care. In fact, Phil Knight, founder and chair of Nike, a firm that in the past has had a less-than-stellar reputation for labor relations in developing countries, recently stated, "The performance of Nike and every other global company in the 21st Century will be measured as much by their impact on quality of life as it is by revenue growth and profit margins."[17]

ASSUMPTIONS, APPROACH AND AIM

The idea that business can be a calling is becoming more widely appreciated and accepted. Yet the question of *what exactly business is a calling to* needs much more exploration. This is the central topic of this book. Based on the contours of a Christian worldview, we hope to address this question by developing a faithful understanding of business at the individual, organizational and systemic/structural levels. In sum, we will be employing wisdom from an ancient tradition in order to contribute to the development of a "new story" of business. Business, we will argue, is a calling to serve the common good through transformational service.

Some of the specific questions we will address include: What implications does the Christian story have for the vision, mission or sense of purpose that shapes business engagement? What parts of business can be affirmed and practiced "as is," and what parts need to be rejected or

---

[15]Steve Crabtree, "Getting Personal in the Workplace," *Gallup Management Journal*, 2004, http://govleaders.org/gallup_article_getting_personal.htm; see also Gunther, *Faith & Fortune*, p. 3.

[16]See, for example, William Werther and David Chandler, *Strategic Corporate Social Responsibility: Stakeholders in a Global Environment* (Thousand Oaks, Calif.: Sage, 2006).

[17]Phil Knight, cited in Jonah Bloom, "Recession Provides a Chance to Build a Better Capitalism," *Advertising Age*, December 8, 2008.

transformed? What challenges exist as attempts are made to live out Christian ideals in a broken world characterized by tight margins, fierce competition and short-term investor pressures? How do Christian values inform specific functional areas of business such as the management of people, marketing and environmental sustainability?

At the outset, it may be helpful to disclose several theological commitments that shape the approach and content of this book. To some readers these may be very familiar and perhaps unnecessary to state. Yet there are subtraditions that hold a variety of beliefs about some of these matters.[18] Furthermore, and more importantly, the *implications* of these commitments for business may not be so obvious.

First, we are operating under a framework that holds to not only the possibility of social transformation but also a belief that a key part of one's calling is to act as a colaborer with God toward this task. We believe that God is active in renewing all of his creation and that we are called to serve as his regents here on earth.

Second, we believe that God works through people of varied (and no) faith backgrounds and through religious and secular institutions and social structures. Whether these phenomena can characterized as a product of natural law or common grace, that which is true, good and beautiful (whether called Christian or not) is a reflection of the Creator. Thus, while followers of Christ should sometimes lead movements or start organizations that reflect higher values, they can, at times, take comfort in joining or affirming existing movements and practices.

Third, a broken world creates complications, sometimes without perfectly clean or clear resolution. While goodness and grace are still present in many forms and places, we are living between the "now" and "not yet" in terms of the full realization of kingdom values in this world. In our current state, wheat and tares often exist side by side. Decisions are often driven by mixed and ambiguous motives, and products and services, and the people, organizations and economic systems (whether religious, Christian, spiritual or secular) that create them can be good *and* bad at the same time.

A broken world may also mean that we may find ourselves operating in

---

[18]See H. Richard Niebuhr, *Christ and Culture* (New York: Harper & Row, 1951).

the very real gap between the normative (what we should do) and the realistic (what we can do). For example, a desire and conviction among many business owners is paying a living wage and providing good benefits. But what if doing so leads to necessary price hikes that renders the business noncompetitive? Sometimes the best we can do is to make a bad situation better or pursue the wisest (versus perfect or optimal) course of action. To be sure, we need ideals to inspire, guide and properly motivate us even though we cannot perfectly achieve them in this world.

Fourth, we believe that faithful Christian living is more complicated than what can be captured by rules or formulas. While a series of checklists to live our lives by might make navigation easier, this does not seem to be God's way. In fact, the absence of ethical guidance in the form of direct commands or casuistic (if-then) type laws given the volume of the Bible is notable.[19] On many matters of import the Scriptures provide us with what might be thought of as fence posts (whether in the form of broad paradigms, commands or principles) or lines we are not to cross. But, within these boundaries, many issues cannot be settled by appeals to simple rules. Navigation requires wisdom and discernment through a relationship with God and a faithful listening community. In the end we may well have to live with legitimate differences in how the paradigms and principles offered by the Scriptures are expressed and applied on the ground.

Taking the relative paucity of rules given in Scripture with the complexity of a broken world, the approach we will take comes in the form of a *framework* for business. In contrast, a formulaic approach to determining the legitimacy of products and services, for example, often oversimplifies what is at stake and overlooks legitimate exceptions.

Fifth, because of its mixed (broken but graced) nature, business is as much a recipient or target as it is an agent for transformation. As N. T. Wright states with respect to human flourishing, "God's new creation not only happens to you, it happens through you."[20] While business already partially reflects divine purposes and aims, it can only grow into a more complete (though still imperfect) fulfillment of its calling through internal

---

[19]Dennis Hollinger, *Choosing the Good: Christian Ethics in a Complex World* (Grand Rapids: Baker Academic, 2002).

[20]N. T. Wright, address given at InterVarsity Christian Fellowship's "Following Christ 2008 Conference," Chicago, December 27-31, 2008.

change and renewal. Our book then is not primarily an apologetic work aimed to defend business against its detractors, nor is it a work that only serves to attack. Rather, we will affirm parts of business *and* call for the reform and transformation of others.

In addition to stating some of our operative beliefs, it might be helpful to clarify how our book is different from other writing that may employ similar language or address similar themes. Some of the topics and aims (e.g., socially responsible, economically and environmentally sustainable transformative businesses) of this book have much in common with writing from and about the business as mission (BAM) (a.k.a. Kingdom Business) movement. We deeply share the movement's conviction that business should be mission driven, and we will say more about this movement in chapter ten.

Although there are some conversations among leaders of the BAM movement to broaden its scope, the writing in the field indicates that the movement is more focused on organizations that are owned or led by Christians, and that target the developing world in the service of missions and with emphasis given to formerly closed countries.[21]

In contrast, our primary (though not exclusive) focus is on the transformation/reform of business overall, particularly in its conventional forms. Although we will use some Christian leaders and Christian-owned organizations as exemplars, and many of the ideas we advance have implications for Christian-owned enterprises, one of our primary audiences comprises those who are working in or intend to work in and lead mainstream secular organizations or industries.

Since we deal with issues with strong values dimensions, this book may also sound a lot like an ethics book. If by *ethics* one means how we have been accustomed to treating the subject in business settings (as resolution of very specific but complicated ethical dilemmas whether through case studies or hypothetical situations), we hope this book will be received in a much different light. However, if by the term one means the older, ancient tradition of addressing much broader goals like the development of

---

[21]See, for example, "Business as Mission," Lausanne Occasional Paper No. 59, 2004 Forum for World Evangelization, Pattaya, Thailand, October 2004; Stephen Rundle and Tom Steffen, *Great Commission Companies* (Downers Grove, Ill.: InterVarsity Press, 2003). See also Tetsunao Yamamori and Kenneth A. Eldred, ͜ ͜ . *Kingdom Business: Transforming Missions Through Entrepreneurial Strategies* (Wheaton, Ill.: Crossway, 2003).

an overarching story or narrative by which to live, then this book is very much about ethics. We would much prefer, however, that this book be seen as a philosophy or, loosely speaking, a theology of business that is built on a faithful representation of a Christian worldview. Our focus then will be bigger-picture questions such as an overall approach and framework. While we will address some issues of implementation, it would far exceed our areas of expertise (and perhaps anyone else's) to address all of the specific how-tos of putting into operation the ideas presented in this book. We do, however, provide some suggested directions and many stories and examples of business leaders who have successfully implemented similar ideals.

This book will unfold along these lines. In the first chapter we examine biblical teaching in order to make a prima facie case for the nobility of all work. We correct some common misconceptions and establish how work, particularly in the "secular" professions, can be an altar (a place of worship), service to and partnership with God to accomplish his purposes in the world. Chapter two builds on this conception of work while extending its central premises to business. We will explore the central issue of what it means to be called to business. To answer this question we will articulate a Christian vision for business as advancing the common good through transformational service.

Chapter three focuses on the rarely examined question of how God can use business as a crucible to transform *us*. While the idea that we should bring our values or our whole selves to work is more common, this chapter explores how the workplace can be used to shape us, particularly our spirituality, in positive ways. We also examine some of the spiritual practices and disciplines we need to guard from overwork or overidentification with work, a very real danger of approaching our work as a calling. In chapter four we look at biblical teaching on wealth, ambition and success, qualities that are potential outcomes of a career in business and that can produce significant tensions with Christian values, such as contentment and the upside-down nature of the kingdom Jesus himself described.

A Christian vision for business in the context of globalization is the subject of chapter five. In particular, we examine the question of whether or not and how we might engage with a global economy that offers unprecedented opportunities for business and for economically impoverished people, yet simultaneously seems to efficiently destroy much of what gets in its way.

Navigating ethical challenges in the workplace is the central focus of chapter six. Short-term market pressures, global competition, survival and greed all play roles in tempting us to cut corners. How should we handle these tests of who we are? And how can organizations curtail unethical activity and encourage good behavior?

Chapter seven focuses on leadership, the use of power and how business can serve employees. Given what the Bible teaches about the value of people and the qualities leaders ought to exhibit, we examine some of the primary implications for the management of business organizations.

Chapter eight takes an in-depth look at what is perhaps the most difficult area of business to see as service to God and neighbor, marketing. Marketing is often seen as the art and science of getting people to purchase things they don't need. We will look at how it can be reenvisioned and reformed in a manner that enables customers to flourish.

In chapter nine we turn our attention to the emerging concerns about the environment and sustainability in an era of rapidly accelerated global economic growth. Just what does the Bible teach about creation care, and what are the implications for how business should be conducted?

Chapter ten discusses several exciting (and very inspiring) ways that emerging practices and organizations are moving business toward becoming proactive and intentional partners in solving social problems. In particular, we look at comprehensive corporate social responsibility (CSR), social entrepreneurship, microfinance and the business as mission movement. We will also explore the very important issue of ownership and control; these factors strongly dictate the freedom and potential for leaders of organizations to engage in transformative work.

1

YOUR WORK IS AN ALTAR

Tom and James, both in their late twenties, are longtime friends. They went to college together and settled in the same city after graduation. Both have been working in the same part of the city for the past few years. Their spouses are good friends, and they get together as couples periodically. Tom works for the consulting division of one of the major international accounting firms, helping companies set up and maintain internal financial control systems. He is on a partnership track, and his work has been well received by the office's partners. Although he finds his work challenging and stimulating, the long hours do get to him sometimes. He often wonders how he will handle the demands now that he and his wife have young children. He sometimes thinks about starting his own business, hoping that might give him more flexibility with his hours. He gets excited about that prospect and likes the idea of being his own boss. He knows some former colleagues who have gone out on their own, and he senses that he has the right mix of people skills, drive and creativity to launch a successful business.

James has been working in business too, but he is in the midst of a major life change. He has been in the software industry since college, and for some time he has worked as a sales representative for a large company in the area. Recently, he began to attend seminary classes part time. He jokingly calls it being on the "eight-year plan" to finish his seminary degree since he can only take a few classes at a time. He and his wife have been volunteering in his church's college ministry for the past few years. He has been leading a small group Bible study for some men, and his wife is leading a group of women. The college pastor gave him several opportunities to speak to the whole college group during their main weekly meeting. He can't remember when he was so nervous or had worked so hard to prepare. This was much more demanding than any sales presentation, but he found the speaking times very satisfying. He also received positive feedback from many in the group. The college pastor has been encouraging him to consider leaving his business to devote himself to local church ministry full time. The church where he is involved would like him on their staff eventually. He is planning on continuing working in sales to pay the bills until he can transition to full-time status with this church or another one in the area.

As they talk about their careers, it becomes clear that they are wrestling with what God is calling them to do with their respective occupations. James believes that entering full-time ministry with his church is the best way to maximize his ability to help advance God's work in the world, certainly better, in his view, than continuing in business, and he encourages Tom to consider similar changes for himself. As Tom hears him talk about this, he has difficulty relating to him because he is very content and senses that his gifts are being best used in business. James recalls for Tom a speaker he heard recently who asked a group of college students and young professionals in the audience this provocative question: "Those of you who are business majors, why don't you get out of the 'ticky-tack' world and do some meaningful work that contributes to other people's lives?" The point he was making is that real impact for God is to be made in church-based work, on the mission field or in a nonprofit organization, not in business. This was very challenging for James and captures the point he is trying to make in his conversation with Tom. Think about how would you respond to the speaker's perspective, and to James if you were in Tom's position.

One way to respond would be by arguing that the church and nonprofit organizations need businesspeople because "ministry" and meeting the needs of others requires capital. Business, then, has value in God's economy in terms of what it can accomplish for "ministry." Or you could insist that if James leaves his business, he loses his strategic platform to live out his faith. You could remind the speaker that most of the people he works with will rarely, if ever, come to church. Those people think that most pastors are not all that relevant to them since they don't live in their world. These responses would illustrate some of the reasons that God calls people to business. That is, business has value in that it is a means to support "ministry" or other good causes and to share one's faith.

Undoubtedly, God may call people to business for these reasons. However, our goal in this chapter is to ask if there is more to the value of work than servicing other ends, such as wealth creation or a strategic platform for living out one's faith. We would suggest that, though valid, these are incomplete reasons for the value of work because they do not uphold the value of work that the Bible assigns. We will argue that work is best seen as having nobility because it is an altar—a significant place at which we devote our time, energy, gifts and skills in service to God, and that work is ministry and has extraordinary value in serving God.

BACKGROUND ON WORK IN BIBLICAL TIMES

The view of work from a Christian worldview stands in sharp contrast both to the classical era (see the discussion of work and leisure in the classical Greek thinkers in chapter three) and to the culture at large today. The Bible has a lot to say about our work, and what we do for a living matters a great deal to God. Jesus spent the vast majority of his earthly life working for a living as a carpenter and spent most of his time around ordinary working people. Many of his parables were drawn from the everyday world of first-century work, such as agriculture and various trades. Even the apostles worked to support themselves so that they would not be a burden to the churches they served.

In biblical times the workplace was a very different place than it is today. Most people worked with their hands in agriculture or some trade or craft. There was no such thing as an industrial system, no stock market and few knowledge-based jobs that would stimulate someone's mind without wearing out his or her body. Unless a person was part of a wealthy class, which was rare, he or she worked very hard to provide a subsistence level of income, and people fortunate enough to practice a trade could rise to something resembling today's lower middle class.

In biblical times people didn't consciously think about their work in the same way we do today. Generally, people did not connect their work to their self-fulfillment, even though honest labor in the fields or in a trade could contribute positively to a person's self-esteem. For the most part work was necessary for survival, and if a worker was aware of how it contributed to a sense of well-being, that was an added bonus. There wasn't a variety of jobs to choose from—people typically went into the occupation that their parents (most likely their father) were in and were trained on the job. There was little opportunity to weigh options about which occupation would provide a meaningful life. Those questions were secondary, if addressed at all. Whereas today, we expect people to be able to articulate how their job fits in with who they are.

In the ancient world most people did not retire voluntarily. They worked until they were not physically able to work any longer and then were taken care of by their extended family. There was no widely available mechanism for people to save and invest for their retirement. The idea that someone could be financially independent and not have to work was limited to a small class of wealthy landowners and political rulers. It was simply not available for the average person. So when the Bible addresses work, the writers assume that people will work for the duration of their lives because it was necessary for them to do so in order to survive in a rough-and-tumble economic environment.

The Bible helps to fill out the view of work that existed in the ancient world. God has a lot to say about *why* we work. The Bible offers a variety of reasons for work—that is, we ought to work because of what work can do for our community and ourselves. But we also work for more significant reasons: work accomplishes God's work and purposes in the world. First, we will focus on the initial reasons, because the Bible takes these very seriously.

WE WORK TO SUPPORT OURSELVES

First, we should work in order to support ourselves and not be a burden on the community. The apostle Paul lays it out pretty clearly to the Thessalonians that everyone has the obligation to work to provide for their own needs. He puts it like this:

> We command you, brothers, to keep away from every brother who is idle and does not live according to the teaching you received from us. For you yourselves know how you ought to follow our example. We were not idle when we were with you, nor did we eat anyone's food without paying for it. On the contrary, we worked night and day, laboring and toiling so that we would not be a burden to any of you. . . . For even when we were with you,

we gave you this rule: "If a man will not work, he shall not eat."

We hear that some among you are idle. . . . Such people we command and urge in the Lord Jesus Christ to settle down and earn the bread they eat. (2 Thess 3:6-8, 10-12)

There were exceptions to this general rule in the church. Those who were unable to work, either through some mental or physical limitation, were entitled to share in the community's goods. Those were the poor of which the Bible speaks, and both Testaments are clear that the community is to take care of the poor (Deut 15:1-11; Lk 3:11; Gal 2:10; Jas 2:15-17). The Old Testament set up a social safety net for the able-bodied poor known as gleaning (Lev 19:9-10). Here the law prohibited a farmer from harvesting all of the crops that grew on his fields. Some had to be left for those who had no land of their own to cultivate. But they still had to take initiative. They had to come to the fields themselves and harvest what they were able. Only those incapable of working, due to physical or mental infirmity, were exempt from the obligation to work.

WE WORK IN ORDER TO TAKE CARE OF OUR FAMILIES AND RELATIVES

The Bible is equally clear on the obligation for adults to provide for the needs of their families. In fact, the New Testament states it bluntly. In writing to Timothy about how to take care of those in need, Paul says, "If anyone does not provide for his relatives, and especially for his immediate family, he has denied the faith" (1 Tim 5:8). It would be difficult to put it more strongly. If someone is able to work, he or she has the obligation to work to provide for the family's needs.

It was assumed that people would continue working until they could no longer do so. At that point their children took on the obligation, according to 1 Timothy 5:4, 8, to provide for parents and other relatives as they had needs. The biblical writers assumed that people would work until they could no longer do so, because it was necessary to provide for their needs.

WE WORK TO CARE FOR THOSE IN NEED

God's command to work isn't only for our and our family's needs. We work in order to have money to be generous to those in need. We don't often think of work in this way, but the Bible is clear that one of the main reasons we work is to help people who are economically poor. Of course, this assumes that we are living within our means and have money available to assist those in need. Paul pointedly says: "He who has been stealing must steal no longer, but must work, doing something useful with his own hands, that he may have something to share with those in need" (Eph 4:28). You'll notice that the passage doesn't say that people are to stop stealing and work so that they can support themselves. That's assumed. The point of the passage is that they would have a surplus of goods left over in order to help those who don't have enough.

The early Christian community was quite poor. It's true that there were some wealthy people, but most were farmers or tradespeople who were not far from poverty, particularly if misfortune struck. The early church was full of people who needed financial assistance, and Paul strikingly calls on the church not only to work hard doing something productive but to share generously with the poor out of their income. The recipients included not only the poor in the immediate community but others with financial needs throughout the ancient world. For example, Paul encourages the Corinthians to give generously out of their abundance to help those in Jerusalem who were the victims of a terrible famine (2 Cor 8:13-15).

Jesus makes it clear why it's so important to be generous to those in need. He puts it in terms of a parable:

> When you give a luncheon or dinner, do not invite your friends, your brothers or relatives, or your rich neighbors; *if you do, they may invite you back and so you will be repaid*. But when you give a banquet, invite the poor, the crippled, the lame, the blind, and you will be blessed. *Although they cannot repay you*, you will be repaid at the resurrection of the righteous. (Lk 14:12-14, emphasis added)

The italicized portions represent the point of Jesus' teaching. We often do things out of our self-interest—in order to gain something for ourselves. But Jesus insists that we do right by the poor even though they can't do anything for us in return. (Jesus is assuming that they can't repay us anything financial.) In fact, the reason he insists on being generous to the poor is precisely *because* they cannot repay us. Think about why Jesus would insist on this. He is calling us to care for the poor unconditionally, without any expectation of getting anything in return. When we are generous to those who can't repay us, it models the unconditional God caring for us. So, our generosity toward the poor and those in need is a mirror of God's love for all his people. This is why the Bible, from cover to cover, places such emphasis on taking care of those in need. We work in order to fulfill this important mandate and reflect God's unconditional love, which is at the core of his character.

WE WORK TO SUPPORT THE CHURCH AND ITS WORK

Not only are Christians obligated to help those in need, they are also to work in order to help support the church and its ministries. The Bible acknowledges that God calls some to gain their livelihood from work in the local church or the mission field. For example, in the Old Testament God called the priests and Levites to perform the priestly services on a full-time basis, earning their living from the tithes of the community. They were dependent on the community that they served for their financial needs. Similarly, in the New Testament era God called the apostles to spend their lives planting churches around the world. The vast majority of the early church's leaders worked to support themselves, and at times the apostles worked too, to avoid being a burden on the churches they served (1 Thess 2:9). Yet they acknowledged the importance of their role as apostles and made it clear that they were entitled to their support from the community they served, even though they voluntarily gave up that right in order to minimize controversy (1 Cor 9:1-15). Their labor for the church entitled them to material support. Throughout the Bible the willingness of the community to support those in full-time church work was considered a barometer of its spiritual health (Mal 3:10). Keep in mind that those who were entitled to earn their living in full-time church service were the exception, not the rule. Most people served God in the course of their day-to-day lives, being obedient to him in the daily routines of work, family and leisure.

WE WORK TO PROVIDE A PLATFORM TO LIVE OUT OUR FAITH

Finally, God calls people to work in order to gain opportunities to proclaim and model the reality of our faith. Through our work we have opportunities to build relationships and to demonstrate care and concern for people with whom we would not likely have contact. These relationships provide a significant means by which God gives us a platform for living out our faith. The New Testament exhorts the early church to continue their diligence at work in order to maintain their respectability in the community. First Thessalonians 4:11-12 puts it this way: "Make it your ambition to lead a quiet life, to mind your own business, and to work with your hands, just as we told you, so that your daily life may win the respect of outsiders and so that you will not be dependent on anybody." Work is an avenue to win the respect of the community. Paul was no doubt assuming that the reasons for a person having respect was to insure that there were no obstacles to a winsome presentation of his or her faith. Most pastors and missionaries would never have the opportunity to credibly communicate spiritual values in our work environment. They don't know the people or the business, can't relate to the day-to-day struggles we face on the job, and would likely be seen as outsiders with little to say. We, on the other hand, know them, work beside them every day, go through difficulties with them and give them the opportunity to see our faith in practice (provided we live it out well) on a daily basis.

THE INTRINSIC VALUE OF WORK

However, there's a lot more to work than just taking care of our financial needs and obligations. *Our work can serve as an altar*—an important arena where we bring our gifts, skills and talents to offer up *in service to God*. When Christians go to work, we are offering ourselves up to God in service to him. When we go to work, we can contribute to God's work in the world. Of course, there are some limits that we will spell out in chapter two. But excluding those exceptions, God calls people to work in arenas like business because it helps to accomplish his work in the world. Business can be the work of God in the world in the same way that being a pastor can be the work of God in the church and in the same way that missionary service can be the work of God on the mission field. All have value to God because of the value of the work done, and work is a good thing that has value when it's done with excellence. The accountant, the manager, the blue-collar worker, the gardener, the janitor and the McDonald's cook can be called by God to their work in the same way the pastor or the missionary is called to his or hers. All of them are capable of doing the work of God in their workplace, both by virtue of the work they do and the way they live out their faith. To take it a step further, God, in his providence, works through our occupations to accomplish his work in the world. This is another point we will develop in more depth in chapter two.

Your work can be an altar because your work has deep-seated value to God. The Bible teaches that work has significant value for three primary reasons: (1) God created work before the intrusion of sin and evil into the world, (2) God designed work for us to fulfill the mandate to "subdue" (exercise stewardship over) the earth, and (3) work is a significant part of what it means to be made in God's image.

WORK WAS INSTITUTED BEFORE THE ENTRANCE OF SIN

Work has great value because God ordained it prior to the entrance of sin and evil into the world. In the Genesis account of creation God commanded Adam and Eve to work the garden before sin entered the picture (Gen 2:15). God did not condemn human beings to work as a consequence of Adam and Eve's decision to disobey. Work is not a punishment for human sin. To be sure, work was affected by the Fall, making it more arduous, stressful and less productive (Gen 3:17-19), but that was not the original design, which was that human beings would spend their lives in productive activity, with regular breaks for leisure, rest and celebration of God's blessing (Ex 20:8-11). Even in the pre-Fall paradise, God put Adam and Eve to work. Work was a part of God's original design for human beings, and because of that it has great value to God.

Work will also be a part of the world after the Lord's return. The prophet Isaiah envisions the world after Christ's return as one in which nations "will beat their swords into plowshares and their spears into pruning hooks" (Is 2:4). The obvious point of the passage is to show that universal peace will characterize the kingdom when it is fulfilled. But what often goes unnoticed is that weapons of war will be transformed *into implements of productive work* (plowshares and pruning hooks). That is, productive work will be part of the program when Christ returns to bring his kingdom in its fullness. So work has high value because it was ordained before the Fall and will be a part of life when the kingdom comes in its fullness. In the paradise settings at the beginning and end of human history, God ordains work.

Work and the Dominion Mandate

What makes work so valuable to God is its connection to another mandate from creation, the command to exercise dominion over the earth. To be clear, dominion is not irresponsible use (see chap. 9). God both commanded and empowered human beings to be responsible stewards over creation (Gen 1:28). They were to function as trustees of the earth, its resources and the environment. Their authority over creation allowed them to use it for their benefit but also made them responsible for managing it for the common good. The Bible is clear that God embedded his wisdom into the creation (Prov 8:22-36) in order to enable human beings to more effectively exercise dominion.[1] God makes his wisdom known through the world, in part, by means of general revelation and common grace. For example, technologies and other discoveries that improve the lot of human beings and help alleviate the effects of sin are the result of God's common grace to human beings. God is not caught off-guard by great scientific or technological discoveries. Human beings don't make these discoveries and apply them to daily life completely on their own. They are utilizing God's common grace to more effectively fulfill the mandate to exercise responsible dominion over creation.

In the Genesis account human beings are given the opportunity and responsibility to rule over creation as trustees. God gave human beings the ability and obligation of stewardship over creation. God ordained the means as well as the ends when it comes to the dominion mandate. Work is the means to fulfilling the human obligation to steward creation. Adam and Eve worked the garden to put it to productive use and reap its fruits. In doing so, they were fulfilling the dominion mandate of Genesis 1:28. Procreation is another means used to fulfill this mandate, thereby establishing a human community to serve as trustees over creation. In Genesis 2, which is a more detailed and complementary account of creation (Genesis 1 being the panoramic overview), God establishes both work (Gen 2:15) and procreation (Gen 2:24) as the primary means by which the dominion mandate would be carried out. Procreation provides the "people power" (of course, that's not the only purpose for procreation), and work provides the direction for fulfilling one of God's principal tasks for human beings. That

---

[1]The Bible clearly teaches that God also uses creation to proclaim his glory (Ps 19).

is, work is one of the primary ways that God had in mind for human beings to do what he commanded them to in the world.

Work is intricately bound up with the dominion mandate over creation. It is not something that we do just to get by or to finance our lifestyles. Work is neither a necessary evil that will be done away with at some point nor what we do in order to enjoy our leisure. Work has great dignity; it is the way God arranged for human beings to fulfill a part of their destiny on earth, that of exercising responsible stewardship over creation. That mandate is still in effect today, and God is still empowering human beings to be effective trustees of his world. Thus work has substantial value because of its connection to the dominion mandate. Adam and Eve were doing God's work in the world by tending the garden and being responsible trustees over creation. We do God's work in the world in our jobs because they are connected with the task assigned to all human beings to exercise dominion over the world.

Some use the term *cocreation* to describe how our work fits with the dominion mandate and to indicate the nobility of work.[2] Though the view we argue for here has much in common with this notion of cocreation, namely, that it involves "working with and under God to care for the creation,"[3] the term may be somewhat misleading. British novelist Dorothy Sayers suggests that our work is a "medium of divine creation," appearing to make it analogous to God's original creation.[4] Some might conclude that this is far too high a view of human beings in the process of creation care. We would suggest that we *cooperate* with God in the advancement of his dominion over the creation, which after the Genesis account of the Fall also involves alleviating the effects of the entrance of sin (evil) into the world.

To be sure, work seems to have lost much of its original dignity. The brokenness of the world results in jobs being dehumanizing, alienating and actually destroying creation instead of protecting and restoring it. We should not underestimate the impact of sin on the workplace in general and on some specific work, which negates our ability to envision how it might fit with the dominion mandate. With some jobs—molecular biolo-

---

[2]Gilbert Meilaender, ed., *Working: Its Meaning and Limits* (Notre Dame, Ind.: University of Notre Dame Press, 2000), pp. 2-6.

[3]Ibid., p. 2.

[4]Dorothy Sayers, quoted in ibid., p. 45. We concur with much of Sayers's view of the intrinsic value of work, based on human beings being made in God's image.

gist, physician and other professions in the sciences—it is not difficult to see the connection. Further, in the helping professions the contribution to the common good and the way that those professions counter some of the effects of sin in the world are also easy to see (though those jobs also reflect the impact of the entrance of sin). But what about more mundane jobs, such as sweatshop labor, assembly line work, janitorial service and flipping burgers? Even though it may be more difficult to see how these fit into a larger purpose, and we should continually endeavor to improve work, they still have nobility because of their contribution to God's work in the world. God, in his providence, is at work in these occupations to accomplish important things.[5] For example, God is at work in every job related to food production and service to accomplish his task of feeding people. Similarly, God is at work in the garment factory to accomplish his task of clothing people. God is at work in construction-related jobs to accomplish his task of housing people. God is also at work in government to accomplish his purpose of maintaining order and justice in the world (Rom 13:1-7). In our work we cooperate and participate with God so that, in his providence, he accomplishes his work in the world. God calls people to business because it has great value in accomplishing his work in the world.

Take the case of Doug and his wife Karen. A few years ago, Karen was diagnosed with a brain tumor and was rushed to a neurosurgeon after she blacked out while getting off a return flight from vacation. The surgeon removed the tumor using the most recent surgical technology, on an out-patient basis, and today Karen suffers no effects of the tumor. Doug marveled at the level of technology now available and the wide variety of products and services that had to be coordinated for Karen's treatment to be effective. He noted the imaging machines, the software needed to run them, the electrical components necessary to run the computers and the service technicians who kept them running effectively. He also was struck by the way business had made these products available to the physician so that they could be used to diagnose and treat Karen's tumor. He commented in the aftermath of her treatment, "I'm sure glad these people didn't feel called to leave their business to 'serve the Lord.'" Through their work those people who know God are obeying his call to business and are helping with the

---

[5]For further discussion of this important point, see Gene Edward Veith, *God at Work: Your Christian Vocation in All of Life* (Wheaton, Ill.: Crossway, 2002).

stewardship of creation. They are serving God in their work and are a part of his work in alleviating the effects of evil (which here took the form of a brain tumor). God was providentially working to heal Karen through the various people involved in her diagnosis and treatment.

So far, this perspective on work and the dominion mandate has focused on how work relates to the order of creation. But how might it relate to the order of redemption, or to the new creation that God is in the process of bringing? Theologian Miroslav Volf has extended the idea of the work and dominion mandate to give it an eschatological dimension.[6] He sees work as one of the places where we can use our spiritual gifts, thus there is a pneumatological component to work. He suggests that the New Testament idea of spiritual gifts is not limited to what he calls "ecclesiastical activity" or church work. Volf argues that in the New Testament era God has "gifted" individuals to prepare his people for works of service (1 Cor 12:7; Eph 4:11-12), both for the church and for the common good, and that works of service cannot be limited to those that occur within the boundaries of the church. Thus all people of God are gifted by the Spirit for specific works of service, both in the church and in the world, of which work is a primary arena.

We cooperate with the Spirit in work just as we cooperate with the Spirit in the rest of our spiritual lives. Volf extends this notion by arguing that the Spirit

> who imparts gifts and acts through them is a guarantee of the realization of the new creation (2 Cor 1:22, which suggests that the Spirit is the deposit, guaranteeing us of the transformation to come; and Rom 8:23, which links the activity of the Spirit with the transformation of the earth). If this is true, then work is actually cooperation with God in is eschatological transformation of the new creation.[7]

Volf summarizes: "As Christians do their mundane work, the Spirit enables them to cooperate with God in the kingdom of God that 'completes creation and renews heaven and earth.'"[8] Thus work is not only a fulfillment of the dominion mandate, but it also is service to God that

---

[6]Miroslav Volf, *Work in the Spirit: Toward a Theology of Work* (New York: Oxford University Press, 1991), pp. 114-18.
[7]Ibid., p. 115.
[8]Ibid.

cooperates with him in the transformation of the world. In other words, work is transformational service to God in his new creation too.

God as a Worker

So work has nobility because it was created before the entrance of sin and is the means by which we cooperate with God in the exercise of dominion over the creation. But there's a more foundational reason why work has value to God. God is a worker and human beings are workers by virtue of being made in God's image. In other words, we work because that's who God is and who we are in his image. Of course, God is much more than a worker and so are we.

Look carefully at the way God is portrayed when it comes to work. One of the first portraits of God in Genesis is as a worker, fashioning the world in his wisdom. God is portrayed as Creator in Genesis 1–2, using initiative, ingenuity, passion and innovation in his work. God is portrayed with what we might call "entrepreneurial" traits. From the beginning of the biblical account God is presented as engaged in productive activity in fashioning and sustaining the good world. And at the end of the creation account God rested "from all his work" (Gen 2:2). God blessed the sabbath (the seventh day) because "he rested from *all the work of creating* that he had done" (Gen 2:3, emphasis added). The pattern for the sabbath is to rest because God rested (Ex 20:11), and conversely to work on the other days because God worked in creation (Ex 20:9). The pattern of creation became the pattern for human beings. We work six days as God did and rest one day as God did. We work to create good because it is part of what it means to be made in God's image. Whenever human beings work to create good, they are imitating God, who creates good in all he does.

The wisdom literature describes the process of God's work in creation guided by wisdom (Prov 8:22-31). The psalmist describes the work of God in creation as the pattern for his ongoing work of providing for the world (Ps 104). He refers to God's past work in creation and the flood (Ps 104:3-9) and then praises God for his work in taking care of his creation (Ps 104:10-31). God provides water and food for both animals and human beings, giving them stable sources of sustenance and security in his world. The psalmist summarizes, "The earth is satisfied by the fruit of his work" (Ps 104:13). The psalm ends with the phrase, "May the Lord rejoice in his works" (Ps 104:31). God works diligently to care for his creation—that's a significant part of who he is. As people made in his image, that is a significant part of who we are too.

This theme is carried throughout the New Testament. In a dispute with religious leaders, Jesus has healed a man on the sabbath and is getting heavy criticism for violating the Pharisees' traditions about the sabbath, though not the sabbath command itself. Jesus makes this remarkable statement that further inflamed the religious leaders when he said, "My father is *always at his work* to this very day, and I, too, am working" (Jn 5:17, emphasis added). Jesus teaches that God is continually at work in the world, accomplishing his purposes. Further, Paul affirms that along with his Father, Jesus is both the Creator and Sustainer of creation (Col 1:15-17). It is a part of who he is. We work because that's who God is, and who we are as made in his image. Dorothy Sayers says, "Work is the natural exercise and function of man—the creature who is made in the image of his Creator. Work is not, primarily, a thing one does to live, but the thing one lives to do."[9] Or as Chuck Colson puts it, "We are indeed 'hardwired' for work," by virtue of being made in God's image.[10]

Work is a fundamental part of who God is and who we are, being made in his image. It is immensely valuable to God because it is the means by which human beings partner with God in exercising dominion over the world. This is why Ecclesiastes proclaims the goodness of work:

> A man can do nothing better than to eat and drink and *find satisfaction in all his work.* This too, I see, is from the hand of God, for without him, who can eat or find enjoyment? (Eccles 2:24-25)

> That everyone may eat and drink, and *find satisfaction in all his toil*—this is the gift of God. (Eccles 3:13)

> So I saw that there is nothing better for a man *than to enjoy his work,* because that is his lot. (Eccles 3:22)

> Then I realized that it is good and proper for a man to eat and drink, *and to*

---

[9]Dorothy L. Sayers, *Creed or Chaos?* (Manchester, N.H.: Sophia Press, 1974), pp. 72-73.
[10]Charles W. Colson and Harold Fickett, *The Good Life: Seeking Purpose, Meaning and Truth in Your Life* (Carol Stream, Ill.: Tyndale House, 2005). See also R. Paul Stevens, *The Other Six Days* (Grand Rapids: Eerdmans, 2000), and *Doing God's Business: Meaning and Motivation for the Marketplace* (Grand Rapids: Eerdmans, 2006); Wayne Grudem, *Business for the Glory of God: The Bible's Teaching on the Moral Goodness of Business* (Wheaton, Ill.: Crossway, 2003).

find satisfaction in his toilsome labor under the sun during the few days of life God has given him—for this is his lot. Moreover, when God gives any man wealth and possessions, and enables him to enjoy them, to accept his lot and *be happy in his work*—this is a gift of God. (Eccles 5:18-19)[11]

All legitimate work has great value to God, and no valid occupation has any more value to God than any other. There is no hierarchy of vocations in God's economy. The work of the plumber, the child-care worker, the salesperson, the executive, the auto mechanic and the pastor are all of great value to God because in their work they are fulfilling the dominion mandate over creation and are reflecting the image of God.

IMPACT OF SIN ON WORK

When sin entered the world, it tarnished everything about God's original design for the world. Instead of human beings living in a close, intimate relationship with God, sin resulted in separation. Instead of people living forever in good health, sin introduced a legacy of death and disease. Instead of living together in harmony and justice, sin introduced conflict, greed and injustice.

When sin entered the world, it had a dramatic and immediate effect on work too. Prior to the entrance of sin, all work was good work, and work was intrinsically good. Sin made most work a mixed blessing, a way to honor God but fraught with numerous and varied possibilities for wrongdoing.[12] In addition, instead of work always being fulfilling and enjoyable, it can be arduous and stressful. As a result of sin Genesis 3:17-19 records that God said to Adam:

> Cursed is the ground because of you;
>> through painful toil you will eat of it
>> all the days of your life.
> It will produce thorns that thistles for you,
>> and you will eat the plants of the field.
> By the sweat of your brow

---

[11]Emphasis added in all Scripture quotations. Ecclesiastes also proclaims the vanity of work, due to the impact of sin. Work is a mixed blessing, involving both satisfaction and pain (Eccles 2:17-23).

[12]See Grudem's *Business for the Glory of God* for more discussion of this point. He argues that business is both a means to honor God and a source of temptation, as a result of both the original goodness of work and the reality of sin affecting work.

> you will eat your food
> until you return to the ground,
>> since from it you were taken;
> for dust you are
>> and to dust you will return.

Sin deeply affected the world of work, transforming God's original design. Sin introduced effort, strain and futility to work that did not exist prior to the entrance of sin. Work included painful toil in which productivity is now mixed with thorns and thistles.

Sin alienates humans from work and the process of work; people feel that they are simply cogs in a corporate machine. It brings a sense of frustration to work; many feel their hard work amounts to little. And it corrupts work, introducing work that is degrading and dehumanizing, and it tarnishes the image of God in human beings. Sin also brings ethical dilemmas and temptations to cut corners to the workplace (see chap. 6). Sin brought about industries and businesses that contribute nothing to the common good. Because of sin work becomes a mixed blessing; its beneficial aspects are combined with significant social and personal costs. Sin tarnishes all the positive elements of God's original design for work. Sin can turn work from being transformational service (to God and others) into self-service.

CAN A JOB JUST BE A JOB?

It is possible that as we look realistically down the road, we will realize that our job is not likely to change, and that it's unlikely to become something we're passionate about. Maybe you've been reading this and are wondering, *Can a job just be a job? Why do I have to earn a living doing something I have a keen interest in?* Of course, ideally we would work at things we are passionate about, where our work is satisfying and gives us a sense of contributing to God's work in the world. But in a fallen world, that is not always an option. Part of the reality of living in a world affected by sin is that not all work is ideal. To be sure, all legitimate work has nobility, whether we experience it as such or not, but sometimes it feels as if it's "just a job." This is likely the case for most people in the developing world, who typically don't have the luxury of seeking fulfilling work (which probably parallels the way it was in the ancient world). Making tents was just a job for the apostle Paul. His passion was planting churches (though he undoubtedly made high-quality tents). Similarly, Jesus' passion was his itinerant teaching; carpentry was his job, though he was good at his craft. Both tent making and carpentry were noble trades for Paul and Jesus, and God clearly called them to their respective trades, but they were not zealous about these things. And it may be the same for us. We realize that to do what we really want to with our life is not possible now—but it may be later, and it's probably worth thinking hard about how God could make it happen for us to make a change.

Even though we may feel that our work is "just a job," in reality it may be much more than that. Remember, work is an altar, a place where we offer ourself to God and participate in his mission of transforming the world. God has invested all legitimate work with great value, and we are doing God's work in the world when we participate in it. Further, we imitate God and fulfill a part of what it means to be made in his image. We also are a part of fulfilling the human mandate to exercise dominion over the creation and are cooperating with God in his eschatological transformation of the world. Our job may not feel like we are doing God's will, but how it feels to us and what it actually is may be two very different things.

For instance, some businesspeople find that an exercise in learning to see the sacred dimensions of their work is helpful. Almost all of the graduate-level (MBA) students I (Kenman) have taught never have thought much about how their work might serve divine (or even greater earthly) purposes. Even the practicing Christians among them have rarely given this much thought and have largely overlooked the idea that their work in business has a deeper meaning than practical considerations.

After spending the first few weeks of class exploring possible and potential links, they are asked to reflect on how their work connects with God's purposes and mission, and the greater contribution their work makes. They often are pleasantly surprised by their answers. The following is just a sampling of their answers:

> I'm a manager for a package delivery company. How I treat my drivers everyday impacts their lives and how they feel about their work. When the holiday season arrives, I help anyway I can to get packages delivered. Often that means driving a truck myself to help relieve the load. This may sound overly sentimental, but honestly nothing puts a smile on my face more than a child's gift delivered on time for Christmas.

I contribute to the efficient production of aircraft. While this may not sound like much in the grand scheme of things, my work makes the world a smaller place by connecting people. Airplanes enable people to travel to conduct business, see family and friends, and for leisure.

Working for a large software company, I have struggled to see my work as a calling. However, in thinking more about it, I realize that my work enables safe and secure commercial transactions on the Internet, giving people more power to shop and save money, with far less threat of having sensitive financial information stolen. While this may be a stretch, Internet commerce may also encourage people to use their vehicles less, contributing to environmental conservation.

I work in accounting. My last company made sports equipment, which to some degree benefits society. I still work as an accountant, but my current employer makes lifesaving medical devices, so without my contributions the company's work would be less efficient, and quite possibly fewer lives would be saved.

To be certain, learning to make these connections also allows us to see limitations and points of tension, places where our work may conflict with a Christian vision for business. Moreover, some people try and can't see how their present position can be reconceptualized at all. Sadly, the only fix may be a change of positions. However, when people are encouraged to see their work as more than making money and to think of ways to encourage human flourishing in their realm of influence, they are often surprised at what comes into focus.

WORK AS SERVICE TO GOD

Regardless of how it feels, the Bible teaches that our work can be an altar, one major aspect of our service to God in the world. The building site for the construction worker, the daycare center for the daycare worker, the office for the administrative assistant, the classroom for the teacher, the pulpit for the pastor, the laboratory for the scientist, the restaurant for the chef are altars where they offer themselves in service to God. All valid work is sacred to God and is a place of sacred service to him. This is the point Paul was making in his charge to believers in the workplace when he said, "Whatever you do, work at it with all your heart, as working for the Lord, not for men. . . . It is the Lord Christ you are serving" (Col 3:23-24). Note that slavery is the context of Paul's teaching here—he encouraging slaves to render faithful service to their masters because they were ultimately serving Christ. That is, they were serving Christ in the mundane, menial work slaves were assigned to.

Each of us serve Christ by doing our work faithfully and with excellence. The plumber serves Christ by fixing leaky pipes; the stockbroker serves Christ when giving investment advice; the waiter serves Christ when serving food; the missionary serves Christ on the mission field; the health care professional serves Christ in the hospital, doctor's office or dental chair; and the software engineer serves Christ at the computer terminal. Paul said that in whatever we do for our work, we are serving Christ. No one serves Christ more or less in one job or another.

Our work can well be our ministry. In fact, the word *ministry* means service. To have a ministry simply means to be in service to God. The term *ministry* comes from the Greek word *diakonia*, which is translated "service," and our word *deacon* is derived from that term. In the New Testament some of the first people described as having a *diakonia* (Acts 6) were those who freed up the apostles to preach, teach and pray. What was their *ministry?* Waiting on tables for the widows in the community. It doesn't sound very spiritual, but it was, and it was an important part of the ministry of the early church. If we're in business, our work may serve as an altar—a part of our service to God, our ministry. It is not our entire ministry, since we're also called to serve God in the church, in our neighborhoods and around the world. But ministry does not stand in contrast to business. Business is ministry, the work of God in the world. All of us are in *full-time* ministry if we are followers of Christ, and we entered full-time service/ministry at the time we came to faith. We all serve God full time, whether it's in the world, in the church or on the mission field. These are simply different arenas of service, and all have significant value to God.

The term *full-time ministry* should be used to refer to one's attitude toward service, more than an arena of service. The term should describe an orientation toward serving God, rather than specific activities (though there are exceptions) that are deemed to be serving God.

This is what Tom Chappell discovered during his business sabbatical. He founded the company Tom's of Maine, a personal-care-products company. He was quite successful, but as a Christian he had a nagging sense that there ought to be more that he could do with his life. So he took a year off from his business to do something very different. He enrolled as a student at Harvard Divinity School in an attempt to "find his calling." At the end of the year of study, he came away convinced that business was his calling, and he went back to his business with a fresh perspective and a new desire to pursue his business, to "work at it with all your heart, as working for the Lord, not men. . . . It is the Lord Christ you are serving" (Col 3:23-24). He realized that running his company was a sacred task God had gifted him for and was using him to make a difference in the world.[13] That is, his office at Tom's of Maine is an altar, the place where he gave himself in transformational service to God. This idea revolutionized how he viewed his work.

BUSINESS AS MINISTRY

But in many of our churches today there seems to be a dichotomy between business and ministry. For example, it is often said that people are "entering the ministry" when they decide to become pastors or missionaries. We refer to church work and missionary service as "ministry," and refer to those who do this as their occupation as being in "full-time ministry," as opposed to those who work in the church or mission field part-time or on a volunteer basis. When someone steps down from a pastoral position or comes home from the mission field and goes into business, we commonly say that they have "left the ministry."

This distinction between business and ministry is at the heart of what we believe is a widespread and erroneous notion in our churches that if people want to maximize their impact for God's kingdom, they need to be in "full-time ministry." Traditionally, ministry is seen as working in a church or parachurch organization. We see the effect of this dichotomy on businesspeople (and increasingly in the nonprofit sector or in the helping professions), which can leave them with the sense that, at best, they play a support role (mostly financial) for those who are working full time in a church or nonprofit organization, and that their work is unrelated to serving God, other than providing necessary financial support.

This distinction between work and ministry has a long history. In the

---

[13]See the account of Tom Chappell's story in his *The Soul of a Business: Managing for Profit and the Common Good* (New York: Bantam Books, 1993).

Middle Ages, priests, nuns and monks, those engaged in "full-time ministry," were seen as doing the most important work of God. But during the Reformation, Martin Luther, John Calvin and other Reformers popularized the idea of "worldly callings." They correctly saw that God called people to a wide variety of occupations, which are sacred callings analogous to those of priests, nuns and monks. They rightly saw the whole world as a theater of God's glory and insisted that working in the world has value to God. This is one of the great legacies of the Reformation: God's call encompasses all legitimate work. Thus Martin Luther even said that a hangman was doing God's work if he did it with excellence. Echoing the idea of work as an altar, Luther said, "The entire world is full of service to God, not only in the churches but also the home, the kitchen, the cellar, the workshop and the field of the townsfolk and farmers." He rejected the dichotomy between the sacred and secular, saying, "Seemingly secular works are a worship of God and an obedience well pleasing to God."[14] Similarly, John Calvin rightly maintained that God could be honored even in the realm of politics. The Reformers' views changed European society profoundly. The idea that a person could have a worldly call provided much of the fertile soil for the industrial revolution and the institution of capitalism to take root in.[15]

The Reformers defined vocation or calling very broadly and emphasized a person's paid occupation as only a part of his or her overall calling. To be clear, the Bible's technical language of calling is reserved for those things that are permanent and irrevocable. God issues a call to salvation, sanctification and service. Those aspects of our call are both permanent and irrevocable. But the Bible does not use the specific language of vocation to refer to a person's occupation, except in rare cases, such as God calling the craftsmen and women to their tasks in building the tabernacle (Ex 35:31–36:1). The language of calling seems to be reserved for the broader aspects of our spiritual lives. We are called to service, but the arena in which we serve God may change. We are not necessarily called to one career or occupation in such a way that we can never change.

---

[14]Martin Luther, cited in Charles Colson and Nancy Pearcey, *How Now Shall We Live?* (Wheaton, Ill.: Tyndale House, 1999), chap. 38.
[15]See the classic work on this topic, Max Weber, *The Protestant Ethic and the Spirit of Capitalism* (New York: Scribner's, 1958).

So we ought to be careful to use the language of calling in the same way the Bible does. What people mean when they say God called them to a certain career is that this arena of service to God is the one that best fits his or her gifts, skills and talents. We use the term *calling* to refer to that niche in which we are a good fit. As long it is understood that the Bible does not use the technical language of calling to refer to one's occupation, the term can be used as a shorthand way to refer to finding the place where a person can maximize his or her gifts, skills and talents, and pursue the specific occupation they believe God is moving them to. Lee Hardy uses the useful categories of "general" and "particular" callings to help draw this important distinction. The former is the calling to what's permanent and applies singularly. With respect to the latter, we can have many at once. For example, we may have particular callings to serve as friends, community members, volunteers, spouses and parents, in addition to our paid work.[16]

Discerning Your Calling

The most pressing question for many people is finding their particular calling in the realm of work. For some, it may be a case of revisioning their current work (as the earlier examples of MBA students shows). For others, it may be a matter of discerning a calling to another position. Discerning our calling can be fraught with difficulty and subjectivity, but here are some guidelines to consider when wrestling with questions of career and occupation.

First, take an inventory of your gifts, skills and talents. What are you good at? What are your strengths? What do you do well and what areas are you not so good at? You can do this more formally with various forms of testing available from career counselors, or more informally by seeking out people who know you, who you trust and who will talk to you honestly about your strengths and weaknesses.

Second, assess your desires, passions or concerns. What kinds of things do you dream of doing? Where is your heart in terms of the various arenas available to do God's work? What do you care deeply about? Are there pressing issues around you that move you to action? Try to evaluate your desires

---

[16]Lee Hardy, *The Fabric of This World* (Grand Rapids: Eerdmans, 1990).

without thinking about the dichotomy between business and ministry.

Third, get some exposure to various careers or occupations where your combination of talents and passions can be applied. Talk to people about what life would be like in a particular occupation, what they do in that occupation and how they envision themselves serving God there. In fact, the criteria of service to God and others should be a primary one to consider, even above pay and job satisfaction. If you can, do an internship or volunteer to help out in some of these areas. We urge churches and other civic institutions to be more helpful in setting up networks for people considering their calling to make it easier to get connected to people who are in various fields. Our churches, in particular, generally have good networks to help people decide whether they want to serve God in the church or the mission field. But we need ways to connect inquiring people with those already established in various occupations that serve God "in the world" too.

Fourth, ask an older, more experienced person to be your mentor as you seek out answers to these questions. This has to be a person who wants to see you succeed and who is willing to meet with you regularly to help you wrestle with these issues. For people in midlife who are revisiting these issues, a support network can be an important source of feedback for you.

Fifth, don't be afraid to make midcourse corrections. Discovering your paid occupational niche can be a long process and may change over time. You may clarify it only by trial and error. In fact, our current roles as college professors represent career shifts for both of us. Don't be afraid to try something out to see if it's a good fit. That may be the only way you'll find out.

God's call to pursue our passion is a spiritual calling from him. God calls people to serve him in the arenas in which their gifts, skills, talents and passions may be of most service. The Reformers taught us that the whole world is the theater of God's glory, and every legitimate occupation is an avenue in which God can be honored and we can do God's work. Our work is an altar and is designed to be God's work in the world. Frederick Buechner offers a nice summary of where to seek our paid vocation: "The place God calls you to is the place where your deep gladness and the world's deep hunger meet."[17]

---

[17]Frederick Buechner, *Wishful Thinking: A Seeker's ABC*, rev. ed. (San Francisco: HarperOne, 1993), p. 95.

CONCLUSION

In this chapter we have tried to make the case for the value of work in God's economy. We have argued that work was ordained by God before the entrance of sin. Work has great value because it is a significant part of the mandate to human beings to exercise responsible dominion over God's creation. Further, work has great value because it reflects who God is and who human beings are as made in God's image. We pointed out that work has been deeply affected by the reality of sin. Sin has not made work evil but has tarnished the original design for work.

We strongly affirm that work can and does still reflect God's original design—as transformational service. We have made the general claim that God ordained work as having great value. Not all work is good, nor is all work of value to God. We are making a prima facie case for the value of work as service to God.

In chapter two, we argue more specifically for business as an avenue of transformational service—to God and to the community—and in chapter three, as an arena of spiritual formation for individuals in the workplace. There we will make a prima facie case as well. We are not insisting that all business is for the common good, but rather that God has ordained it to be service to him and the community. We will provide some parameters and guidelines within which business must operate in order to maintain its ordained role as transformational service. These will not function as rigid checklists but rather as guiding principles to aid in the exercise of wisdom. Similarly, in chapter three we make the case that business is a crucible in which spiritual formation occurs, but it can also be an arena in which a person succumbs to a variety of temptations.

2

The Shape of a
Calling to Business

At thirty-eight, Anne has recently made a midcareer shift from social services into banking.[1] Anne was drawn into the industry through a family connection—her retired father had a long, successful career as a small-town bank manager. Her goal is to move into the managerial ranks as soon as possible, but in order to get her foot in the door Anne has accepted a position in the consumer lending division of a large, established institution. Anne was attracted to this particular organization because customer care is a regular emphasis in its promotional campaigns.

After six months in her position, Anne receives her first performance review. With high marks nearly across the board, she is told that if her current level of achievement is maintained, she will be a sure candidate to get onto the managerial fast track. The only item that could hold her back is the size of her loan portfolio. She is then encouraged by her supervisor to make a big push to bring in more clients or pursue follow-up loans with existing customers.

One afternoon, Anne receives an interesting phone call. A man calls to inquire about taking out a loan in order to finance the purchase of an automobile for someone he has met over the Internet. Anne agrees to meet with him the next morning. She finds that simply out of the goodness of his heart, the man is simply trying to help a woman he has been corresponding with via e-mail.

From his appearance and their ensuing conversation, Anne concludes

---

[1]While her name has been changed and her story modified slightly for illustrative purposes, Anne's story is real to life.

that the potential customer may not be "all there" mentally and emotionally. While he is clearly competent enough to understand the terms of the loan and has the financial ability to service it, she is concerned that he might be a potential scam victim or may be making a decision that will jeopardize his own financial future. The man is older and also seems lonely; Anne notes that parts of the conversation that should end quickly seem to go on and on. Even though Anne tries to dissuade him from taking the loan, the man leaves, stating that he intends to come back later that afternoon with some financial records in order to finalize the transaction.

Anne is very concerned about the matter and brings it to the attention of her supervisor, who urges Anne to make the loan. "Anne," she says, "we are in the loan *business*, not social services. Besides," she adds, lowering her voice to a whisper, "your career prospects, and mine, and, I might add, our bonuses, and our firm's quarterly numbers rest on new loan generation. Unless he is somehow financially unqualified, I expect you to be a team player and finalize that loan when he returns this afternoon. Otherwise, I will close the deal myself."

Anne leaves the conversation with her supervisor in a troubled frame of mind. Anne's Christian values helped draw her into banking, which, as modeled by her father, seemed like a good way to earn a living while also helping others achieve their dreams through the provision of sound financial services. Never did she imagine that her career advancement and the restfulness of her conscience could be threatened by refusing to make a loan that might wind up hurting someone. Anne quickly realizes that if this is going to be a common occurrence, she will soon be at another career crossroads.

Anne's disagreement with her supervisor is based, in no small part, on some important foundational issues surrounding the fundamental purpose of business. Whose interests should it serve? Should business exist only to make money or to help others live better lives along the way? By implication, what purposes should Anne's job as a banker (and her bank, and other businesses) serve?

Chapter one built a case for the general nobility of work. In this chapter we will look more specifically at the content of the call to work in business. After examining some common perspectives on the core purposes of business, we will look to Scripture for guidance on the shape of a Christian perspective on the purpose of business. We will argue that business (on both institutional and individual levels) should serve as a sacred partnership to help achieve divine purposes in this world. Simply put, business is a calling to help transform society, the lives of others and ourselves in ways that reflect God's intended patterns for living.

COMMON STORIES OF BUSINESS

Several dominant views or stories of business have served to shape many key assumptions and practices. While the following is not meant to be an exhaustive list, one common perspective is that business should serve the aim of making money alone. While any profession can be approached from this perspective, business seems to be an especially acute case. At an *individual* level this view is reflected in the pragmatism with which many business professionals describe their vocational path. A career in business mostly serves the purpose of earning income to pay bills and support other areas of life where real significance is to be found. As some of our graduate students have put it, "If life were free of charge, I would have done something with more personal meaning, like becoming a musician or a high school teacher. But living is expensive, and I knew that one day I would have a family to support, so I just sort of fell into a business career. I try to do my work honestly and with a good attitude, but most of the things I am really passionately devoted to are outside of my work." Taking this view to heart, someone like Anne would have to compartmentalize her life—by treating "work as work" or "business as business" and nothing more—if she hopes to earn a living and advance her career without a troubled conscience.

Others are bolder in stating that business is the best avenue to achieve their materialistic ambitions. Through the years we have had more than a few students unabashedly describe their attraction to a business career as one in which they will have the best chance to earn an income that will support "a comfortable, upscale lifestyle." More stark, perhaps, is the quest of some already wealthy businesspeople who have millions of dollars in various holdings, and in some cases, billions, but want more just to know what it feels like to be "really rich." An extreme but vivid example is entrepreneur Jim Clark, the founder of Netscape. The following is author Jim Collins's commentary on an account of Clark in Michael Lewis's book *The New New Thing:*

Despite his impressive résumé, Clark comes across as a man who is stuck on a monetary treadmill: He seems addicted to running after more and more, and then more still, without ever stopping to ask why. Late in the book, Lewis describes a scene in which he presses Clark on this very issue. Earlier, Clark had said that he would retire after he became "a real after-tax billionaire." Now he was worth $3 billion. What about his plans for retiring? "I just want to have more money than Larry Ellison," he says. "I don't know why. But once I have more money than Larry Ellison, I'll be satisfied."

But Lewis pressed further. In about six months, Clark would surpass Ellison in terms of net worth. Then what? Did Clark want more money than, say, Bill Gates? Lewis writes, " 'Oh, no,' Clark said, waving my question to the side of the room where the ridiculous ideas gather to commiserate with each other. 'That'll never happen.' A few minutes later, after the conversation had turned to other matters, he came clean. 'You know,' he said, 'just for one moment, I would kind of like to have the most. Just for one tiny moment.' "[2]

Many of us may marvel at Clark's insatiable quest for more, yet on a scaled-down level, haven't we all had similar thoughts? Happiness always seems to be just around the corner. Of course, this holds true regardless of what our current level of financial wealth may be.

At an *institutional* level, the view that business exists for the singular purpose of making money has nearly achieved the status of unquestioned, cultural assumption. Anne's supervisor, in the opening illustration, clearly holds it. The television show *The Apprentice* (with the opening theme song "For the Love of Money" by the O'Jays) shouts it from the rooftop. Profit is the primary criteria used to judge weekly contests and to settle the dramatic question of who "gets fired" in the dreaded boardroom face-off with the show's star, Donald Trump.

Beyond popular culture, this view has serious philosophical support and is the conventional view within the fields of finance and economics. The late Nobel Laureate in Economics, Milton Friedman, popularized the idea when he argued in a *New York Times Magazine* essay (1970) that the only legitimate purpose and aim of business, particularly publicly held corporations, is to maximize profits for its owners, the shareholders. As

---

[2]Jim Collins, "Built to Flip," *Fast Company* 32 (2000). Available at www.fastcompany.com/magazine/32/builttoflip.html.

long as a corporation is acting lawfully and within "ethical custom," achieving other objectives, even "noble" ones like care for an elderly customer, employee development or environmental protection (unless the bottom line is somehow enhanced long-term) is tantamount to theft from the owners.[3] Friedman's view is still widely held (and debated) today.[4] From this perspective Anne may want to consider shifting to a career in financial counseling for a *nonprofit* organization if helping others is her primary motivation. At the end of the day business should be driven by value creation as defined by economic measures alone, and she should expect that situations like the one in front of her will likely repeat themselves over and over again if she stays.

To be clear, Friedman's argument is not an endorsement of short-term greed. His perspective comes from a philosophical orientation that believes that society runs best if the "market" (versus government regulation) is left alone to sort things out, private property (wealth) rights are protected and self-interest is accounted for as a primary motivational force behind human behavior. It is also important to note that Friedman does not extend his argument to privately held companies, who may be purposed in whatever direction the owners wish, including charitable ones.

In contrast to the profit maximization perspective, an increasingly popular view holds that corporations should create both economic and social value for a broad range of "stakeholders," including owners, customers, suppliers, surrounding communities and the environment. Corporations need to make a profit for shareholders, but strategic decisions must be balanced with advancing the interests of other groups who also have a stake in the organization.[5]

---

[3]See Milton Friedman, "The Social Responsibility of Business Is to Increase Its Profits," *New York Times Magazine* (1970), in Scott B. Rae and Kenman L. Wong, *Beyond Integrity: A Judeo-Christian Approach to Business Ethics*, 2nd ed. (Grand Rapids: Zondervan, 2004), pp. 131-35.

[4]See, for example, Milton Friedman, John Mackey and T. J. Rodgers, "Rethinking the Social Responsibilities of Business: A Reason Debate," *Reason.com,* October 2005, www.reason.com/archives/2005/10/01/rethinking-the-social-responsi.

[5]Our point here is to dialogue with the dominant views as practiced by current organizations rather than to be exhaustive in our treatment of available theoretical approaches. In addition to stakeholder theory or, more accurately, theories, a variety of views have been proposed. As examples, Thomas Dunfee and Thomas Donaldson have proposed a social contract approach (see their *Ties That Bind: A Social Contracts Approach to Business Ethics* [Boston: Harvard University Press, 1999], and Helen Alford and Michael Naughton propose a common goods approach (see their *Managing As If Faith Mattered* [Notre Dame, Ind.: University of Notre Dame Press, 2001]).

"Stakeholder theory" may be supported and shaped by various philosophical orientations or "normative cores" that serve as compasses. One version, as developed by Whole Foods founder and CEO John Mackey is based on a relaxed view of ownership rights and more positive appraisals of human nature. Private wealth, according to this view, should be used more intentionally for public benefit, and building entire economic systems on the basis of narrow, self-interested assumptions about people has a predictable effect—people act in increasingly narrow, self-interested ways. In contrast, assuming the best about people might just lead to better social outcomes.[6] A stakeholder-oriented view of business might serve to relax the tension Anne is currently facing, though it still would not answer the more immediate question of what a balance would precisely look like.

These are just a sampling of the prevailing views of business that exist. Some of them (particularly the "making money" ones) are so steeped in our cultural values that it's challenging to find much wrong with them. After all, money is necessary for living, and the acquisition of the finer (material) things in life seems to be just a part of the American (and increasingly, the global) dream. Furthermore, how else might a business be determined a success if not for the amount of money it makes?

Perspectives such as these are not so much wrong (though a *love* of material things may be) as they are terribly incomplete. With respect to the broader category of work, viewing business as only a means to an end falls short (see chap. 1). Such an approach reflects a split that some researchers have documented as a "Sunday-Monday gap" between work and the values that shape meaning in the rest of one's life. Moreover, such a view focuses solely on the "external goods" of business, while neglecting the value of the work itself and the possible broader contributions business can make.[7]

---

[6]See John Mackey's response to Friedman in Friedman, Mackey and Rodgers, "Rethinking the Social Responsibilities of Business: A Reason Debate." For other formulations of stakeholder theory, particularly from an academic perspective, see R. Edward Freeman, *Strategic Management: A Stakeholder Approach* (Boston: Pitman Harper & Row, 1984). This text is regarded as a seminal work in the formation of stakeholder theory. Also see Brad Agle et al., "Towards Superior Stakeholder Theory," *Business Ethics Quarterly* 18 (2008): 153-90; also see Jeffrey S. Harrison and R. Edward Freeman, "Stakeholders, Social Responsibility, and Performance: Empirical Evidence and Theoretical Perspectives," *Academy of Management Journal* 42 (1999): 479-87.

[7]For thoughtful discussions on how business tends to value external goods at the expense of internal ones, see Alasdair MacIntyre, *After Virtue*, 2nd ed. (Notre Dame, Ind.: University of Notre Dame Press, 1984); and Scott Waalkes, "Money or Business: A Case Study of Christian Virtue Ethics in Corporate Work," *Christian Scholars Review*, fall 2008. See also Alford and

While we will have more to say on this later, the existing institutional perspectives on business, particularly the profit maximization view, fall short for similar reasons, namely, too narrow a focus on a singular end result.

FOUNDATIONS FOR A CHRISTIAN VISION FOR BUSINESS

A Christian vision of business (on both individual and institutional levels) differs markedly from the views just described on both the levels of foundational worldview and ultimate aims. Such a vision is grounded in and modeled after divine patterns for living as shaped by God's purposes for his creation. In order to arrive at a deeper understanding of these patterns, it is important to explore several important theological ideas, including the purpose, content and scope of God's mission in the world; the human role within this agenda; and the nature of people, institutions and social structures.

The Bible tells us that God's ultimate purpose or mission is to bring glory to himself by the redemption of *all* creation. Both the overall "creation, Fall, redemption and consummation" narrative structure and specific passages reveal that the scope of his redemptive mission is holistic (multidimensional)—physical, spiritual, material (economic) and social. In sum, God desires for human beings to flourish by being in relationship with him (Deut 6:4-6; Mt 22:34-46; Jn 15:4), to have physical abundance (Ex 3:8; Eccles 2:24; 3:12; Joel 3:18; 1 Tim 6:17) and to live in a spirit of true harmony with others and with the earth (Jn 13:35; Rom 12:18; Col 3:12-15).

Some Christians in the pietist tradition limit God's mission of reconciliation (and thereby the scope of human flourishing) to the relationship between himself and humankind ("spiritual" transformation alone). This restriction often leads to the view that our work on earth (whether in business or not) should serve the primary purpose of evangelism. Someone holding such a view might say, "Why should we work to make business (or anything else on earth) better when it will all be destroyed someday anyway? God cares about our souls, and our only mission should be to lead people heavenward!"[8]

A careful look at the Bible reveals that the content of God's redemptive

---

Naughton, *Managing As If Faith Mattered.*
[8]See further discussion of this point in chap. 10.

mission is much broader. For instance, the Hebrew word *shalom* captures the core essence of God's mission. Sar Shalom (Prince of Peace) is one of the Old Testament names used to describe the ministry of the Messiah (Is 9:6). A word study of *shalom* reveals that it signifies wholeness, health, peace, welfare, prosperity, rest, harmony, and the absence of agitation or discord. Furthermore, many of the Hebraic laws prescribe individual and communal practices that insured that physical needs were met and that relationships with neighbors, those outside of the community and the land reflected justice and mercy (Ex 22:25-27; 23:10-11; Lev 19:33-34; 25; Deut 15:1-18; 16:18-20; 24:17-22).

Jesus' own life as recorded in the New Testament reflects similarly holistic concerns (Mt 11:2-4; 25:31-46; Lk 4:16-21). As Ken Eldred puts it, "The ministry of Jesus demonstrates that God cares about transforming people's spiritual, economic and social conditions. He fed the hungry, called people to personal holiness, healed the sick, taught in the synagogue, preached to thousands and affirmed the social outcasts."[9]

While God extends his reconciliatory efforts to all people, the Bible indicates that he has a special place in his heart for the marginalized. Building on a theme touched on in chapter one, this concern is reflected in places such as the exodus story and many Hebraic laws that protected the poor, widowed and orphaned. The prophets also connected the pursuit of social and communal justice with something close to the heart of God. Isaiah 58:5-8 makes clear the importance of loosening the chains of the oppressed and sharing food with the hungry by connecting these practices with proper religious disciplines such as fasting and inward character traits such as righteousness. Likewise, Jeremiah 22:16 equates defending the cause of the poor and needy with what it means to know God.[10] This teaching is echoed in both the Psalms (Ps 10:17-18; 82:2-4) and wisdom books (Prov 14:31; 22:2).

The content of Jesus' teaching, particularly his proclamation of the kingdom of God, is consistent with these themes. In the Sermon on the Mount (Mt 5–7) Jesus clarifies that the nature of God's kingdom or reign

---

[9]Ken Eldred, *God Is at Work* (Ventura, Calif.: Regal Books, 2005), p. 67.

[10]For a thoughtful and well-developed account of biblical justice and God's concern for the poor, see Stephen C. Mott and Ronald J. Sider, "Economic Justice: A Biblical Paradigm," in *Toward a Just and Caring Society: Christian Responses to Poverty in America*, ed. David P. Gushee (Grand Rapids: Baker, 1999), pp. 15-45.

represents a great reversal of worldly values.[11] In sum, the divine kingdom is an inclusive one in which the first shall be last, the undesirable are welcomed at a banquet spread for all, and no one, not even those who are seen as losers, will be beyond blessing (Lk 14:10-14). This theme is continued in the later letters of the New Testament. For example, the mark of true religion, according to James, is taking care of widows and orphans in their distress (Jas 1:27). Orphans and widows are used here as figures of speech to represent the most vulnerable and marginalized in the culture, and include other classes of the traditionally oppressed. These characteristics or marks of the kingdom are especially important for the task before us as it relates to business and serving the broader community. Glen Stassen and David Gushee note, *"What its [the kingdom's] characteristics are* is crucial for Christian ethics, for Christian discipleship, for Christian living and for the response of faith(fullness)."[12]

In addition to its holistic content and special consideration of the marginalized, the *scope* of God's mission includes the transformation of individuals, social institutions (like business organizations) and structures (like global economic systems) to more closely reflect the fullness of shalom. It is important to note that various traditions (e.g., Reformed and Anabaptist) disagree with respect to the amount of change and transformation that is possible and over the means to use (e.g., direct engagement versus modeling an alternative reality). However, most would agree that although the kingdom will not realize its fullness until a future time, we are still to work in the present with a hopeful nod to the future.

Some Christians live with the assumption that transformation is limited to individual people and translate this belief into the workplace by focusing on matters of personal integrity and laboring with the right attitude alone. Human experience tells us that broken institutions and structures act as "principalities and powers" (Eph 6:12) and limit our ability to make the world a better place. Anne's situation is a good illustration. The fact that she has to choose between upholding important values and being "successful" speaks to the broken nature of the broader context in which

---

[11]For further discussion of this important topic in the teaching of Jesus, see Allen Verhey, *The Great Reversal: Ethics and the New Testament* (Grand Rapids: Eerdmans, 1984).

[12]Glen H. Stassen and David P. Gushee, *Kingdom Ethics: Following Jesus in Contemporary Context* (Downers Grove, Ill.: InterVarsity Press, 2003), pp. 20-21.

she is operating. Likewise, in many headlining scandals, such as subprime mortgages, it is clear that people or organizations that worked with integrity found themselves at a significant financial disadvantage, at least in the more immediate time horizon.

Scripture reveals that institutional and structural change is well within the scope of God's intentions. While not be applied literally today, the Hebraic law had a clear social dimension and was intended as much more than an individual moral code. It was designed to transform Israel into a "kingdom of priests and a holy nation" (Ex 19:5-6). The law was intended for the transformation of the *community*, not just the lives of individuals. The law actually structured ancient Israel's society and institutions. For example, Leviticus 25 structured how real estate, virtually the only productive capital in biblical times, was transacted. It set up the Year of Jubilee as well as the law of redemption, both of which functioned to insure that people were not left without an opportunity to provide for themselves (see chap. 4). The Jubilee mandated that all land revert to its original owners and all slaves be released on the fiftieth year. The law of redemption had more immediate effect, requiring that land sold due to economic hardship be bought back by a relative and returned to the owner, so he or she was not precluded from the means to provide for his or her family.

This emphasis is further captured in the prophets' vision of the kingdom, which includes individual transformation and a proper ordering of society. For example, a part of the portrait of the Messiah is that he comes to bring justice to the nations, in addition to his coming to provide individual salvation. In Isaiah 42:1-4, the Servant of Yahweh (the Messiah) promises to bring justice, which refers to an ordering of society in which the injustices, oppression and marginalization of the vulnerable will no longer be. That is, the kingdom that the prophets envision has both an individual and social component—individual in that people will be spiritually renewed, and social in that the society will reflect God's righteousness in relationships and institutions. Likewise, in the New Testament book of Ephesians, the apostle Paul informs us that our struggle is not just against human forces but also "against principalities and powers." Max Stackhouse points out, "The Greek term for the powers *(exousia)* . . . is often linked with official leaders, but more often with the symbolic power of the offices and roles they play in the common life—that is, with principalities, authorities, or dominions."[13]

While the concept of human flourishing is far too complicated to capture in short space, we will proceed on a working definition that human flourishing is captured by the full meaning of shalom, is holistic in nature (physical, emotional, spiritual, social) and broad in scope (individual, communal and systemic).

Once we have a sense of the content, aims and scope of God's mission, understanding our role is another foundational concept necessary to developing a Christian vision for business. God has extended a generous invitation to be his junior partners in achieving his goals. We can see in the Genesis creation narrative that human beings are given dominion and stewardship over the earth, and also the important role of regent or God's earthly representative (Gen 1:28; 2:15). Moreover, the role offered to us is so prominent that our work on earth will last into eternity. Theologian Miroslav Volf argues that in fashioning a "new heaven and earth" God will not destroy everything and begin anew (creation *ex nihilo*) but will take what we have done in this world as building blocks and perfect it (transformation *mundi*).[14]

Another foundational concept is an understanding of the nature of people, organizations and social structures or systems. This gives us a deep sense of context and provides implications about realistic expectations for change. Humans are broken people with a proclivity toward vices such as selfishness, pride and greed. However, the Bible teaches that we are also made in God's image *(imago Dei)* and are therefore capable of moral good, rational thought, creativity and relationality. In sum, we are made in God's image but marred and broken at the same time. So, we are neither evil nor angelic but both. Economic systems and business practices must account for this dual reality. To emphasize only the worst aspects of humanity expects too little of people and may well encourage narrowly self-interested and even selfish behavior. In contrast, emphasiz-

---

[13]Max L. Stackhouse and Peter Paris, eds., *Religion and the Powers of the Common Life*, vol. 1 of *God and Globalization* (Harrisburg, Penn.: Trinity Press International, 2000), p. 35. Also see Hendrik Berkhof, *Christ and the Powers* (Scottdale, Penn.: Herald, 1962).

[14]Miroslav Volf, *Work in the Spirit: Toward a Theology of Work* (New York: Oxford University Press, 1991). Similar lines of thought can be found in the work of theologians such as Richard Mouw, *When the Kings Come Marching In: Isaiah and the New Jerusalem* (Grand Rapids: Eerdmans, 1983), and Darrell Cosden, *The Heavenly Good of Earthly Work* (Peabody, Mass.: Hendrickson, 2006).

ing only the divine aspects of human nature ignores the reality that, at least in part, humans are motivated by self-interest, and typically results in a lack of accountability.

While they are not literally created in the image of God, organizations similarly reflect this duality. There are no perfect business organizations, and even the ones that may be considered the most broken will have elements that may be surprisingly redemptive. For example, a family-owned company that gets regular recognition for being one of the Seattle area's best employers is in the payday lending business, controversial for its high (some would say usurious) interest rates charged to customers who are among the most vulnerable and least able to pay.

Social structures, like the global economy, also produce a mixed blessing. While these points will be discussed at further length in chapter five, the global economy does a lot of good by producing great wealth and material abundance. However, at the same time, people's lives are affected by tremendous amounts of risk, uncertainty and disruption, and by ecological and cultural damage.

Our aim in presenting the dual nature inherent in earthly things is not to confuse good and evil, nor is it to argue that we shouldn't attempt to draw lines between them. Rather, we are simply shedding light on the complex context we operate in. Sometimes we are left with imperfect, complex choices. Our current task must be to use careful discernment in promoting aspects of business that reflect God's intentions, and boldly and creatively work to transform the parts that do not. William Schweiker keenly observes:

> The reduction of the meaning of the "world" to any single appraisal—to say, "the world is utterly fallen"; "the world is obviously 'God's body'"—falls below the complexity of Christian thinking as well as actual experience. . . . A properly Christian response to social and cultural existence will endorse its goodness as created, resist it as fallen, work for its transformation, and hope in its salvation.[15]

---

[15]William Schweiker, "Responsibility in the World of Mammon: Theology, Justice, and Transnational Corporations," in *Religion and the Powers of the Common Life*, ed. Max L. Stackhouse and Peter Paris, vol. 1 of *God and Globalization* (Harrisburg, Penn.: Trinity Press International, 2000), p. 111.

BUSINESS AS TRANSFORMATIONAL SERVICE

Based on the foundational concepts just described, we can now begin to sketch the contours of a Christian vision for business. Simply put, becoming an active and intentional partner in God's mission, business (as both an institution and a profession) must continually act in ways that contribute to human flourishing. Products and services should primarily improve the lives of users and the broader community. Humans are to be treated with dignity (and not as economic units or simply as laborers) because we are made in God's image and have eternal value. Creation should be responsibly stewarded because God made nature and desires that humans live in harmony with it, and because it affects our well-being (see chap. 9). Because God cares for the marginalized, global economic structures and more immediate business decisions must be scrutinized to make sure we don't "trample on the heads" of the voiceless (Amos 2:6-7).

To be certain, business cannot "solve all of the world's problems," as the title of a recent book suggests.[16] Although a highly powerful force, business must act in cooperation with other people, institutions and structures. Moreover, as we will note in more detail, business takes place in a context shaped by competitive realities, pressures from various stakeholders and limits on time and capital, so at times a gap will exist between what we should do and what we can do, and we may be forced to choose the wise (versus perfect) course of action or live with a tolerable harmony.

We propose "transformational service for the common good" as one way to capture the shape of a calling to business. Both *transformational* and *service* are key biblical concepts deeply rooted in God's mission. When combined, the terms offer a normative perspective for business (and perhaps many other professions and social institutions).

The term *transformation* implies positive change toward ourselves, others and our social institutions to reflect human flourishing. *Transform* (versus *rebuild*) also connotes that business already reflects God's intentions to some degree. While perhaps overstating it, Robert Sirico argues that we shouldn't seek to "bring Christ into the workplace, but to discover his presence already there."[17] So, in many cases our task is more

---

[16]Michael Strong, *Be the Solution: How Entrepreneurs and Conscious Capitalists Can Solve All the World's Problems* (Hoboken, N.J.: John Wiley, 2009).

[17]Robert Sirico, "The Entrepreneurial Vocation," in *Beyond Integrity: A Judeo-Christian Approach*

akin to remodeling a house than tearing one down and completely rebuilding it, though some parts may need total demolition and ground up reconstruction.

The word *service* fits well from a look at the overarching theme of the Scriptures. Isaiah 53 depicts the coming Messiah as a suffering servant. The idea that "the first shall be last" is a key part of the kingdom Jesus described in Matthew 19–20. The Gospels record that Jesus modeled "servanthood" through his life (see chap. 7). When people expected the Messiah to come in earthly glory, he was born in a manger, lived under humble circumstances and was put to death in a manner befitting a common criminal.

For Christ's followers service is not just a moral obligation or an orientation toward others, it is also a practice or spiritual discipline that provides a pathway to a life of true abundance. In fact, the emerging field of positive psychology gives scientific support to biblical wisdom on the abundant life, including the role of serving others. Consistent with the spirit of Jesus' statement that "whoever loses his life for my sake will find it" (Mt 10:39; 16:25), research has found that acts of gratitude, kindness and altruism (and not necessarily higher incomes) are among actions that can boost human happiness, which in turn can influence our physical well-being.[18]

Service is a term used often in business as an orientation toward customers and to describe an approach to leadership (servant leadership). However, with roots in the Latin word for slavery—*servitium*—the term can imply passivity and simply doing what another wishes. As such, questions like service to whom, appropriateness of the service offered and the legitimacy of the greater purpose may be overlooked. Some needs and wants of consumers or employees (those that may be harmful to themselves or others) should *not* be served or met. Given the nature of God's primary mission, the central quality or shape of the service offered must be characterized by *transformation* of human lives and institutions that allows flourishing in all the ways God has intended.

---

to *Business Ethics*, ed. Scott B. Rae and Kenman L. Wong, 2nd ed. (Grand Rapids: Zondervan, 2004), pp. 60-66.

[18]Claudia Willis, "The New Science of Human Happiness," *Time*, January 9, 2005, citing the work of Sarah Lyubomirksi, Robert Emmons and Martin Seligman.

Once we have acquired a sense of the broad shape of a Christian vision for business, we must allow it to change our thinking and approach to business. Change begins with the transformation of our outlook. On an *individual* level this means changing our reasons and motivations for being in a business career. While not to be dismissed, the pragmatic reason of paying bills, the chance to demonstrate a life of faith, or an opportunity to use one's gifts are all well intentioned and noble, but incomplete, as we stated earlier. They must be placed in the proper context of service to God and neighbor.

A repurposing must also occur on an *institutional* level. The traditional purpose and philosophy of profit maximization and the emerging alternative of balancing stakeholder interests both fall short. Profit maximization as the sole measurement of business success is reductionistic because it fails to account for how well other objectives are being met. Stakeholder theory gets closer to the ideal, but terms like *advancing* and *balancing* (used to describe obligations to stakeholders) are vague and not self-defining without the benefit of a larger story, values framework or worldview for guidance. Rightly understood, transformational service for the common good can provide such a guiding narrative.

An important question to examine is how profit fits into this vision. In fact, some readers may object to the devaluing of profit and may wonder if service isn't something we do without regard to self-interest or financial gain. After all, isn't it the proper role of government and nonprofit organizations, and not business, to offer services without the prospect of financial gain? Coming from the other direction, some may wonder why profit is necessary at all. For example, we have both been part of business and theology faculty gatherings in which the latter will say at the end, "While we have come to appreciate business more, we still don't see why making a profit is necessary."

We can see several legitimate perspectives (not mutually exclusive) on profit as *one* objective of business that would fit well under the auspices of a Christian vision for business. To begin with, profit can legitimately be seen as a *means* of providing the financial resources necessary to sustain the other service objectives of the organization. For example, Max De Pree, author and former CEO of furniture manufacturer Herman Miller (a Fortune 500 company), states that "the primary function of profit is to fund the future of the company."[19] Similarly, Whole Foods CEO John Mackey observes:

> Making high profits is the means to the end of fulfilling Whole Foods' core business mission. We want to improve the health and well-being of everyone on the planet through higher-quality foods and better nutrition, and we can't fulfill this mission unless we are highly profitable. High profits are necessary to fuel our growth across the United States and the world. Just as people cannot live without eating, so a business cannot live without profits. But most people don't live to eat, and neither must a business live just to make profits.[20]

Without the prospect of profit, maintaining the health of a business becomes much more challenging. For example, unless a company shows a healthy profit, its cost of capital will likely increase, negatively affecting the organization's ability to meet its other objectives. "no margin, no mission," as the old saying goes.

Second, profit can also be seen as a byproduct or *reward*. Rather than focusing on profit, a business that meets its core objectives—such as developing excellent products or services, serving customers, treating employees with respect and dignity, carefully managing its finances, and serving its community—may well find that profit will come as a result. An excellent example is Johnson & Johnson's credo, which in sum acknowledges a fair return to stockholders as a "final responsibility," *after* obligations to doctors, nurses, patients, employees and the community.[21]

Finally, earning profit can be seen as a direct means of *service* to the owners or shareholders, who have risked their capital for the growth and development of the enterprise. Profit does not have to be associated with something unseemly, such as greed. Many shareholders (or the institutions managing their money) invest for noble purpose, such as retirement or sending their children to college. Others donate company stock to charitable causes. Charitable institutions themselves invest money in the stock market in order to maximize the dollars available for their core service

---

[19]Max De Pree, cited in Sarah Jio, "Good Business," *Seattle Pacific University Response Magazine* 26, no. 5 (2004). Available at www.spu.edu/depts/uc/response/winter2k4/goodbusiness.html.

[20]Friedman, Mackey and Rodgers, "Rethinking the Social Responsibilities of Business: A Reason Debate."

[21]Found at www.jnj.com/connect/about-jnj/jnj-credo/.

missions. Increasing the economic value of investments then is a direct form of service to investors.

Once we have a renewed sense of purpose, including a proper view of profit, we can then allow it to spread across and seep down the entire landscape of business. Nothing should be held back from such scrutiny. Transformational service needs to be holistic in scope. For example, we may treat our customers well but squeeze our employees or source goods, strongly suspecting that someone may be exploited along the supply chain. We may visibly give to charitable causes but ignore the fact that our products or services contribute to environmental decay. As much as possible these types of disconnects must be seamlessly brought together.

Likewise, business as transformational service affects not just how we do business but *what business we are in*. While we noted in chapter one that a vocational approach to work signifies more of an attitude than an arena, our *specific* place of operation does matter. Do our products or services improve the lives of their users and the broader community? There are many profitable products and services available in the marketplace that are downright damaging. Many "goods" on the market contribute to conspicuous consumption (and thereby divide people along economic lines) by playing too much on status and being envied. Others are cheaply made, disposable and pollute our landfills. Even if made with exploitation-free labor and marketed with the utmost transparency, the question of whether they should be made at all needs to be considered. Lee Hardy states in *The Fabric of This World*:

> Even when we move into the realm of the morally unobjectionable, however, clearly some jobs—given the priorities of the kingdom of God—are to be preferred over others. Here all things may be permissible but not all things are expedient. In some jobs my neighbor is less well served than others. . . . Simply having the right attitude, the Christian attitude is not enough. One must also take into consideration the social content of one's work: am I, in my job, making a positive contribution to community, am I helping to meet legitimate needs, am I somehow enhancing what is true, what is noble, and what is worthy in human life?[22]

---

[22]Lee Hardy, *The Fabric of This World: Inquiries into Calling, Career Design and the Design of Human Work* (Grand Rapids: Eerdmans, 1990), p. 95.

Of course, these categories are not always easily decipherable, and we can easily slip into the territory of judgmental legalism in placing an industry, a product or a service into the category of "unacceptable." Most things in our complex world cannot be so neatly separated, and formulas often overlook legitimate exceptions. Faithfully asking honest questions (like the ones that come later in this chapter) and pursuing the ideals as best as we can is probably more realistic and what is required of us.

It is also important to hold out the possibility that people can be strategically called to work in and help change imperfect sectors of the world. We are aware of professionals who are working for transformation in what seem to be less than savory industries and organizations. One serves in an executive role at a hip-hop record company led by a well-known and controversial figure, and the other began his film-making career directing movies in the horror genre. They are not alone as far as historical precedent. Many Old Testament biblical figures (e.g., Joseph and Daniel) who are cited for their faithfulness worked for "organizations" and leaders that would not do very well if measured by their encouragement of human flourishing. Within the Bible is a long record of how God uses imperfect people, institutions and systems to accomplish his purposes.

Finally, business must develop an acute sensitivity to how its actions affect the voiceless. Given God's concern for the marginalized, the structure of economic systems and actual business decisions and processes (versus just giving to charity or volunteer work) should give special consideration for the poor and vulnerable, be they employees at the lowest status and pay levels, or members of the external community). While financial gain is not the point, a lengthy study of companies that invest in employees at the lowest levels of their organizations led the researchers to the conclusion that the companies actually increased their profitably by doing so. This goes against conventional wisdom that employees at these levels are readily replaceable or are not as essential to profitability.[23]

How Wide a Gap?

At this juncture, it is reasonable to wonder if there is anything redemptive about business as it exists. Doesn't business already create a lot of value for

---

[23]Jody Heymann and Magda Barrera, *Profit at the Bottom of the Ladder: Creating Value by Investing in Your Work Force* (Boston: Harvard Business Press, 2010).

people and communities? Undoubtedly, we would be remiss in overlooking the positive side of the ledger or the ways business already reflects divine intentions and that deserve affirmation. Business partially promotes human flourishing in ways that go well beyond making money. In particular, by engaging in lasting tasks such as creating, sustaining, providing and stewarding, business helps to serve the vision of transformational service.

Businesspeople and organizations mirror God's creativity in inventing, manufacturing and distributing many necessary goods and services.[24] In most cases business achieves these tasks far more effectively, efficiently and perhaps even fairly than the simple bartering systems of old, and the government and nonprofit organizations of today. The fact that people and communities could obtain the goods they needed without violence is of relatively recent origin, owing to the advent of market-based economic systems.

Business invents and makes products such as lifesaving medical devices, computers, airplanes, iPods and ovens. Many of these products require large amounts of capital to fund research and development, amounts that would be difficult to secure through donations or taxation. Business is also heavily involved in publishing books, making films and recording and distributing music, and also provides "third places" (places that are not home or work, like coffee shops) where people can meet and build community.[25]

Business also mirrors God's provisional activity by creating wealth and opportunities for employment. While we will comment further on this point in chapter five, market-based economies (and the critical role that business plays within it) represent the only known system that can actually create the new financial wealth to lift people out of economic poverty. On a more immediate scale, business also engages in the task of provision by creating many jobs that sustain people economically through high wages and good benefits. Business is said to employ approximately 55 percent of the American workforce, with small business serving as the primary ve-

---

[24]Michael Novak, *The Fire of Invention* (Lanham, Md.: Rowman & Littlefield, 1997). See also Sirico, "The Entrepreneurial Vocation," pp. 60-66; and R. Paul Stevens, *Doing God's Business* (Grand Rapids: Eerdmans, 2006).

[25]Other forms of flourishing or well-being, namely, spiritual and social, have arguably suffered because of our "needs" getting out of hand and our increasing technological dependency. However, a counterargument is that life would not be as idyllic as some might imagine without some of the modern conveniences available to us.

hicle for new jobs.[26] Job creation also has a multiplier effect. Economists tell us that for every well-paying new job in some sectors (such as technology), another two to three jobs are created in other industries, government and the nonprofit sector.

Beyond just providing the opportunity to earn wages, business is also responsible for creating many "good jobs" that offer challenge, opportunities for personal development and at least partially fulfill the human needs for achievement and community by providing the opportunity to use ingenuity, creativity and collaborate with others on tasks.

Business also helps build a tax base for communities, which pay for many government services, and contributes countless dollars and volunteer hours to charitable and social causes. While some, and perhaps even most, of this "giving" is no doubt motivated by public relations motives and might be properly characterized as investment, communities do benefit. For example, Home Depot often partners with KaBOOM! to build playgrounds on a voluntary basis. Home Depot benefits by having an additional venue to train its workers, acquiring good publicity and making itself more attractive as a place to work, but there should be no doubt that the community enjoys new play structures.

Additionally, the role that business plays in community building and peace and civility should not be underestimated. Countries and regions of the world that engage in trade with one another have more incentives to peacefully resolve conflicts rather than go to war.[27]

At the same time that business is doing so much good in the world, however, there is much to it that runs counter to shalom/kingdom ideals. For example, a strong argument could be made that the global economic system we have is so flawed that vibrant economic growth actually depends on the promotion of wasteful, conspicuous consumption (which leads to social, spiritual and environmental problems).

Many parts of business operate under and promote a worldview or value system that runs on a reversal of God's ordering of human life and its institutions. Revealing its distance from God's kingdom, in which the last shall be

---

[26]Donald Schmeltekopf, "The Moral Context of Business," address given to business students and faculty at Baylor University, Waco, Texas, on October 20, 2003. Available at www.baylor .edu/business/news.php?action=story&story=34170.

[27]See for example Timothy Fort, *Prophets, Profits and Peace: The Positive Role of Business in Promoting Religious Tolerance* (New Haven, Conn.: Yale University Press, 2008), p. 25.

first, the powerful are usually first in line in the world of business. For instance, in almost every situation with negative economic news, some of the already wealthy find a way to manipulate markets and further enrich themselves. In any "bubble," whether it's real estate, technology stocks or mortgages, for example, the powerful make their money and get out, vacating the space long before the collapse occurs, leaving taxpayers and small investors with losses and financial burden. Restitution is rarely, if ever, made.

Likewise, powerful executives often tilt the distribution of results in an inequitable direction. Often there is no relationship between what executives and employees are paid. Organizational leaders can also protect themselves against any possible contingency. Golden parachutes ensure an attractive landing in case their companies get bought and the leaders are let go. Employment contracts guarantee a large payout even if leaders are fired for failing to do their jobs well, whereas rank-and-file employees, who also contribute to an organization's success, are usually left without such benefits. In contrast to a vision of justice, shalom and the upside-down nature of the kingdom, business often operates on opposite principles. Blessed are the proud, powerful and wealthy!

Other examples of this in business are even less visible. For example, many businesses may claim to serve others but are really out to serve themselves. They may talk about business as service only because it is what is expected or it brings a net gain on the bottom line. They may treat employees well not because it is right to do so but because they want to get more out of them. Some businesses may go green simply to bring in the "green," as environmentally friendly products may now return high margins.

Likewise, many conventional management theories rely on materialistic and individualistic underpinnings that assume the worst about human nature, leading to motivational techniques and incentive systems that emphasize material rewards alone, all the while ignoring and even undermining other dimensions of human well-being (i.e., psychological, spiritual, ecological).[28]

---

[28]For an interesting critique of management theories, see Bruno Dyck and David Schroeder, "Management, Theology and Moral Points of View: Towards an Alternative to the Conventional Materialist-Individualist Ideal-Type of Management," *Journal of Management Studies* 42 (2005): 705-35. Also see Fabrizio Ferraro, Jeffrey Pfeffer and Robert I. Sutton, "Economics Language and Assumptions: How Theories Can Become Self-Fulfilling," *Academy of Management Review* 30 (2005): 8-24.

Table 1. Business for the Common Good Framework

	Resist/Reform	Tolerate	Ideal/Affirm
Mission/Purpose	Short-term wealth attainment. Abundance is gained at the expense of other stakeholders or other measures of well-being.		Lasting and holistic value creation optimized for all stakeholders. Purpose is embedded and reflected seamlessly across all functions and decisions (sourcing, manufacturing, marketing, accounting, etc.).
Relationships (with God, others, self)	Others are treated as though they only exist to service our purposes or as objects to be moved. Vulnerable people remain invisible and voiceless. This divides people needlessly, creates or promotes envy and strife. Greed, dishonesty and dehumanizing others is encouraged. This harms a healthy sense of self. Material objects, individual financial success, ambition, self and power are worshiped more as a result.		Others are treated with dignity and respect and have a deepened sense of purpose. The vulnerable are given a voice. People are brought together in a spirit of reconciliation and harmony. Generosity, care, honesty and humility are cultivated. A healthy sense of self is enhanced. God is worshiped more and the beauty of others is enhanced.
Resources (economic, physical, etc.)	Managed carelessly or without regard for long-term impact.		Managed in ways that honor the spirit of stewardship and trusteeship. There is a deep concern for long-term impact and the lives of future generations.
Products/Services (what business we are in)	Products and services that have little or no regard for enhancing life and are not respectful of our physical environment.		Products/services that enhance life and enable truth, beauty, goodness and reconciliation to flourish in people's lives.
Methods (how we do business)	Dishonest, manipulative and unjust. Disrespectful of self and others. We would not want to switch places with a customer, employee, supplier, shareholder or community member.		Honest, dignified and respectful. Treating others like we would members of our own family. We would gladly switch places with other stakeholders.

Guidelines

Given the fact that business is both good and broken, how should we engage it? How can we begin to draw distinctions between the types of business activities that promote the goals established by a vision of the common good rather than work against it? Table 1 is offered as guiding framework, and the descriptors should be seen as on a continuum. (Column 2 is left blank deliberately for readers to fill in.) We strongly emphasize that we do not intend this framework to be used as a checklist or a formula. Moreover, we realize these are ideals that no business, product or service can achieve in their entirety. However, we must set goals according to God's expectations and not whether or not we can reach them.

The following are a few more questions to complement table 1.

Mission/purpose. Why does our business exist? Is it to "make money" or to enhance people's lives? How is a greater purpose reflected in all that we do?

Relationships. Who or what do people tend more to worship as a result of involvement in our business?[29] How do our decisions and actions affect the internal qualities of the people with whom we come into contact?

Are people involved (employees, suppliers, customers, shareholders, etc.) treated with respect, dignity and fairness?

Does our business enable people to live more harmoniously with each other? For example, do the ways we have designed jobs and compensation systems create trust and teamwork or cutthroat competition and envy among employees? Does our marketing divide people unnecessarily by appealing to status or insecurity?

How do our actions enhance or harm the lives of those who are affected but have little power to advocate for themselves? Would we switch positions with them and put one of our loved family members in their place?

Is our communication honest and directed toward constituents to enable them to make informed decisions, or does our communication mostly spin half-truths in our favor without regard for the well-being of others?

Resources. Are our resources (physical, natural, financial, etc.) managed in a way that honors divine intentions? Are we fair (and even generous)

---

[29]We are indebted to Tim Dearborn and Chris Shore for this particular question and for their influence on some of the other questions in our framework. See Tim Dearborn and Chris Shore, *Doing Business in the Kingdom of God* (Monrovia, Calif.: World Vision, 2006).

with respect to wages, value provided for the customer, return on investment, community service and so forth?

Do our products, services and operations interact with nature in a way that honors our role as trustees/stewards versus owners, and protects human well-being, especially for future generations?

Products/services. Do our products and services enhance human well-being? Are they purposefully designed with this end in mind?

Methods. Do we treat others with integrity, respect and dignity? Would we gladly trade places with employees, customers, suppliers and others we deal with? Are we proud to share how we did business at the end of every day with our spouse, children, friends and others who look to us for guidance?

THE "REAL WORLD"

To be sure, the vision we describe is a bold one. Legitimate questions can and should be asked about whether or not such a vision can be lived in the real world of global competition and short-term financial pressures. Will those who try to incorporate such goals be successful, or will they be greeted by a rude awakening in the form of either a lost job or a crushed business? Aren't the issues of firm ownership and control the real bottom-line determinants of the ability to act in the ways we have suggested versus pursuing decisions that maximize profit?

Undoubtedly, firm ownership, control and capitalization structure matter greatly. Pressures from both institutional and individual investors to generate high levels of quarterly financial return (genuine or "managed") and "hit the numbers" are very real. Reduce profit for the sake of achieving social goals and the wrath of Wall Street will be quickly felt. At a minimum some investors will flee, and in theory (and sometimes in practice) a lawsuit could be triggered under corporate law for breach of fiduciary duty to the shareholders.

Further, it would be naive to expect that large shareholder-owned secular corporations will change their mission statements to include references such as "service to God and neighbor." While we will say more about some innovations in firm ownership in chapter ten, there are small but hopeful signs within conventional ownership structures. An increasing number of publicly (shareholder) held companies in a wide range of industries have stated purposes in their charters and mission statements that go well beyond profit making and engage in practices that contribute to human flourishing. Many of these firms are highly financially successful too. Some researchers, like Collins and Porras, argue that these organizations are successful precisely *because* they don't just focus on the financial bottom line but have a much greater sense of purpose and mission (core values).[30] Indeed, an example of one such organization (Herman Miller) is given toward the end of this chapter, while others that fit this description are used as examples throughout this book.

Several leaders of these types of organizations have boldly stated that if investors are not happy with their decisions to consider stakeholders in their decisions, they can invest elsewhere.[31] Moreover, the "socially responsible" and "social" investment sectors are growing. Many private and some institutional investors are seeking both a financial return and to make a positive (or at least to refrain from making a negative) social impact with their investment dollars. Organizations that create economic and social value are more attractive to these type of investors. Some research indicates that investors—even involved, educated ones—may not be motivated solely by the financial bottom line.[32] Some investors are willing to make the tradeoff of less financial return for the sake of social impact, giving managers more leeway to pursue activities that don't necessarily pay financially. Likewise some consumers are willing to pay more for socially responsible products (such as fair trade coffee), and a growing number of employees want to work at firms that share their values. In theory, a firm that can attract these types of stakeholders may even wind up enjoying some financial advantages in the marketplace through the formation of a "virtuous [versus vicious] circle."

Of course, organizations, industries and public expectations can and do change over time, so we must also exercise influence by being these types

---

[30]Jim Collins and Jerry Porras, *Built to Last: Successful Habits of Visionary Companies* (New York: HarperCollins, 1994).

[31]See, for example, Mike Volkema, CEO of Herman Miller, quoted in Gunther, *Faith and Fortune*, p. 177. See also Friedman, Mackey and Rodgers, "Rethinking the Social Responsibility of Business: A Reason Debate," in which Mackey makes a similar claim.

[32]Pietra Rivoli, "Ethical Aspects of Investor Behavior," *Journal of Business Ethics* 14 (1995): 265-77.

of stakeholders ourselves. We can be intentional in terms of where we shop, what we purchase, where we invest and where we work.

STAYING FAITHFUL TO THE CHRISTIAN VISION

We will close this chapter with examples of organizations that have been able to achieve worldly measures of success while staying faithful to convictions that are consistent with a Christian vision for business. To be clear, we are not holding these examples out as formulas for financial success or to support the argument that "God will bless you if you are faithful." We must be honest in pointing out that advancing this vision will present difficult challenges, and quite possibly sacrificed profits. We do believe that God will bless your faithfulness, however, the blessing may not come in the form of greater earnings.

Kiel Mortgage. "Big enough to do the job, small enough to care" is a throwback-style radio jingle that is often heard on western Washington airwaves promoting Kiel Mortgage, a brokerage based in the Seattle suburb of Kent, Washington. Owned and operated by a Christian family since its inception in 1996, Kiel has been recognized for its high standards of ethics and community involvement.

Citing faith as a motivating force, Kiel is actively managed in a way that places values before profits. Unlike many of its competitors, Kiel has always tried to place the interests of its customers first. While other mortgage lenders were making outrageous sums of money by advertising teaser rates (which would quickly reset) to get customers in the door, Kiel refused on the basis that such loans would be misleading to customers. Kiel also stayed away from highly profitable (at least short term) subprime loans that got many borrowers in over their heads and that were sometimes supported by fraudulent income claims or home value appraisals. In an environment in which many competitors were getting rich quick and where sticking to principles might mean losing employees who could see the size of commissions earned at competing places of employment, the pressure to sway from such values is enormous.

Based on the company's practices, Laura Kiel, the company's cofounder and president, served as a commissioner on the Washington State Mortgage Broker Commission that developed and helped pass model consumer protection legislation and mortgage regulations. Kiel is also well known for its charitable community endeavors and values a strong sense of camaraderie in the workplace. The company recently built an additional wing to its building so that all employees could eat lunch together on a weekly basis.[33]

Herman Miller. Several years ago, senior executives at Fortune 500 company Herman Miller, one of the world's largest office furniture manufacturers, were faced with a crisis. As reported in *Business Week*, a research manager pointed out that the raw materials used to make its signature product, the Eames Chair, was made from tropical hardwoods. The company's president remarked that changing the wood to more environmentally responsible species would "kill that chair." Even though the company was (and is) publicly held, corporate executives went ahead and made the change consistent with the company's heritage and values, including a strong commitment to the environment.

Founded by devout Christians in western Michigan, where it is still headquartered, Herman Miller is an illustration of a company that has worked hard to uphold its core values, even when doing so was not necessarily good for profits. Other examples include a strong commitment to ethics and a participatory management style. Under legendary former CEO Max De Pree (son of the company's founder), the company instituted employee stock ownership plans that effectively functioned as "silver parachutes" (versus executives' "golden parachutes") so that employees would have to be bought out in the case of an unfriendly takeover.[34]

To be certain, upholding values has its costs. The company's commitments have not been a magic blueprint for financial success. Some shareholders have not been very happy with their financial returns, and the company conducted significant numbers of employee layoffs in 2002 due to decreasing profits resulting from the dot-com meltdown. The Aeron Chair was very popular with new economy dot-com technology companies, and when many of them crashed, so did the market for the chair.

About More Than Money

In reducing the institution of business (and our involvement within it) as an engine to make money (whether for shareholders, to pay bills or to get

---

[33]Hsin-Hsiang Hung, "Kiel Mortgage: Interview with Brent Abrams," MBA class project for Christian Ethics and Values in the Marketplace, Seattle Pacific University, March 2008.
[34]See Jio, "Good Business."

rich), we greatly underestimate its value, both in social and spiritual terms. God intends business to be much more life-giving than a chase for financial gain.

Reducing business to profit is like reducing the human body to blood or oxygen, or as John Mackey stated earlier, "living to eat."[35] Using the human body as a metaphor for business, blood, oxygen and nutrition are necessary for life. However, thinking about our blood, oxygen or food all day long would be quite odd, unless we are driven to do so by disease or illness. Reducing human beings to their blood, oxygen or their need to consume food overlooks our splendid capacities, namely, physical activity, creativity, rational thought and relationships.

Yet business is too often reduced to its barest level, profit, rather than enlarged to include all of the other good things it does and is capable of doing. Dave Packard, cofounder of Hewlett-Packard once stated:

> I think many people assume, wrongly, that a company exists simply to make money. While this is an important result of a company's existence, we have to go deeper and find the real reasons for our being. As we investigate this, we inevitably come to the conclusion that a group of people get together and exist as an institution that we call a company so that they are able to accomplish something collectively that they could not separately—they make a contribution to society, a phrase which sounds trite but is fundamental.[36]

This chapter began with the story of Anne, who wound up leaving banking and the business world altogether because her treasured value of serving others could not be reconciled with her work. While it is unrealistic to expect that the types of tension she faced will disappear altogether, surely they can be lessened, and people like Anne could work with a far greater amount of passion and purpose if business is reenvisioned (and reshaped) in a manner that reflects a sacred partnership with God.

---

[35]In addition to John Mackey, Ken Eldred and Don Flow also make this point. See Eldred, *God Is at Work*, p. 68; and Don Flow, "Christianity, Informing, Infusing and Reforming Business," a speech given at the "Bridging Sunday and Monday Conference," Seattle Pacific University, October 5, 2007.

[36]Dave Packard, cited in Charles Handy, "What's a Business For?" *Harvard Business Review,* December 2002, p. 54. Also see David Packard, *The HP Way: How Bill Hewlett and I Built Our Company* (New York: Harper Business, 1995).

3

BUSINESS AND
SPIRITUAL FORMATION

Barry Rowan was about to face the most significant challenge of his twenty-five years in business. After earning an MBA at Harvard and beginning his career at Hewlett-Packard, he'd had two very successful runs as a senior executive with technology companies, one venture capital-backed and the other publicly traded. He'd served as CFO and then president at one, and CFO and subsequently division manager at the other. He had been recently hired as CFO for a telecom company providing wireless phone service to both residential and corporate customers in Latin America. He was later appointed CEO of the Brazilian subsidiary of that company, charged with turning around a troubled situation.

The subsidiary had won the license to compete with the national phone company to provide services in a vastly underpenetrated market. The project turned out to be a massive undertaking, since in order to win the license, the company had committed to turning on service in eighty cities (roughly 125 million people) in a two-year period, half in the first year and half in the second. To do this it created a joint venture with two other phone companies to access the expertise and the multibillion dollars of capital required to make it all work. They hired a staff of four thousand people to roll out this service, and the project took off like a rocket. Once they turned on service, they put on half a million customers in the first ten months, making it one of the fastest-growing competitive local exchange carriers in the world at the time. The stock price of the main company more than tripled during Rowan's first year, going from three dollars to ten dollars per share.

According to Rowan, things looked like they were going smoothly, but underneath the surface some cracks began to appear in the operations. The CEO was terminated, and the shareholders recruited Rowan to be the replacement. He moved to Brazil and entered a business setting very different from anything he'd ever experienced before. For starters, he had a bodyguard and a bulletproof car. About two weeks after he got there, the capital markets were starting to tighten up significantly, which made further expansion very challenging. One of the company's partners decided not to fund the next level of capital, leaving a gaping $110 million funding hole in the business plan. It became clear that they weren't going to achieve the results they had promised. About this time, Rowan also learned that many of the customers couldn't pay their bills. Of the five hundred thousand customers they had signed up for the service, ultimately two hundred thousand had to be written off—fully 40 percent of them. The credit screening had been too lax. He assumed the CEO position and moved to Brazil right in the midst of discovering the bad debt, when one of the major partners decided not to fund the next project and as the capital markets were crashing, including the NASDAQ dropping by 50 percent.

Rowan realized quickly that a massive financial and operational restructuring would be required to save the company. He describes arriving at the decision this way: "When I was down there in Brazil, first I thought, *We're going to fix this company.* We had to lay off 1,500 of the 4,000 people, but I thought, *We can get it reorganized and back on track.* After I was there about four months, it dawned on me that *this thing could crater. Not only will the stock potentially not go up, it could go to zero.* It just stunned me that this could happen, and I was just blown away by the prospect of that failure. I had failed in small ways before but never anything as cataclysmic as this." The stress of going to work each day in such a difficult time made him almost physically sick. By his account, as his bodyguard pulled the bulletproof car into the underground parking lot at the office each morning, he felt like he wanted to throw up.

As Rowan reflected on that difficult time, he understood that God was powerfully at work, using the challenges of his business life to shape his soul. In thinking back on it, he realizes that this was one of the most significant times of spiritual growth in his life. He said, "So as I was in these very, very challenging circumstances, God was showing me what was really going on. As painful as the dramatic business failure was, it paled in comparison to the anguish in my soul. God showed me in the midst of the pain, and continuing in the solitude of the ensuing months, the reason I was so distraught and in such a spiritual funk. I had made achievement my god. It wasn't until the achievement went away, that I realized a part of my god also went away."

According to Rowan, God continued to use the experience in Brazil to shape him ever more deeply as he tried to make sense of the experience. "In the pit of despair, my soul was pierced by Jesus' words, 'Any of you who does not give up everything he has cannot be my disciple.' I cried out to God, 'How can I give up anything else when I have nothing left to give?' I began to come to the frightening conclusion, that what he was asking of me was to surrender even more. Was I willing to give up any claim to my own future? Instead of following the admonitions of my education and our culture to 'Plan your work and work your plan,' and to 'Start with the end in mind,' was I willing to live fully in the present moment and let God unfold the pattern of my life as he saw fit? While my life with God began with surrender, albeit with heel marks in the sand as I relinquished my life to him, this was a level of abandonment to him that was unfathomable and frightening to me."

With the benefit of five years' perspective, he describes the experience this way, "Through that painful experience, God completely reoriented my perspective of time. He showed me that my call was not to live in my plans for the future or memories of the past, but to be fully present to the present moment. I began to see each moment as a sacrament. It became a kind of second conversion for me. The remarkable part was that after coming into this recognition and confessing that I had made achievement my god—which took months to recognize—I came into a place of profound joy and freedom. The truth was I *had* made achievement my god. I lived for the adrenaline rush of success, but I had been blind to this truth for decades. As God revealed this reality to me through the pain and the failure, it set me free. As much as I pleaded for him to do otherwise, God didn't deliver me from my circumstances. He delivered me through them."

He adds this spiritual perspective. "Jesus calls his disciples with the words, 'Come follow me.' He is just beckoning us to come with him on the greatest adventure life has to offer. But it must be on his terms, not ours. For me, he was saying, 'Come follow me to this next level of abandonment and surrender. Give up everything you have.' As he has continued to draw me into deeper levels of relinquishment, I realize that it takes much more strength to let go than to hang on. Witness Jesus' own experience in the garden. But through our surrender to him, Jesus draws us into this profound intimacy with him and a freedom and joy I had heard about but had never really tasted. Out of a darkness that grew blacker than black for me, God brought me into a freedom and a lightness of soul I didn't know were possible. It is a country I'd only rarely visited before, and if I had, it was only for brief periods. I experienced God through the pain of Brazil. Nothing the world has to offer compares to the inexpressible joy that comes from experiencing the tender intimacy with God for which we are designed."

"My career has been the crucible for the formation of my soul, and this experience in Brazil is one of the more dramatic examples I can give you of how this has been true in my life. Yet, I increasingly see every moment charged with his presence that would shape us into who he has in mind for us to become. We have but to look for him and to submit to his work in our souls. His current work in me is to teach me about love. Not the limited love of man, but the pure love of God. This one might take him awhile."[1]

Rowan's experience and reflections help illustrate a powerful truth that we want to make explicit in this chapter: God can employ business as an arena to transform us. Business (and all arenas of work) is a critical area that can be used by God to shape our character and spirituality.[2]

Involvement in business is a crucible in which many important character traits are nurtured and a person's daily intimacy with God is cultivated. As Rowan put it, "For me, part of the pruning shears that God has used [to shape my soul] have been the challenges of my involvement in business."

SPIRITUAL FORMATION AT WORK

The predominant understanding of how faith and business relate has been as a one-way relationship, that is, we bring our faith and values to shape our workplace. Far less obvious and less frequently explored, however, are the ways that business can be used in a reciprocal (though not always com-

---

[1]Personal interview with Barry L. Rowan, April 7, 2009. All quotations from Mr. Rowan come from this interview.

[2]For further reading on this important topic, see Laura Nash, *Believers in Business: Resolving the Tensions Between Christian Faith, Business Ethics, Competition and Our Definitions of Success* (Nashville: Thomas Nelson, 1994).

fortable) manner to shape *us* in positive ways. To be certain, business can also ensnare us in a variety of vices (e.g., greed and idolatry) and deform our character (see chap. 4).

Each person's experience with God shaping his or her character through business is different, with various traits or virtues being developed through involvement in specific situations, making it difficult to generalize. Certainly, people's responses to the challenges of business are also quite different—some, such as Rowan, find their faith deepened, character sharpened and intimacy with God intensified. Others may respond to similar experiences very differently and find their faith abandoned, character development short-circuited and intimacy with God turned to spiritual complacency.

What we propose here are some conceptions about character and virtue development that successful involvement in business both requires and nurtures. While the following is not meant to be an exhaustive study, we consider first how God can use business to help develop some important character traits and virtues. In a later section we will examine some important spiritual practices that if practiced serve as antidotes to overwork or overidentification with work, a possible dark side to approaching our work as a calling (as opposed to a job or career).

Consider first the virtue of service. Business, especially when approached from the framework we outlined in chapter two, requires that people and organizations serve their constituencies well in order to thrive. Companies must be committed to serving their customers, meeting their needs, listening carefully to their criticisms and treating them fairly. If customers are not well served, they will take their business to someone who will serve them more effectively. George Mason University economist Walter Williams observes, "You don't have to like your fellow-man, but you have to serve him."[3] Further, employees must serve their companies; team members must learn how to serve each other and become more interdependent; managers must serve those who report to them and those they manage; and executives are responsible for serving the entire organization they lead. (We'll take up servant leadership in chapter seven.) If leaders and managers don't serve well those who report to them, morale suffers and employees become less productive. In general, business both requires

---

[3]Walter Williams, cited in John Stossel, *Give Me a Break* (New York: Perennial Currents, 2005), p. 244.

and cultivates an orientation toward serving others. Of course, this is not to suggest that there are no limits or boundaries on one's service to any given constituency. It is true that in most contexts and certainly in biblical times, servants did not have the prerogative of setting boundaries with their masters, because they did not have any individual rights at all. That's where the imagery of the servant cannot be justifiably extended, since Jesus, the ultimate servant, also put boundaries on his service, at times walking away from serving the masses in order to secure time with his disciples or personal time with God. Thus the virtue of service and the existence of boundaries can coexist. In fact, we can make a good case that within proper boundaries the virtue of service is actually more meaningful when the person is serving out a choice and less out of a compulsion.[4]

Business also requires and cultivates the virtues of *trust, trustworthiness* and *fairness*. For the vast majority of businesses that are dependent on repeat customers for their success, trust and fairness are critical to keeping customers. Think about how quickly people take their business elsewhere when trust is missing and they are being treated unfairly. It is not uncommon for people to go out of their way to do business with companies and individuals they trust. It is even more common for people to go out of their way *to avoid* doing business with those whom they do not trust. There are many examples of companies acting in untrustworthy ways. But when that becomes public knowledge, it is common for the company to lose business as a result. Within an organization trust (teamwork) is critical in fostering prosperity. Where trust is low, the cost of doing business increases due to costly monitoring and compliance mechanisms that are required. In addition, where trust is low, there are intangible costs such as a decrease in employees' commitment to work and eagerness to accept change. The costs of low morale and high turnover suggest that treating people with *dignity* and *respect* is critical to good leadership and a significant part of effective management. Business both requires and cultivates trust, fairness and respect.

Business also fosters the virtues of *initiative* and *perseverance*. Business encourages what some call "entrepreneurial traits, which also includes

---

[4]For further discussion of the place of boundaries with the virtue of service, see Henry Cloud and John S. Townsend, *Boundaries* (Grand Rapids: Zondervan, 1992).

creativity."[5] Long-run success in business requires creative solutions to complex problems. It further demands that people exercise persistence in order to accomplish significant business goals that can take months if not years to achieve. For example, men and women in sales are required to take initiative on a daily basis and persevere with potential customers or clients until the sale is complete. This is characteristic of business in general, for if companies don't take initiative to lower their costs, increase their market share, seek out new customers and keep their employees' morale high, they will suffer decline. Executives must be able to think creatively about bringing new products and services to the market, anticipating their customers' needs, maintaining the right level of employment and insuring adequate financing for their future. This kind of creativity is essential to leadership, and without it companies are ill-equipped to deal with the uncertainties of the constantly changing global economy. *Perseverance* is likewise critical to long-term success in business, and without it companies and individuals both tend to give up when persistence would enable a breakthrough to be made. For example, most start-up companies face very difficult obstacles to becoming established companies, and it is common for entrepreneurs to testify of how their determination made the difference between success and failure.

With persistence comes the *ability to deal with adversity*. With this, we move into the area of how God uses business to cultivate a person's relationship with him. James 1:2-5 indicates that adversity is a regular part of the Christian's life, and business is one of the primary crucibles in which both character and intimacy with God are forged by overcoming hardships and difficulty. Anyone who has been laid off knows what this is like—and anyone who has to lay off employees or close down plants knows how painful this can be. In addition, dealing with general economic downturns provides difficult, though beneficial, opportunities to deal with adversity and to nurture the humility, wisdom and persistence that accompany it. It further develops a person's *trust in God*, to enable him or her to build reliance on God for personal security and well-being, and the company's stability. A businessperson's intimacy with God is

---

[5]For further discussion of this see Robert Sirico, "The Entrepreneurial Vocation," in *Beyond Integrity: A Judeo-Christian Approach to Business Ethics*, ed. Scott B. Rae and Kenman L. Wong, 2nd ed. (Grand Rapids: Zondervan, 2004), pp. 60-66.

often nurtured by having to wrestle with the prospect of failure, potential layoffs or ethical dilemmas, both in the request for wisdom and for the strength to follow one's moral convictions. For example, in her extensive interviews of Christian CEOs, Laura Nash found that dealing with adversity or ethical dilemmas drove these men and women to frequent prayer. They cited prayer as a critical component that often emerged from these situations, and at times the conviction that developed from those times of prayer actually provided answers to the difficult issues that were on the table at that time.[6]

Dealing with adversity was a major part of the story of Barry Rowan. He made it clear that business in general, and adversity in particular, have been crucibles that God used to shape him spiritually. His business challenges have nurtured what he calls "surrendered leadership," and have moved him away from what he calls "an idea of self-sufficiency and to interdependence." He sees this as having significant ramifications for what it means to lead an organization. He says, "It now means that it's not about being in charge and doing things well myself. It's about releasing the potential of other people to grow into what God has in mind for them to become. So I think that's an example of a character dimension that God has grown out of this self-sufficiency into interdependence and recognizing the value of everybody, which I think leads to another one. God is bringing me into an authentic humility."

Some additional virtues nourished by business actually can help prevent having to face difficult times. To be sure, adversity is due to circumstances beyond our control. But sometimes difficulties come as a result of something preventable. The proverbs are clear that laziness, or a lack of diligence, can contribute to economic misfortune (Prov 6:6-11; 10:4-5; 12:11, 14, 24; 13:11; 24:30-34). Business demands *diligence* and *discipline*, where we learn that "you reap what you sow." Popular business author Stephen Covey describes "the law of the farm" as a lesson that to succeed a person must engage in advance planning, give daily attention to the work and not put off the important work until the deadline approaches. He insists that if we ignore the law of the farm, we will not reap a successful harvest.[7] Though it is true that some people succeed without hard work, that is

---

[6]See Nash, *Believers in Business*, for further discussion on this.
[7]Stephen A. Covey, *The Seven Habits of Highly Successful People* (New York: Free Press, 1989).

certainly not the norm. In general, business both requires and cultivates diligence, and discourages laziness and a lack of discipline.

SPIRITUAL PRACTICES AND THE DARK SIDE OF CALLING

While business can be used as a crucible to develop our faith, spirituality and character, it can also shape us in negative ways, if we aren't exceedingly careful. In addition to the historically described business vices (e.g., greed and avariciousness), very real "shadow sides" to the case we have made for approaching business as a calling (chaps. 1-2) are overwork and overidentification with work.

While there are many reasons behind these problems, including global competition, employer expectations, fear, greed, technology ("crackberries"), identifying our paid work as a calling (particularly when stripped of its broader spiritual context [see chap. 1]—work as *one* of many callings) may certainly be a contributor.

Current research suggests that people tend to see their work as either jobs, careers or callings. This tripartite way of seeing work was popularized in the influential work of Robert Bellah and associates in *Habits of the Heart*.[8] Their research suggests that people see their work typically as (1) *jobs*, that is, strictly as a means to providing for what a person does away from the work, (2) *careers*, which involve a higher degree of commitment but are focused on financial progress and movement up the ladder, or (3) *callings*, in which the satisfaction, perceived value of the work and social purpose of the work are the most important elements. Although subsequent research indicates that those who view their work as a calling tend to have higher job satisfaction, a danger might be that work is too closely intertwined with their entire life. For example, Amy Wrznesiewski and her colleagues suggest that "people with a calling find their work inseparable from their life." While the overall effects are positive (i.e., higher job and life satisfaction), those with callings also tend to put in longer hours.[9]

Many (though not all) studies report that Americans are working considerably longer hours than just a decade or two ago. Most of us can name

---

[8]Robert N. Bellah et al., *Habits of the Heart: Individualism and Commitment in American Life* (Berkeley: University of California Press, 1985).
[9]Amy Wrznesiewski et al., "Jobs, Car.... ...nd Callings: People's Relations to Their Work," *Journal of Research in Personality* 31 (1997): 22.

a coworker or two who continuously keep their vacation banks at the maximum number of hours by refusing to use the time. Moreover, stories of older executives who have had successful business careers while alienating almost all of their family and friends, and who now cannot retire for fear of losing everything that matters to them are well circulated.

As antidotes to overwork and overidentification with work, the Bible provides several measures that can be broadly categorized as spiritual practices. While the practices that follow are by no means exhaustive, they are habits, both of mind and of action, which are actively nurtured in order to cooperate with God in the process of spiritual formation. Dallas Willard observes that "spiritual growth and vitality stem from what we actually do with our lives, from the habits we form, and from the character that results." In simple form, spiritual disciplines and practices can be seen as "taking appropriate measures" toward spiritual growth and character development.[10] Richard Foster describes them as means to break free from "ingrained habits."[11]

While there are many spiritual practices (e.g., prayer, solitude, simplicity) that are important and pertinent to our formation, three stand out as particularly relevant for preventing overidentification with work: (1) remembering the sabbath, (2) redeeming the time and (3) keeping work in proper perspective.

Remembering the Sabbath

By way of background there were some important differences between the ancient world and today that have a bearing on the discussion to follow. First, there was little separation between the workplace and the home in biblical times. There was not much of a dichotomy between work and home since most work occurred in or around the home. Agriculture and trades dominated the ancient economy, and parents did much of their parenting on the job. As a result, balancing work and family was not that difficult because there was so much overlap between the two. But with the industrial revolution, work became increasingly separate from home, as people, mostly men, left home during the day to go to work. More re-

---

[10]Dallas Willard, *The Spirit of the Disciplines* (New York: HarperCollins, 1988), pp. 20, 153.
[11]Richard Foster, *Celebration of Discipline: The Path to Spiritual Growth* (New York: HarperCollins, 1978), p. 3.

cently, as women have entered the workforce in unprecedented numbers, they too wrestle with the dual demands of work and family. This tension is more acute for women, particularly in some Christian circles, which may hold a more traditional view of family life, in which men are "the bread-winners" and women stay home to rear children. More women are working but the demands of parenting are still there for them. It is well documented that in dual-career families women bear more of the burden for the "second shift" of domestic duties.

Further, with more and more people working from remote locations and being constantly reachable by technological devices, people are finding that drawing a boundary between work and home can be more difficult than even a decade ago. It may be that work is returning to actually look more like it did in ancient times, with less separation between home and the workplace.

A second difference has to do with the way leisure was viewed in the ancient world vis-à-vis work. For example, the classical Greeks related work and leisure in a way quite different from today. In his *Nicomachean Ethics*, Aristotle insisted that leisure was primary and work was subordinate to it.[12] This is very different from the contemporary view that leisure is what you do when you are not working. In both classical and contemporary periods, leisure is preferred over work and is actually the goal; work is simply a means to that end. The Greek term for leisure is *scholē*, from which we get our words *scholarship* and *school*. Work was defined as *the absence of leisure*, and the Greeks used the term *ascholia* to define it. That is, work was secondary to leisure and was something to be done when one was not at leisure. This is an important difference between the view of work and leisure in the ancient world and today. Today, particularly in the West, we largely view work as primary and leisure as secondary—that is, we define leisure in terms of work, not the other way around.[13]

In addition, the view of what constituted leisure was very different in the ancient world. Leisure referred not to rest from occupation or enter-

---

[12]Gilbert C. Meilaender, ed., *Working: Its Meaning and Limits* (Notre Dame, Ind.: University of Notre Dame Press, 2000), p. 7.

[13]For historical material of the relationship between work and leisure, see Josef Pieper, *Leisure: The Basis of Culture* (New York: St. Augustine's Press, 1998). Pieper's original publication in German was in two works: *Musse und Kult* and *Was heisst Pholosophieren* (Berlin: Kosel-Verlag, 1948).

tainment, both of which Aristotle called "play," but rather to the time away from work to cultivate the life of the mind and to give oneself to intellectual pursuits, which he held were intrinsically valuable and essential to having a good life. This type of leisure was quite different from the leisure of today and involved cultivation of the intellectual virtues and the contemplative side of life, without which, according to Aristotle, true happiness was not possible. To be sure, Aristotle's view was not the hedonistic "working for the weekend" of today.

However, there is one similarity in the ancient view of work and leisure that resonates with some in today's culture. That is, the ancients saw work solely as a means to providing for one's leisure, leaving work as simply a means to an end and without the intrinsic nobility to it that is characteristic of a Christian view of work. Aristotle argued first that a modicum of earthly goods was necessary to attain happiness, and work was necessary to attain such goods. But, second, he insisted that work is what makes leisure possible. Thus, for Aristotle work has instrumental value only— value in terms of what it can provide in terms of leisure. Granted that what constitutes leisure is very different today compared to the classical era, nevertheless, Aristotle viewed work as strictly a means to an end. This parallels the view of many in our culture that work is valuable only because it earns people the opportunity to do the things that matter most to them, whether it is training for a triathlon, spending time with family, pursuing additional education or volunteering. It is what we do when we are not at play or leisure. This contrasts sharply from the view of work we presented in chapters one and two, where work has intrinsic value, regardless of what else it accomplishes.[14]

Scripture spoke into this background of the ancient world when it addressed these critical notions of work and leisure. From the beginning God designed human beings to live in ways that would contribute to their flourishing. One of the primary concerns addressed in Scripture, as early as Genesis 1, is the need to bring work and leisure together. Both are essential to becoming the person God designed human beings to be. In fact, God felt so strongly about it that he modeled it in creation and legislated

---

[14]For further discussion of this relationship between work and leisure in the ancient world, see Leland Ryken, *Redeeming the Time: The Christian Approach to Work and Leisure* (Grand Rapids: Baker, 1995).

it in the Ten Commandments. Although handed down as a commandment it was intended as and often received as a gift. God instituted a sabbath day in order to insure that people kept their work from taking over
their lives. In Exodus 20:8-11, God ordained a rhythmic pattern of one
day in seven for human beings to rest—that is, to stop working and give
attention to other aspects of life, namely, the contemplative and worship
components, and to put aside all the occupational obstacles that get in the
way of nurturing our soul and our relationship to God. The Hebrew term
shabbat simply means "stop and rest." God intended through observing
the sabbath that people put away their to-do lists and do those things that
refresh them, giving particular attention to worship, reflection and our
relationship to God. God felt so strongly about this that he repeated this
command periodically throughout Israel's history. For example, in the
book of Deuteronomy, when God repeated the Ten Commandments just
before Israel entered the Promised Land, God reissued the sabbath command, but with a different basis. In Deuteronomy 5:12-15, God reminded
Israel of the sabbath, but this time it was based on their experience of
slavery in Egypt. God encouraged them to "remember that you were
slaves in Egypt and that the LORD your God brought you out of there
with a mighty hand and outstretched arm. Therefore, the LORD your
God has commanded you to observe the Sabbath day" (v. 15). Because of
their four hundred years of slavery in Egypt, God commanded them to
keep the sabbath.

What's the connection between their sojourn in Egypt and the need to
keep the sabbath? When they were slaves in Egypt, there was no rest from
work—it consumed their lives. In fact, when they requested rest, their
taskmasters put even more taxing demands on them, requiring even more
time and effort. God is affirming to the Israelites that they are no longer
slaves, and they should not live as though they are. Refusal to keep the
sabbath meant that people were enslaved to their work. The sabbath command was designed to remind them that they were not to live like they
were enslaved to their jobs. Moreover, it should be noted that the sabbath
was not created in the service of work. In other words, sabbath observation
was not for the purpose (so commonly accepted today for taking time off)
of "recharging our batteries" or becoming more effective workers. It was
and is simply a gift to be received.

Keeping the sabbath was also an exercise of faith. Refusal to keep it meant that people were not willing to trust God for their income. In Exodus 31:12-17 God indicates that the sabbath is a sign of his covenant with Israel—that by keeping it they communicate that they trust him to take care of them, according to their covenant relationship. God emphasizes this even more strongly when he specifies that the sabbath must be kept even during harvest and planting times (Ex 34:21). In an agricultural society these were the two busiest times of the year, times when taking time off would mean loss of income. That would be like telling a CPA to be sure to follow the sabbath even in the few weeks before April 15, or college students to keep the sabbath just before final exams start.

The point of the sabbath command is a loving reminder that there's more to life than work; we are more than laborers. Of course, for people who don't like their jobs or are just grinding away at them, there is little temptation to work too much. But for many business and professional men and women who are driven to succeed, or for people who work in very demanding, high stress occupations, the pressure of work can be overwhelming. This is particularly the case today when people are more frequently expected to be constantly available to work, even when not in the office, and increasingly often, even while on vacation. The sabbath command reminds us that *we are not our work*, and that work, though a significant part of our lives, does not ultimately define us and is not the primary place we get our identity. The ability to take regular time off affirms to ourselves and to our community, that life is bigger than work.

But, some may object, the sabbath was for the Old Testament, for Israel, not for today. And they are right, to a point. In the New Testament era the church is not under the law of Moses like the nation of Israel was. We are not obligated to keep the sabbath command literally today. That is, we don't have to take one day off per week literally like Israel did. That's not to say that it wouldn't be a good idea! But we are not under the law in that way.

However, there is surely a more general principle, or principles, that are bound up with the sabbath command that we ought to take seriously today. Because the sabbath command is ultimately grounded in the order of creation (Gen 2:2-3; Ex 20:11), from the beginning, and prior to the entrance of sin into the world, God designed us to regularly cease from our work. God still desires that we trust him for our income, and taking regular time off indicates that we trust him, though it is not the technical sign of our covenant with him. And God still desires that our work not consume us. Taking regular time off still indicates that we are not our work. Though we are not under the command to take literally one day in seven off from work, the reasons for giving the sabbath command are still relevant today and suggest that we develop a *sabbath outlook and lifestyle.* Even though our work is our altar, that doesn't mean that we have to spend all of our time there. Nor does it mean that we are called to worship our work. Of course, a sabbath lifestyle is not just an individual matter. It is also a communal and institutional affair. It was originally designed to be celebrated in community, not in isolation or alone. Unless the organizations we are a part of respect a sabbath outlook (whether or not they call it such), it is much more difficult for individuals to practice a rhythmic pattern of life.

The book of Ecclesiastes commends the enjoyment of all of life, including both work and leisure, as God's good gift. We mentioned these passages in chapter one and made the case that God blessed work as intrinsically good. But we didn't point out that leisure is also blessed as a good thing. Ecclesiastes makes that clear too. For example, Ecclesiastes 8:15 says, "So I commend the enjoyment of life, because nothing is better than for a man under the sun than to eat and drink and be glad. Then joy will accompany him in his work in all the days of the life God has given him under the sun." We suggest that passages like this teach that we should keep life in proper perspective, with commitments to enjoy both work and leisure, without either one defining who we are.[15]

REDEEMING THE TIME

It's one thing to realize that Scripture strongly encourages us to create space for acknowledging and appreciating the spiritual transformation that is taking place through our work, but quite another to practice that

---

[15]This section is not intended to be an exhaustive study of the sabbath institution. For further reading on this see Marva Dawn, *Keeping the Sabbath Wholly: Ceasing, Resting, Embracing, Feasting* (Grand Rapids: Eerdmans, 1989), and *The Sense of the Call: A Sabbath Way of Life for Those Who Serve God, the Church and the World* (Grand Rapids: Eerdmans, 2006); and Mark Buchanan, *The Rest of God: Restoring Your Soul by Restoring Sabbath* (Nashville: Thomas Nelson, 2006).

regularly. This is especially difficult in a culture where working people are increasingly expected to be reachable for work, through technology. Keeping work and leisure in symmetry, from a Christian worldview, involves a *distinctive view of time*. A part of life after the Fall is that life is too short and the days move ahead too quickly. In view of this the Bible counsels us to "number our days" (Ps 90:12), and to "make the most of the time" (Eph 5:15-16; Col 4:5 NRSV), that is, to use our time wisely.

When most people hear phrases like this, they commonly take it as a mandate to "get busy for God's kingdom," to stop wasting time, to make every moment count and to have all of our time accounted for in some productive way. It doesn't look all that different from what the time management experts for business tell us. That view of time comes more from business school than from the Bible. The Bible is full of admonitions to get your time in order, but it is not necessarily telling you to get busy filling up your day with productive activity. It may actually be advising you to do less, not more, in order to be faithful to God's view of time.

Take the phrase of the psalmist, to "number our days" (Ps 90:12). Moses wrote Psalm 90 while in the wilderness, in the years prior to the nation Israel entering the Promised Land. During that time, Moses saw firsthand how short and fleeting our lifespan is on earth. During his tenure leading the people in the wilderness, Moses witnessed an entire generation of roughly two million people die, which on average amounted to dozens of people every day. Moses was familiar with how quickly our time goes. He was well positioned to advise us on our time from a biblical worldview.

In the early parts of the psalm he comments on how quickly our normal lifespan can end. He says,

> You sweep men away in the sleep of death;
>> they are like the new grass of the morning—
> though in the morning it springs up new,
>> by evening it is dry and withered. (Ps 90:5-6)

Moses saw on a daily basis the grass in the desert, and he saw the application of this law of nature applied to human beings. He goes on to describe how hastily our lives move ahead:

> The length of our days is seventy years—
>> or eighty, if we have the strength;

yet their span is but trouble and sorrow,
    for they quickly pass, and we fly away. (Ps 90:10)

With this backdrop Moses makes the request that God "teach us to number our days aright, that we may gain a heart of wisdom" (Ps 90:12). Numbering our days correctly is connected to living life wisely. But what exactly does it mean to "number our days aright"? Literally, the term means to "count our days." So let's take this literally and count our days. Moses has already indicated that the normal lifespan is between seventy and eighty years. Since they didn't have medical technology in the ancient world, let's take the upper limit of eighty years as our starting point. Eighty years at 365 days per year amounts to a total of 29,200 days that constitute life. For this example we'll use a person at age fifty. This means that person has already lived a total of 18,250 days, which leaves him or her with a total remaining days of 10,950 days. (We would encourage you to replicate this assignment and calculate it with your current age.) If that person at age fifty were us, we would be alarmed at how much of life has passed so quickly and how little remains in comparison. (If you really want to get serious about numbering your days, at the end of each month, subtract another 30-31 days, or if that's too convicting, at the end of each year, subtract 365 days.) Moses' point is not that we simply engage in this counting exercise, but to make sure that we catch *the effect of the count*. That feeling of being startled at how our life has passed and the sense of urgency it creates to use our time wisely—that's the point of Moses' advice. It's to change our view of our time, not to give us specific time management strategies. We are to count our days in order that our days will count.

It's not hard to see how we could take the admonition to "number our days" and turn it into an order to fill our time with meaningful tasks—that is, to get busy and get to it! It's easy to see this view of time reinforced by the New Testament command to "make the most of the time" (Eph 5:16; Col 4:5 NRSV). But what exactly does this mean? In the New Testament there are actually two different words for time. *Chronos*, from which we get our term *chronological*, describes clock time. This is the notion of time we most commonly think of when we think about how we use our time, and clearly what the corporate time-management consultants have in mind. But the New Testament uses another term to refer to time, *kairos*, which is used in both Ephesians 5 and Colossians 4, and means "opportunity." That's why it is often translated with the phrase "make the most of every opportunity."

The Greeks had a very interesting myth behind this idea of *kairos*.[16] In Greek literature Kairos was a god who was short, very fast, and bald, except for a long patch of hair at the back of his head. Kairos would rush at people and they would try to capture him by grasping him by the hair. Of course, he came so quickly that many people failed to grasp him, but those who did were said to have "captured time." That is, they grabbed the opportunity before it quickly passed them by. This is why many translations of Ephesians 5 and Colossians 4 render the command to "redeem the time" with the phrase "making the most of every opportunity." In both of these passages, as in Psalm 90, using our time well is a significant part of living a good life and living it wisely.

In the New Testament, using our time well has little do with traditional time management—that's the *chronos* view of time. It has more to do with taking advantage of the opportunities God brings to us. It may be that some people need to stop wasting time. But we suspect that for many of us redeeming the time actually means slowing down, not speeding up. We need to have a margin of available time for things that truly matter. For example, to take advantage of the opportunities God brings to us with our children, we who are parents need to be there for them and to be somewhat unscheduled, so we can be truly present with our children and utilize teachable moments (which are rarely scheduled). Similarly for our neighbors, our coworkers and our employees, we may need to slow down so that we can take advantage of the opportunities God brings us to serve them, show them Christ's love and perhaps have a chance to have a conversation about things that matter. We suspect that many of us move through life so quickly that we fail to notice, much less take advantage of, the occasions God brings to us to contribute to his kingdom.

KEEPING WORK IN PERSPECTIVE

Nowhere in the Bible is the subject of work in a broken world addressed more directly than in the book of Ecclesiastes. Solomon is reflecting on life on this side of eternity. It is a book of sobering reality, yet good, wise

---

[16]"Kairos," in *Theological Dictionary of the New Testament*, ed. Gerhard Kittel, trans. Geoffrey W. Bromiley (Grand Rapids: Eerdmans, 1965), 3:457.

advice about how to live in a world that has lost its moorings. Solomon addresses a variety of subjects—among them wisdom, wealth and work— and describes all of them as "vanity" or "meaninglessness." In fact, some might think that Solomon's view of work as vanity is a good counterargument to our view of work having intrinsic value. But Solomon does not intend to say that work (and the other pursuits he discusses) are meaningless in an absolute sense, since the rest of the Bible affirms the intrinsic goodness of wisdom (Prov 8), wealth (1 Tim 6:17-19) and work (Gen 2:15). Rather, these things are meaningless *in the sense Solomon is using them*, as the component that gives ultimate meaning and coherence to life. None of the areas Solomon addresses in Ecclesiastes are capable of providing the key that unlocks the door to life's meaning.[17]

Consider Solomon's advice about approaching work in a fallen world. In Ecclesiastes 2:18-26, Solomon gives his readers three sobering realities to consider when it comes to work. First, *we don't know who will inherit our work when we are done*. He puts it like this: "I hated all the things I had toiled for under the sun, because I must leave them to the one who comes after me. And who knows whether he will be a wise man or a fool? Yet he will have control over all the work into which I have poured my effort and skill under the sun" (Eccles 2:18). That is, we don't know what will happen to our work after we are gone, and what kind of person will continue the investment we have made. For example, my best friend and I (Scott) started and ran a summer basketball camp when we were in college and graduate school. When it was time for us to get "real jobs," we sold the camp to a friend, who promptly changed jobs himself, leaving him unable to continue to run the camp. He folded it without ever conducting it at all. All our emotional investment in the business came to nothing in a short time after turning it over to him.

Second, though there may be uncertainty about who will follow in our footsteps, Solomon points out that *our successor may have less ownership in our work than we did*. The reason for this is that he or she wasn't there when we began and fought through many of our hard struggles. Solomon puts it this way: "So my heart began to despair over all my toilsome labor

[17]For more detail on this view of Ecclesiastes, see J. Stafford Wright, "The Interpretation of Ecclesiastes," in *Classical Evangelical Essays in Old Testament Interpretation*, ed. Walter C. Kaiser (Grand Rapids: Baker, 1972), pp. 133-50.

under the sun. For a man may do his work with wisdom, knowledge and skill, and then he must leave all he owns to someone who has not worked for it" (Eccles 2:20-21). This person is reaping the benefits of our hard work, perhaps without the same level of commitment that we had when you began it. We see this repeatedly when entrepreneurs leave their companies to their kids or to someone they sold the business to. Consider the entrepreneur who starts her own business. She pours her life into it, often risking all of her assets to get it off the ground. In many cases, it becomes almost like another child she nurtures and care for. When the day comes to sell it, it is often painful to see the successors treat it as just a job and simply as a source of income. But Solomon insists that this makes a lot of sense in a fallen world. The entrepreneur could not have reasonably expected the people who succeeded her to have the same passion for the business as she did. After all, she started it, put life savings on the line to do so and devoted her life and energy to it for many years in order for it to succeed. Solomon experienced this firsthand too, turning his kingdom over to his son, Rehoboam, who promptly mismanaged it, leading to a split of the nation into Israel and Judah, all in his lifetime (1 Kings 12).

Finally, Solomon's counsel for work *cautions the workaholic* about what failing to put work in perspective will do to life. He puts it this way, "What does a man get for all his toil and anxious striving with which he labors under the sun? All his days his work is pain and grief; even at night his mind does not rest" (Eccles 2:22-23). This is describing the hard-driving type-A person who is on a performance treadmill—he or she seems to never get or take a break from the pressures of work. Sometimes those pressures come from the demanding environment a person works in, but frequently those pressures come from inside. These people have an internal engine driving them continually to live up to higher and higher expectations. Many very successful people are wired this way. But they often don't realize the costs of their workaholism. What begins as the sweet taste of achievement becomes a trap. Keeping up past standards of performance can become a cruel taskmaster. The toll it takes on them physically, emotionally and relationally can be substantial. Their drivenness keeps them from recognizing these costs. In some cases, driven people make changes only when their bodies force them to through heart attacks, depression or exhaustion. In fact, it has been said that for much of our society, battling cancer has become the only legitimate excuse to take time off from work.

To summarize, in this passage Solomon paints a realistic picture of work under the curse of sin. Of course, the Bible in general and Solomon in specific paint a picture of work as having great value and nobility, balancing the original intention for work with the reality of work in a fallen world. But Solomon is not content to let this disheartening view of work be the last word. He has some good advice for how to live in a world where work has both dignity because of God's design and indignity because of the reality of sin. He urges a commitment to both work and leisure, and an attitude of enjoying both as gifts of the good God. He counsels: "A man can do nothing better than to eat and drink [figures of speech for rest and leisure] and find satisfaction in his work. This too, I see, is from the hand of God, for without him, who can eat or find enjoyment?" (Eccles 2:24-25).

LIFE IS FULL OF TRADEOFFS

Our culture has falsely advertised that we can have it all. From a Christian perspective the only place we can have it all is in heaven. Life on this side of eternity, under the reality of sin, is a series of tradeoffs. Choices have consequences and involve costs that need to be considered, no more so than when it comes to keeping perspective on work and family and personal life. This does not mean that a person should automatically reject many demanding careers with their time-intensive requirements, such as medicine, pastoral ministry or many business tracks. It does mean that the costs of those pursuits must be seriously weighed, and that keeping life in perspective in the midst of these demanding careers is challenging.

Take the case of my (Scott's) friend Jim. He started out of college with a high-powered advertising agency in New York City that required long hours and lots of travel. The schedule was fine as long as Jim was single and in the early years of his marriage. He was promoted on schedule, and with each promotion his responsibilities increased, as did the hours and travel. He didn't think much of it because that was the norm in his industry. Everyone worked long hours and the job came first.

Then he and his wife started having kids. Prior to starting a family, his wife had arguably a more stressful job than Jim did—she was a corporate lawyer in New York, where she was told that if she wanted a family life, this job was not for her. She agreed, and when their first child came along, she decided to work at home as a full-time parent.

Jim, on the other hand, kept moving up and eventually started traveling more internationally. He was eventually put in charge of the firm's European operations, which took him overseas even more. One year he traveled internationally 272 days. One occasion called attention to the growing problem. He was in Asia visiting a client and called home on Halloween, on the second week of a three-week trip. His wife and kids had just returned home from trick-or-treating in the neighborhood and his daughter, who was three at the time, said to her mom, "*If Daddy ever comes home*, can he see me in my costume?" Understandably, Jim was very troubled by this, but was stuck in a very demanding job and had no feasible way to get his life back under control.

I met Jim when he moved to Southern California to head up his agency's office in the area. He was being groomed for a top position in the New York office in the firm, and this was to be a proving ground to see if he could effectively run the office. His two-year assignment stretched into five years, and during that time he and family fell in love with California and lost any desire to return to New York. However, the firm was expecting him to come back and return to the high stress, long hours and long commuting pace that was the norm for the firm's New York top management.

Jim was not looking forward to the day when it was time to return to the New York office. He had grown accustomed to a somewhat slower pace in California and to his five-minute commute to the office from home. While in California, he felt like he had balanced work and family well for the first time. And Jim said no to the demand that he come back to New York, astounding his colleagues but delighting his family. He quit his job with the firm and went to work with a smaller, local advertising agency that no one in New York had ever heard of. "I want a life," he said.

Jim realized that there were tradeoffs that had to be made—that he could not have it all, at least not in the way he thought of his life before moving to California. He realized that to be responsible for his family, he could not travel as much, nor could he put in the long hours he had when they lived in New York. He took a 50 percent cut in pay, and though he is still doing very well, he is no longer on the fast track to the top in the advertising business. There is no doubt that this was a very difficult choice. But Jim believes he made a good choice.

It may be that after his kids are in college and more on their own, Jim may return to New York and take up a more time-intensive position in advertising. His choice to prioritize his family does not mean that Christians should necessarily avoid highly demanding careers, especially if they desire to fulfill a task of transformational service. But the costs should be counted carefully as these decisions are made. We suggest that a person does not have to be a workaholic in order to view his or her work as transformational service, nor does being successful require ruining one's personal life.

CONCLUSION

Business is an environment that both reveals and refines a person's character and spirituality. We have argued that involvement in business both requires and nurtures virtues such as service, trust and perseverance. It further functions as a crucible in which spiritual formation occurs, most commonly in dealing with the adversity that inevitably comes with business. In order to maximize the role of the workplace in a person's spiritual formation, we have suggested some spiritual practices and ways of thinking that help place work in perspective with other important aspects of life. We will extend this argument in chapters four and seven—there we will suggest more specifically that what makes business such a significant contributor to a person's spiritual formation is the connection with money and power. The Bible is clear that both these components are critical indicators of a person's spiritual maturity. Jesus teaches that money is a barometer that reveals the condition of a person's inner life (Mt 6:19-24). In addition, the Bible cautions against the abuse of power, since it is inconsistent with the concept of greatness in the kingdom (Lk 22:24-26). We will take up the subjects of wealth and success in chapter four, and the exercise of power in chapter seven.

4

WEALTH, SUCCESS
AND AMBITION

The drive toward wealth, success and ambition permeates business. This should come as no surprise—we live in a culture driven by the desire to realize a dream that is most often defined in terms of a financial fortune. Yet the Bible directly warns of the dangers of pursuing these. How, then, can a Christian simultaneously be successful in business and remain faithful as a disciple?

Since we are both full-time professors, from time to time we like to exercise our professorial prerogatives and give surprise quizzes. Usually we do this to get people thinking about the subject at hand. That's our purpose here—to stimulate your thinking about the material in this chapter. This quiz is about the Bible's views on money, success and ambition. They are all true-false questions. Try to answer them now, and we'll provide hints to the answers as the chapter progresses. We would encourage you to retake this quiz, which reappears at the end of the chapter (with the answers), after reading the chapter.

1. The Bible has more to say about money than it does about heaven and hell. T / F

2. The Bible teaches that it is wrong to accumulate wealth for yourself beyond what you need. T / F

3. Ambition is not encouraged in the Bible, because it is the opposite of contentment. T / F

4. Jesus and the disciples were from very poor backgrounds, making it easier for them to identify with those in poverty. T / F

5. The Bible teaches that poverty is a virtue that helps people understand what it means to trust God. T / F

6. The Bible connects a person's attitude about money with his or her overall spiritual health. T / F

7. It is not possible to faithfully follow God without an attitude of care for the poor and needy. T / F

8. The early church held all their possessions in common, divesting themselves of all earthly goods. T / F

9. Jesus' advice to the rich young ruler to "sell all you have and give it to the poor" is the norm for the Christian today. T / F

10. A person whose goal is to be CEO of his or her company is being too ambitious and lacks the virtue of contentment. T / F

11. It is possible to be successful in business without compromising your integrity or your faith. T / F

12. A person cannot be wealthy without succumbing to the temptations (greed, idolatry and envy) the Bible warns about. T / F

These are complex questions. If work is a place where we give ourselves in service to God, then we can't escape considering issues of ambition, success and money. In many cases they accompany working with excellence and faithfulness, because work that is done well often leads to the prospect of getting ahead. In fact, most people expect both advancement and social mobility as a reward for hard work and productivity. This expectation raises some tough questions for the person attempting to integrate work with the Bible's teaching on contentment and materialism. A person's attitude toward wealth and success is a key indicator of his or her level of spiritual maturity (quiz question 6).

Our discussion in this chapter continues the general theme of business and spirituality that began in chapter three, where we argued that business is a crucible in which a person's spiritual life can be challenged and developed. We now take this further and maintain that the struggle to curb materialism and check the influence of wealth potentially *nurtures* spiritual growth and *reflects* spiritual maturity.

WEALTH AND SUCCESS IN THE ANCIENT WORLD

In terms of money and economics it would be hard to overestimate the differences between the ancient world and today. The ancient economy was characterized by extremes of wealth and poverty, often existing side by side, with some lower-middle-class people working in the trades. It appears that Jesus was among that lower middle class, since his family, being carpenters, was not dependent solely on agriculture but had a somewhat marketable trade (quiz question 4). The disciples appeared to be of some moderate financial means, since their plea that they had left everything (their business and livelihood) to follow Jesus would make little sense if they had been very poor (Mt 19:27). The majority of the economic activity centered around subsistence-level agriculture, herding and some trades, where farmland was the primary productive asset. The vast majority of the population worked to provide for their basic self-sufficiency, and a small number of elites controlled most of the wealth, resulting in significant social and economic disparities between the land-owning elites and the masses.[1] As a result, the majority of the population regularly was subjected to economic injustice and lived on the edge of economic vulnerability.

For the most part the ancient economy was what economists describe as "zero sum" in nature. That is, the pool of economic resources was relatively fixed, and to get ahead a person usually had to do so at someone else's expense. Historian Douglas Oakman says, "Low productivity and social inequities encouraged a notion of *limited good*, in which the goods of life were believed to have been distributed and could not be increased absolutely."[2] It was as though the economy was like a pie; if someone got a bigger piece, someone else got a smaller one. There was more of a cause-and-effect relationship between economic winners and losers, and as the rich got richer, usually the poor got poorer. In most cases the wealth of the rich was obtained at the expense of the poor. This is why, in the ancient world, the accumulation of wealth itself could be problematic, because it correlated more closely with someone else's poverty than it does today,

---

[1]Douglas E. Oakman, "Economics of Palestine," in *Dictionary of New Testament Background*, ed. Craig A. Evans and Stanley E. Porter (Downers Grove, Ill.: InterVarsity Press, 2000), pp. 304-5.
[2]Ibid., p. 305.

particularly since those extremes of wealth and poverty often existed closely side by side.[3]

This also partially explains why the Old Testament prophets had strong words of rebuke for those who oppressed the poor by taking advantage of their vulnerability. For example, Amos spoke out against the rich in ancient Israel:

> For three sins of Israel,
>   even for four, I will not turn my back [my wrath].
> They sell the righteous for silver,
>   and the needy for a pair of sandals.
> They trample on the heads of the poor
>   as upon the dust of the ground
>   and deny justice to the oppressed. (Amos 2:6-7)

Or as Jeremiah put it:

> Woe to him who builds his palace by unrighteousness,
>   his upper rooms by injustice;
> making his countrymen work for nothing,
>   not paying them for their labor. . . .
>
> But your eyes and your heart
>   are set only on dishonest gain,
> on shedding innocent blood
>   and on oppression and extortion. (Jer 22:13, 17)

By contrast, those who take care of the poor are praised. Jeremiah affirms that

> "He defended the cause of the poor and needy
>   and so it all went well.
> Is this not what it means to know me?"
>   declares the Lord. (Jer 22:16)

Proverbs pointedly affirms this point:

---

[3]John R. Schneider, *The Good of Affluence: Seeking God in a Culture of Wealth* (Grand Rapids: Eerdmans, 2002), pp. 31-32. Schneider points out that enjoying one's affluence could be just as problematic because "when someone consumed a non-essential item, he or she was depriving someone else of the only means available for assistance" (pp. 31-32). Given the close proximity of the rich and poor and the ancient world, the person who was deprived could be your neighbor.

He who oppresses the poor shows contempt for their Maker,
  but whoever is kind to the needy honors God. (Prov 14:31).

Here is an example of how someone could oppress the poor and take advantage of their vulnerability. Suppose a man owned a piece of land and was farming it for his family. As a result of drought, mismanagement or laziness, he came into hard times and could not support his family any longer. Then someone with financial resources offered to loan the man some money to get him through the difficult times, but it would be at exorbitant rates, thereby insuring that he would eventually default on the loan. And, of course, his land was the collateral for the loan, since that was the only piece of valuable property he owned. When he could no longer pay the money back, the lender took his property, and the man then became a tenant farmer working for the lender, keeping a subsistence level of the produce for his family and turning the rest over to the new owner.

This is but one example of the rich taking advantage of the poor.[4] This practice seems to be what the prophet Isaiah condemns when he says,

What sorrow for you who buy up house after house and field
    after field,
  until everyone is evicted
  and you live alone in the land. (Is 5:8 NLT, emphasis added)

This is also why the Old Testament law had a provision that obligated the next of kin to buy back the property and return it to the original owner. Thus that person's family would not be without a means of making a living (Lev 25:25-28). This part of the law insured that the poor would not be victimized and presumed that land ownership was the primary link to economic stability.[5] This may also account for the prohibition on usury, related

---

[4]This practice continued into the New Testament era. Frequently the poor had to sell their land outright and thus became tenant farmers. In other cases they borrowed money, using their land as collateral and eventually forfeiting it (see Schneider, *Good of Affluence*, pp. 120-21; and Justo Gonzales, *Faith and Wealth: A History of Early Christian Ideas on the Origin, Significance and Use of Money* [San Francisco: Harper & Row, 1990], pp. 73-75). Of course, there were a variety of other factors that often separated families from their land, including temporary occupation of parts of the land by foreign nations, high levels of taxation that forced families to sell their land and the increasing concentration of wealth in the hands of a few (see Christopher J. H. Wright, *God's People in God's Land: Family, Land and Property in the Old Testament* [Grand Rapids: Eerdmans, 1990], pp. 106-9).

[5]For further discussion of this connection between ownership of land and wealth creation in the ancient world, see Wright, *God's People in God's Land*, pp. 115-80. The right to private property

not to commercial lending but to charging interest to people who were purchasing items necessary for their survival. In other words, a person's dire economic conditions were not to be seen as opportunities for business, in which their vulnerability would likely be taken advantage of. Rather, they were to be considered candidates for charitable care.[6]

In the ancient world there were few legitimate ways a person could accumulate wealth. Frequently people acquired wealth through taxation, by using positions of political power to extort money from the general populace. The rulers gained wealth this way, as did the tax collectors in Jesus' time. Solomon initiated an extensive taxation and forced-labor program in order to finance his empire during his reign. People also acquired wealth through theft. Or they could acquire additional wealth through oppression of the poor. There were relatively few ways that people could become wealthy through trades or commerce, though some did, such as Job and Abraham. But they were the exception, not the rule, in the ancient world. People most often got wealthy at the expense of others, often through morally questionable means.[7] This is one of the reasons that the Bible counsels people not to chase after wealth because of the temptation it brings (1 Tim 6:9). The pursuit of wealth brought the prospects of falling into a moral trap because, in the ancient world, there were so few ways to become wealthy without resorting to immoral practices. This is one of the reasons why the Bible views wealth somewhat skeptically. Not that there is anything inherently wrong with wealth, but because the means used to acquire it so frequently involved moral and spiritual compromise.[8]

The same is true of ambition. There were not many opportunities for people to get ahead in the ancient world. For the most part a person's socioeconomic position was fixed by virtue of the family he or she was

---

in the Old Testament was not absolute, since land could not be permanently bought or sold (since it ultimately belonged to God [Lev 25:23]). The law was structured so that land would stay in the family and provide family stability.

[6]This discussion of the taking of interest should be seen in the larger context of structures that were in place to prevent inordinate accumulation of wealth—such as the Year of Jubilee, limits on the kinds of pledges taken as security for debt and laws against the removal of boundary stones (see Christopher J. H. Wright, *Old Testament Ethics for the People of God* [Downers Grove, Ill.: InterVarsity Press, 2004], pp. 164-66).

[7]Brian Griffiths, *The Creation of Wealth* (Downers Grove, Ill.: InterVarsity Press, 1985), pp. 25-31; Schneider, *Good of Affluence*, pp. 31-32.

[8]Of course, the temptation to idolatry was also a significant concern—people would trust in their wealth instead of God for their security.

born into.[9] There was very little social mobility and few legitimate avenues for ambition to be realized. This is one reason why the Bible places so much emphasis on contentment, and why the opposite of contentment is envy, not ambition (quiz question 3). For example, Paul counsels the Thessalonians to "make it your ambition to lead a quiet life, to mind your own business and to work with your hands" (1 Thess 4:11). Part of the reason for this is that contentment signified that a person was ultimately dependent on God for his or her needs, because God could be trusted to adequately meet those needs. This is the basis for the prohibition on envy, since the ban on covetousness (Ex 20:17; Deut 5:21) presumes that God supplies a sufficient portion of material goods. But beyond that, ambition for socioeconomic advancement generally could not be fulfilled without getting involved with immoral people and questionable practices.

In the ancient world the idea of going from "rags to riches" was virtually unheard of. The scenario in which a person could do well financially and do good at the same time was very difficult to achieve. However, with the advent of industrial capitalism, the economic system changed radically and the zero-sum game mostly became a thing of the past. Today, when someone or some company makes a profit legitimately, the size of the pie increases. By definition, profit is the creation of wealth. Someone like Bill Gates or Warren Buffet simply having extraordinary wealth does not mean that others are necessarily worse off economically.[10] Nor does it necessarily follow that Gates's or Buffet's wealth was gained at the expense of someone else. In a modern market economy, wealth is constantly being created, so that it is possible for someone to become wealthy without necessarily

---

[9]There was some limited social mobility in the time of Jesus, usually as a result of marriage to someone in a higher class, or as a result of patronage, that is, being sponsored by a wealthy patron who recognized a person's personal achievements. It was not normally as a result of working hard at one's occupation (D. F. Watson, "Roman Social Classes," in *Dictionary of New Testament Background*, ed. Craig A. Evans and Stanley E. Porter [Downers Grove, Ill.: InterVarsity Press, 2000], p. 1003).

[10]Silicon Valley businessman T. J. Rodgers, in an interview with Dinesh D'Souza, pointed out that Bill Gates had done much more than charity organizations like Mother Teresa's to eradicate poverty in the undeveloped world. Without disparaging the heroic work of Mother Teresa and the sisters who carry on her work, it seems clear that capitalism and technology have done a significant work in lifting roughly half the world's population out of poverty. It should also be noted that much of the funding for charities focused on the poor comes from the wealth created by capitalism. See more detailed discussion of this in chap. 5. The interview is cited in Dinesh D'Souza, *The Virtue of Prosperity: Finding Values in an Age of Techno-Affluence* (New York: Free Press, 2000), p. 124.

succumbing to the temptations about which Scripture warns (quiz question 11). Our market economy makes it far easier to be wealthy and virtuous than did the agricultural subsistence economy of the ancient world. There are, however, some countries, most notably in the developing world, that still resemble the economic life of the ancient world. In these places the zero-sum game would still apply to some degree. In those parts of the world, people are more routinely subjected to economic injustice, and many live in perilous poverty without hope of bettering their conditions. Extremes of wealth and poverty do exist side by side in many parts of the developing world, a feature that more resembles the ancient economy.

Today, in countries where market capitalism is thriving, rags-to-riches is no longer a rare exception. Social mobility is widely available today, given hard work and education. Though a segment of the population is trapped in poverty, today it is quite possible, and in many cases expected, for someone to work him- or herself out of poverty and into the middle class. Today, it is more the norm in market-oriented economies that people who become wealthy do so without resorting to theft, taxation or oppression. Numerous businesses succeed because they provide a needed and legitimate product or service, a morally legitimate avenue to acquiring wealth. Of course, there are still avenues in which wealth is acquired through illegal or immoral means. Further, it is possible to become wealthy in a legitimate business but with exploitive business practices or elaborate and deceptive financial schemes. In addition, it is certainly the case that people sometimes cut corners ethically to get ahead. But today legitimate business, hard work and ambition can and generally do lead to social mobility and the accumulation of some wealth.

WEALTH AND A CHRISTIAN WORLDVIEW

Given the many differences in economic life between the ancient world and today, understanding the Bible's teaching on wealth and possessions can be a bit complicated. Part of what contributes to this complexity is the abundance of biblical material that addresses the issue—there's more material in the Bible on money than on heaven and hell combined (quiz question 1). Often when people read the Bible on economic matters, they naively assume that since materialism is fundamentally a matter of the heart and that the heart has not changed in more than two thousand years, then the

Bible's teaching on money directly applies to today. However, it's critical to read the Bible in the context of these differences between the ancient economy and the modern information-age economy. Many of the Bible's specific commands about economic life are difficult to apply directly today. For example, laws governing the disposition of land (the Year of Jubilee and the redemption of the land) presumed simple ownership by extended families and were designed to keep land in these families. It is very difficult to see how those laws could be applied to a complex real estate market or account for new forms of ownership, such as intellectual property, which is the reason why no one seriously proposes returning to the Jubilee or the law of redemption. Or take the mandate for manual labor by Paul when he instructs people to "work with their hands" as a sign of their diligence (1 Thess 4:11), which cannot be applied literally in an information age economy, in which people work with their minds and a minority of the workforce is engaged in manual labor. With much of the Bible's teaching on money, we need to search out general principles that transcend culture and context, and that we can apply to a very different socioeconomic setting. What follows is our suggestion of the elements that form the biblical parameters for our understanding of money, wealth and ambition.[11]

1. God is the final and ultimate owner of all our material possessions. Everything we own ultimately belongs to God. The psalmist says: "The earth is the LORD's, and everything in it" (Ps 24:1). Our wealth and possessions are his good gifts to us (Ps 115:16). In the Old Testament one way that this principle was embodied was in the way Israel transacted real estate, the primary economic asset in the ancient world. Land could not be permanently bought or sold—it could only be leased, and in the Year of Jubilee it was to be returned to its original owners. The rationale was spelled out clearly: "The land must not be sold permanently, *because the land is mine* and you are but aliens and my tenants" (Lev 25:23, emphasis added).[12] What-

---

[11]The material on this subject is voluminous, and we can only summarize the main contours of the Bible's teaching on wealth. For further discussion in this area, see Schneider, *Good of Affluence;* Craig L. Blomberg, *Neither Poverty Nor Riches: A Biblical Theology of Possessions* (Downers Grove, Ill.: InterVarsity Press, 2001); Wesley K. Willmer, *God and Your Stuff: The Vital Link Between Your Possessions and Your Soul* (Colorado Springs: NavPress, 2002); Ronald J. Sider, *Rich Christians in an Age of Poverty: Moving from Affluence to Generosity,* 5th ed. (Nashville: Thomas Nelson, 2005); Gonzales, *Faith and Wealth.*

[12]Wright, *God's People in God's Land,* pp. 58-65, 119-28. Leviticus 25:23 affirms not only God's ownership of the land but also the people's status as aliens and tenants—not permanent residents.

ever wealth we have is God's good gift to us (Eccles 5:19-20; 1 Tim 6:17), which we are to enjoy, and of which we are to be responsible trustees.

This idea that we are stewards, not owners of our possessions, is a powerful theme in the Bible. Stewardship of our resources is a constant theme in both Old and New Testaments, with Jesus' parable of the talents being one of the principal illustrations (Mt 25:14-30). In it the master entrusts resources to each of his servants, and on his return he holds them responsible for using the resources productively. The point of the parable is that the master expects us to put his resources to productive use while he is away, and that there is nothing wrong with the master profiting from the use of these resources. Though the resources in question are broader than simply money, there is no doubt in the parable that the talents do not belong to the servants—they are but stewards of those resources entrusted to them and are responsible for their proper use on the master's behalf.

2. There's more to life than that which a person accumulates. Jesus put this very clearly when he said, "A man's life does not consist in the abundance of his possessions" (Lk 12:15). He admonishes people who are pursuing wealth to remember that we are to "seek first his kingdom and his righteousness, and all these things [material needs] will be given to you as well" (Mt 6:33).

I (Scott) got a sobering lesson in this in the process of taking care of the possessions of a couple of deceased relatives. After they died, it fell to my wife and me to dispose of all their estate. With one particular relative, who did not own much, we kept a suitcase full of old photographs and called the haulers to literally take all of her possessions and dispose of them. With a second relative, virtually everything he owned was either given away, sold at a substantial discount or thrown away. We kept only the items that had sentimental value. What was remarkable about the process was how dispassionately we disposed of the things these people had worked their lives to accumulate. It was a powerful reminder of how insignificant possessions are in the big picture of a person's life. We kept what was of value—the things that embodied memories of the person and his or her life. Paul's statement that we enter the world with nothing and depart in the same way (1 Tim 6:7) was vividly illustrated to us.

3. Hold your wealth and possessions loosely and give with open-handed generosity. If everything a person possesses ultimately belongs to God, and there's more to life than what we own, then holding our possessions loosely seems to logically follow. The Bible is clear that generosity is to characterize God's people (1 Tim 6:18). Giving is to be done willingly and gladly, not under compulsion (2 Cor 9:7). There is a special emphasis on giving to the poor and taking care of their needs (Eph 4:28). The way people handle their money, particularly how generous they are with it, is considered a barometer of their spiritual lives. Jesus makes it clear that our hearts follow our money, that is, we can tell a lot about where our heart is by where we invest our money (Mt 6:19-21; quiz question 6). This is the reason why Jesus tells the rich young ruler to give all his money away. But this is not necessarily the norm today—there were a variety of wealthy people who followed Jesus and formed the early church, which suggests that the accumulation of wealth is not by itself prohibited in the Bible (quiz question 9). However, in the example of the rich young ruler, his wealth was a indication of the condition of his heart, and the only way to deal adequately with the issue was to divest himself of his wealth.

The church in the early parts of Acts appeared to hold all goods in common (Acts 2:44) and some have suggested that the church was an early form of communal living. Though renunciation of all earthly goods was not the norm, it is clear that the church held their goods very loosely in order to meet its members' substantial financial needs. Acts 2:42 makes it clear that the early church members sold their possessions not for the principle of renunciation *but for the sake of those who had immediate needs.*[13] The early church did not practice divestment of all earthly goods, though they were exceedingly generous in meeting numerous pressing economic needs. The early church was always generous, sometimes extending that generosity to needs in other parts of the world (Acts 11:27-30; 2 Cor 8:1-12). However, the apostles also emphasized that each person was responsible for working in order to provide for self, family and the poor (Eph 4:28; 2 Thess 3:6-10). If someone was not willing to work, that person was not entitled to a share in the community's resources.

The Bible puts a special emphasis on generosity to the poor and the economically vulnerable. Throughout Scripture a person's attitude toward

---

[13]Gonzales, *Faith and Wealth*, p. 82.

the poor was considered an important measurement of spirituality (quiz question 7). The prophets linked a person's care for the poor individually and Israel's care for the poor nationally with spiritual commitment. For example, Isaiah maintains that true religious observance does not consist in ritual and ceremony but in tangible care for the poor and the pursuit of economic justice. He says,

> Is this not the kind of fasting I have chosen:
> to loose the chains of injustice,
>   and untie the cords of the yoke,
> to set the oppressed free
>   and break every yoke?
> Is it not to share your food with the hungry,
>   and to provide the poor wanderer with shelter—
> when you see the naked, to clothe him? (Is 58:6-7)

Earlier in this chapter we pointed out that Jeremiah linked a person's care for the poor with what it means to know God ("'He defended the cause of the poor and needy, and so all went well. *Is that not what it means to know me?*" declares the LORD" [Jer 22:16, emphasis added]), and Proverbs teaches us that it honors God ("whoever is kind to the needy honors God" [Prov 14:31]).

Jesus continues this priority on care for the poor by making it one of the distinguishing marks of his earthly ministry. In fact, Jesus identifies his care for the poor as one of the primary pieces of evidence that he has inaugurated the kingdom. In Luke's account of his first public ministry, Jesus spoke of his mission: to "preach good news to the poor . . . proclaim freedom for the prisoners and recovery of sight for the blind, to release the oppressed" (Lk 4:18). Jesus' ministry among the marginalized in his day was considered fulfillment of prophecy about the Messiah's coming. Similarly, when followers of John the Baptist asked Jesus directly whether or not he was the Messiah, he replied, "Go back and report to John what you hear and see: The blind receive sight, the lame walk, those who have leprosy are cured, the deaf hear, the dead are raised, and the good news is preached to the poor" (Mt 11:4-5). The Bible is clear that we are to cultivate generosity in general. But the Bible's teaching specifically and repeatedly mentions the poor as one of the primary objects of our generosity. James repeats the Old Testament priority on this when he says,

Religion that God our Father accepts as pure and faultless is this: to look after widows and orphans in their distress [figures of speech representing some of the most economically vulnerable groups in the ancient world] and to keep oneself from being polluted by the world. (Jas 1:27)

4. The Bible sanctions enjoying one's life and resources as God's good gift. Our prosperity is ultimately the result of God's blessing in our lives. The Bible makes it clear that our diligence also plays a part (Prov 10:4), but ultimately, all that a person accumulates comes from God. There is nothing inherently wrong with having wealth and enjoying it as God's good gift, as long as it is earned legitimately and we are generous with it (quiz questions 2, 12). Ecclesiastes affirms that "when God gives any man wealth and possessions, and enables him to enjoy them, to accept his lot and be happy in his work—*this is a gift of God*" (Eccles 5:19, emphasis added).[14] God promised the nation of Israel a "land overflowing with milk and honey," figurative language for the abundance of his blessing.[15] God clearly intended his people to enjoy the abundance of his blessing in the land. In addition, the biblical descriptions of the Garden of Eden in Genesis and the new Jerusalem in Revelation echo this same vision of God providing abundance. Though his blessing today is not tied to national prosperity, as it was under the Mosaic law, the principle of God intending abundance for his people seems clear. Of course, this is balanced by mandates for generosity and compassion toward those who are in need. This emphasis on enjoying life as God's good gift is not to suggest anything like a prosperity theology, in which God necessarily rewards righteousness and faithfulness with material prosperity. God does indeed reward faithfulness with his blessing, but it is not necessarily or even normally a financial blessing. Today there is no necessary connection between a person's wealth and his or her faithfulness to God.

---

[14]It should be noted that Solomon also affirms the vanity of wealth—that it cannot provide ultimate satisfaction, nor is it a substitute for God (Eccles 5:8-20; 6:1-12). These are not mutually exclusive propositions, since wealth can be God's good gift without making it akin to idolatry. Solomon is suggesting that wealth can be a gift without it being so highly valued that it is seen as the key to fitting the pieces of life's puzzle together into a coherent whole.

[15]Schneider, *Good of Affluence*, pp. 70-74. Of course, with the blessing of abundance came the responsibility of generosity, especially toward the poor, which Schneider also affirms. See Sider, *Rich Christians*, for further discussion of these responsibilities toward the poor. See also Ron Sider, *Just Generosity: A New Vision for Overcoming Poverty in America* (Grand Rapids: Baker, 1999).

Neither is poverty a virtue in the Bible. The poor and poor in spirit are blessed not because they are poor but because theirs is the kingdom of heaven (Mt 5:3; Lk 6:20; quiz question 5).[16] In the wisdom literature poverty is often associated with a lack of diligence, wisdom and moral character (Prov 6:6-11; 10:4; 24:30-34), though today there are also systemic causes of poverty that have nothing to do with a person's character. Neither wealth nor poverty per se is a necessary indication of a person's spirituality. Throughout the Bible the wicked prosper and the righteous often suffer poverty for reasons that may have little to do with their spiritual maturity or lack of it. For example, the psalmist laments the ease and wealth of the wicked:

> For I envied the arrogant
>   when I saw the prosperity of the wicked. . . .
> This is what the wicked are like—
>   always carefree, they increase in wealth. (Ps 73:3, 12)

The New Testament also affirms the enjoyment of life as God's provision for his people. For example, Paul commands Timothy to pass along his teaching that "those who are rich in this world [are] not to be arrogant nor to put their hope in wealth, . . . but to put their hope in God, who richly provides us with everything for our enjoyment" (1 Tim 6:17; quiz questions 2, 12). God commands *contentment* (defined as "wanting what you have"); *trust in him*, not money, for security; and *generosity* with one's wealth to balance the mandate to enjoy life as God's good gift.

5. A person's ultimate source of trust for security and identity is God and his provision, not money. Though the Bible affirms wealth as God's good gift, this does not mean that either its pursuit or its possession is free from temptation. One of the dangers of wealth that the Bible frequently mentions is the connection between wealth and idolatry. Though it is not a necessary connection, since there do seem to be wealthy people who faithfully follow both Jesus and the apostles, it is a common cause for caution. To succumb to idolatry in any of its various forms is a serious problem, and it is a temptation not difficult to fall into for wealth to become a substitute for God. The Bible repeatedly cautions against trusting in wealth for our

---

[16]For more on this view of the Beatitudes, see Dallas Willard, *The Divine Conspiracy* (New York: HarperCollins, 1998).

economic security. The psalmist laments the person who trusts in riches, suggesting that it is futile to do so because money can't save our life before God (Ps 49:6-7). Further, the prophets urge people to trust in God, not wealth, wisdom or power for their ultimate sense of security in the world (Jer 9:23). The New Testament cautions against trusting in wealth instead of God, since wealth is so unreliable and God is entirely faithful to take care of our needs (1 Tim 6:17). Jesus makes it clear that wealth can be a hindrance to entering the kingdom (Mk 10:24), not only because it so often involved immoral activity but also because of the spiritual danger to use our wealth as a substitute for trust in God.

Neither should a person's balance sheet be used as a source of identity or security.[17] The danger, suggests Craig Gay, is that money "has become a kind of end in itself and indeed the final purpose for a great many people."[18] Thus the notion of someone's net worth is very problematic, since it tends to measure worth in strictly financial terms, reducing the person's value to what can be quantified in a financial statement. Gay suggests that part of the danger of the dominance of money on a person's worldview is "life it-self comes to be experienced as a kind of malleable mélange of commodi-fied meaning, values and significations," that everything is valued in the quantifiable terms of money.[19] Sociologist Robert Wuthnow echoes this when he concludes that "money is subjectively linked with our self-identity" and thus becomes an important determinant of how a person views him- or herself.[20]

Nor are people to be identified by what they purchase, whether it is the size or location of their home, type of car driven or any other posses-sion that a culture deems makes a person valuable.[21] This is perhaps

---

[17]For further reading on this important basis for a person's security and identity, see the insight-ful book by Craig M. Gay, *Cash Values: Money and the Erosion of Meaning in Today's Society* (Grand Rapids: Eerdmans, 2004).

[18]Ibid., p. 90. For further discussion of the critique of materialism, see Robert Wuthnow, ed., *Rethinking Materialism: Perspectives on the Spiritual Dimension of Economic Life* (Grand Rapids: Eerdmans, 1995); and Robert Wuthnow, *God and Mammon in America* (New York: Free Press, 1994).

[19]Gay, *Cash Values*, p. 68.

[20]Robert Wuthnow, *Poor Richard's Principle: Recovering the American Dream Through the Moral Dimensions of Work, Business and Money* (Princeton, N.J.: Princeton University Press, 1996), p. 153.

[21]For further discussion of this point, see Tom Boudoin, *Consuming Faith: Integrating Who We Are with What We Buy* (Lanham, Md.: Sheed & Ward, 2003); and Rodney Clapp, ed., *The*

more subtle than might be first realized, since the consumer culture has
become so identified by what is known as "branding" (see chap. 8).
Branding refers to the way consumers identify with particular brands of
products, whether clothes, cars, electronics or other consumer items the
culture values. Catholic theologian Tom Boudoin points out that branding can affect the way consumers identify themselves, determine their fit
in a particular group or subculture, and even shape their definition of
success. He suggests that various brands can communicate meaning and
identity, especially for younger adults and teens in formative stages of
developing their identity. In what others call "branding for life," Boudoin points out that "if young adults get settled into certain brands
through which they declare their self-identity, those brands will more likely
be a part of that person's identity ensemble as they move into adulthood
and middle age."[22] This is one of the long-term goals of advertising, to
help consumers attach personal meaning to product brands—advertisers
know that they have succeeded when they bring consumers to self-iden-
tify with their products.[23]

Part of the solution to the materialism endemic to our culture is to approach money with what Gay calls "lightheartedness" that comes ultimately
from our trust in God for our provision. The late Catholic theologian Richard John Neuhaus suggests taking a "whimsical" view of wealth:

> The point is that wealth—having or producing it—really does not matter
> that much. This point is missed by both the avaricious, who become captive
> to their possessions, and by religiously driven ideologues promoting designs
> for a just economic order. Both take wealth too seriously. A theologically
> informed appreciation of economic life and the production of wealth should
> be marked by a sense of whimsy and wonder in the face of the fortuitous,
> contingent, chancy and unpredictable realities of economic life.[24]

Consuming Passion: Christianity and the Consumer Culture (Downers Grove, Ill.: InterVarsity
Press, 1998).

[22]Boudoin, *Consuming Faith*, pp. 7-8 (emphasis added). He further suggests that "branding offers a consistent, coherent identity, in which you are told about your true self; it offers mem-
bership in a community; it issues an invitation to unconditional trust; it offers the promise of
conversion and a new life" (ibid., p. 44).

[23]For further reading on this as one of the goals of advertising, see Howard J. Blumenthal,
Branded for Life: How American Are Brainwashed by the Brands We Love (Cincinnati: Emmis
Books, 2005).

[24]Richard John Neuhaus, "Wealth and Whimsy: On Economic Creativity," *First Things*,
August-September (1990), p. 29.

Of course, this is more challenging during difficult economic times, but no less important, and does not diminish the importance of diligence and responsibility in taking care of yourself and your dependents.

SUCCESS AND AMBITION WITHIN A CHRISTIAN WORLDVIEW

At first glance the Bible appears to downplay ambition. Paul commands the church to "make it your ambition to lead a quiet life" (1 Thess 4:11). The only place where ambition is praised is when Paul commends people for their desire to be an overseer of the church (1 Tim 3:1). In the context of the ancient world this is not surprising since there were few valid outlets for someone to pursue economic ambition. But that does not mean that the Bible does not have advice for people today who are working hard to succeed. Just because there were few categories for socioeconomic mobility in the first century doesn't mean that the Bible looks down on those who want to pursue success in their business (quiz questions 3, 10). After all, there were some notable examples of virtuous "worldly" success in the Scripture. Abraham and Job were wealthy men; Joseph rose to the position of prime minister of Egypt; Nehemiah was a high-ranking official in postexile Persia; Daniel thrived in the culture of Babylon and virtually ran the empire for various kings over roughly sixty years of service; and there was a small cadre of successful, wealthy people who supported Jesus and the apostles during the New Testament era. There does not seem to be anything intrinsically problematic about people being faithful to God and being successful or ambitious at the same time, assuming their motives are consistent with the Bible's teaching (quiz question 11).

But we should be clear on what constitutes success from a Christian worldview. To be sure, it is not necessarily connected with a person's balance sheet. Neither is it necessarily connected with having a position of influence. Nor does being famous or well known necessarily connect with success. After all, someone could be well known for many things, some of which would land a person in jail! These are all false measures, though they are commonly held cultural assumptions. If your work is an altar, a place of transformational service to God, then how you measure your success will not be according to earthly standards.

When he began his legal career, my (Scott's) friend Ben worked for one of the most prominent, wealthy and well-known trial lawyers in the country. This person was the envy of the legal community, and many lawyers in the firm aspired to his level of professional and financial success. But the more Ben got to know him, the more he realized that his personal life was hardly something to admire. He was a thoroughgoing workaholic, and as a result he had no personal life outside his work, he experienced several broken marriages and was estranged from all of his children. In fact, when he was discharged from the hospital after a heart attack, the only person who was willing and available to take him home was his secretary. No one from his family was available or wanted to bring him home. While he was successful by the criteria of the culture, he is a good example of someone who climbed the ladder of success only to find out that it was leaning against the wrong wall!

Similarly, out-of-control ambition nearly ruined the life of Dominic Orr, whose story was the focus of a provocative *Fortune* magazine cover story titled "Confessions of a CEO." Self-described as "ruthlessly aggressive," Orr was a classic workaholic. He was a successful CEO, taking two Silicon Valley tech companies public, but costing him his marriage and nearly permanently alienating his two children. A painful nine-year journey that involved therapy, depression and extended time out of the workplace eventually helped Orr regain perspective. He returned to be CEO of another start-up company, chastened by his past hard-driving ways. What finally made him realize that his life was careening out of control was when his son took a fireplace poker and his skateboard to Orr's car. His son said, "I tried to destroy something that mattered to him." Orr eventually realized that even though he was at the top of the corporate world, he was at the bottom of his personal life. He did make painful changes to his work life and has regained his relationship with his two children, though his marriage was irreparable.[25]

By contrast, consider Mother Teresa, arguably one of the most universally admired figures in the world, and her legacy lives on since her death. For most of her life she labored in obscurity, serving the poorest of the poor in the slums of Calcutta. Toward the end of her life Mother Teresa began to receive recognition for her decades of selfless service and even won the Nobel Prize (she gave the money away!). She achieved nothing of what our

---

[25]For more on the story of Dominic Orr, see Stephanie Mehta, "Confessions of a CEO," *Fortune*, November 2, 2007.

culture considers success—not wealth, position or fame (though she did become famous toward the end of her life, and somewhat against her will). From our cultural view of success we would conclude that she wasted her life. But from a Christian perspective, her life was anything but a waste. She actually was very ambitious to advance the work of God she was called to, but she clearly rejected all of the cultural criteria for success.

We have argued that business is an arena a person can do God's work in the world by being engaged in transformational service. We suggest that ambition to advance God's rule in the world through business is an appropriate form of ambition, in which title and position come about as a byproduct of a person's pursuit of excellence. But to seek the title and position with little regard to service represents naked ambition and confuses the goal with the byproduct. The goal for the person in business is transformational service, and the position or title is the byproduct, not vice versa.

When we ask students who have entrepreneurial goals what they want to do in business, they often reply, "I want to run my own company." When we inquire further about what kind of company they want to start, they frequently haven't given that much thought. Their goal is to get to run their own company, but what the company does is less important than the fact that it gives them the chance to run their own business and "be their own boss." What the company does and how it does it matter far more than whether a person runs the company.

The Bible has two primary criteria for measuring success—*excellence* and *faithfulness*. The Bible commands a commitment to excellence because our ultimate boss is God, and we are aiming to please him. If our work is an altar, then we ought to do our work with a quality that adds true, long-term value to our organization and to the broader community. Remember Paul's statement in Colossians 3:23-24: "Whatever you do, work at it with all your heart, as working for the Lord, not for men. . . . It is the Lord Christ whom you serve."

We also pursue excellence because *God is our model.* The creation that God made was very good (Gen 1:31). Work that is not up to standard is not pleasing to God, nor does it model anything attractive about a relationship with God. Someone who is settling for mediocrity generally doesn't have much of a platform at work to make a significant difference. The Bible commands diligence and perseverance in our pursuit of excellence (Prov 10:4-5; 20:4). The contrast between the wise person and the sluggard is a constant theme in the Proverbs, and it is clear that working hard is virtuous, while laziness leads to hard times (Prov 6:6-11; 24:30-34).

But many times whether we are successful is out of our control. To be sure, there is often a connection between success and hard work, but ultimately what we accomplish comes from God (Eccles 5:19). Our wealth is God's gift, our position is often a reward for our faithfulness, and any fame we achieve clearly comes from God. Though there is nothing intrinsically wrong with wealth, position or fame, these are byproducts of a life of faithfully pursuing excellence in our work. The Bible puts the *faithful* person on a pedestal to be admired. Proverbs states that "the faithful man will be richly blessed" (Prov 28:20). Jesus praises the "good and faithful servant," who was faithful in lesser matters and will be entrusted with more responsibility (Mt 25:21; Lk 19:17). It is required of a person not that he or she is found successful in the eyes of the culture but found *faithful* (1 Cor 4:2). To be faithful involves perseverance in the work God has called a person to, doing that work with integrity and excellence, and using work as an avenue to live out our faith. In chapter three we mentioned the research of both Robert Bellah and Amy Wrznesiewski, who described three categories of how people approach their work: jobs, careers or callings.[26] They conclude that people who are pursuing wealth, position or fame generally have *careers*, in which the ascent up the ladder is foremost, and what they do in order to achieve that is not as important. People who are committed to excellence and faithfulness are generally pursuing *callings*, in which what they do is paramount. By extension, promotion or advancement, if it happens, is seen as a byproduct. If our work is our altar and business is approached as transformational service, then what we do counts far more than how quickly or how far we advance professionally.

Ultimately, success from a Christian perspective is more about *who a person is* than what he or she accomplishes. This is at the heart of the notion of business and spiritual transformation. Jesus put this pointedly when

[26]Robert N. Bellah et al., *Habits of the Heart: Individualism and Commitment in American Life* (Berkeley: University of California Press, 1985); and Amy Wrznesiewski et al., "Jobs, Careers and Callings: People's Relations to Their Work," *Journal of Research in Personality* 31 (1997): 22. For a discussion of the context in which work has meaning, see Wuthnow, *Poor Richard's Principle*, pp. 95-137.

he asked the disciples, "What good is it for a man to gain the whole world and forfeit his soul? Or what can a man give in exchange for his soul?" (Mk 8:36-37). In other words, if a person achieves all the success he or she can muster, but does so at the expense of his or her character and quality of life, nothing has ultimately been gained. This is echoed by many of the ancient philosophers who understood "the good life" as something well beyond material aspirations. Aristotle, for example, connected happiness with being a good person, saying, "Happiness is an activity of the soul *in accordance with virtue.*" The ancient philosopher Epicurus similarly said, "It is not possible to live pleasantly without living prudently, honorably, and justly."

CONCLUSION

Are you ready to take the quiz again? Compare your answers from the first time you took it.

1. The Bible has more to say about money than it does about your eternal destiny. T / F

   If you check a concordance, you will find that Jesus had more to say about money than about heaven and hell combined. This ought to help us understand why this topic is so important for ordering a person's spiritual life today. (True)

2. The Bible teaches that it is wrong to accumulate wealth for yourself beyond what you need. T / F

   The Bible condemns greed and commands generosity, but also commends the enjoyment of life as God's good gift. Ecclesiastes teaches that both wealth and the enjoyment of it are gifts from God. The New Testament also affirms enjoying one's prosperity as God's good gift (1 Tim 6:17). (False)

3. Ambition is not encouraged in the Bible because it is the opposite of contentment. T / F

   Ambition is not emphasized in the Bible because there were so few morally legitimate avenues for a person to realize economic aspirations. This is why contentment is such an important theme in the Bible. The opposite of contentment is not ambition but envy. Ambition does, however, need to be defined on kingdom terms. (False)

4. Jesus and the disciples were from very poor backgrounds, making it easier for them to identify with those in poverty. T / F

   Jesus and his disciples did not grow up as street kids in grinding poverty. They were not wealthy either, but because of their trades they were likely in the lower middle class. The disciples evidently had some financial means, otherwise Jesus' admonition for them to leave everything to follow him would have lost its impact. (False)

5. The Bible teaches that poverty is a virtue that helps people understand what it means to trust God. T / F

   Though poverty may help people understand what it means to trust God, the Bible also emphasizes the need to work to provide for oneself and one's family. The poor are blessed because theirs is the kingdom, not because they are poor. There were also many wealthy and righteous people throughout the Bible. (False)

6. The Bible connects a person's attitude about money with that person's overall spiritual health. T / F

   Jesus is very clear about this: a person's heart and possessions are linked, and what people do with money reveals their heart (Mt 6:19-21). (True)

7. It is not possible to faithfully follow God without an attitude of care for the poor and needy. T / F

   This is a key part of Jesus' teaching that reflects the Old Testament prophets who linked care for the poor with genuinely knowing God (Is 58:6-7; Jer 22:16). (True)

8. The early church held all their possessions in common, divesting themselves of all earthly goods. T / F

   The early church did not practice divestment, but they did display an extraordinary degree of generosity toward others in need. This generosity was balanced by Paul's admonition that "if you don't work, you don't eat" (2 Thess 3:6-10). (False)

9. Jesus advice to the rich young ruler "to sell all you have and give it to the poor" is the norm for the Christian today. T / F

This is not a norm for today since there were some very influential wealthy people who were some of the closest followers of Christ. No suggestion is ever made in the Bible that they were less than full followers because of their wealth. (False)

10. A person whose goal is to be CEO of a company is being too ambitious and lacks the virtue of contentment. T / F

   A person with this goal is not necessarily overly ambitious and lacking contentment. There is nothing wrong in aspiring to be CEO as long as it is properly motivated. Contentment and ambition are not mutually exclusive. (False)

11. It is possible to be successful in business without compromising your integrity or your faith. T / F

   In the ancient world a person was far less likely succeed without oppressing the poor or abusing power. But today it is possible, perhaps even the norm in industrial capitalism, to do well financially and do good at the same time. (True)

12. A person cannot be wealthy without succumbing to the temptations (greed, idolatry and envy) which the Bible warns about. T / F

   There were righteous and wealthy people throughout the Bible, even among the closest followers of Jesus. However, we should not underestimate the difficulty of having wealth and resisting those temptations at the same time. (False)

5

Business and
the Global Economy

During an otherwise quiet November evening in laid-back Seattle in 1999, orange-tinted smoke, backlit from the setting sun, could be seen billowing from the ground between tall silhouetted buildings. Thunderous blasts from the firing of tear gas canisters and the rapid fire of rubber bullets interrupted screaming as chaos and violence broke out on normally placid downtown streets. Precisely orchestrated protests, including attempts to physically block World Trade Organization (WTO) delegates from assembling, quickly turned into clashes with riot-geared police, abruptly forcing the word *globalization* into public awareness.

Many of us then observing were surprised that a meeting of representatives of a then-obscure organization could inspire such controversy and passionate opposition, and turn a normally peaceful event into physical confrontations, burned dumpsters and smashed windows. What could cause a gathering of bureaucrats discussing normally bland topics such as the setting of international trade quotas to evolve into an incendiary debate that inspired in the now infamous "Battle in Seattle" and incite similar protests at many subsequent gatherings?

The meeting's planners, participants and the local police were all caught off-guard by the turn of events as the WTO meetings had turned into a lightning rod for all that was deemed wrong with globalization. The vast majority of protestors were nonviolent and represented diverse interests, including environmental, labor and developing country concerns. Instead of being *antiglobalization*, as they were commonly labeled, many of the protestors were emphatic that they were advocating for a different vision for globalization.[1] Energizing their defiance was a common belief that corporate financial pursuits were much too influential in the setting of policies that would dramatically affect the lives of scores of people, most of whom did not have their interests represented in any meaningful way.

Surrounding the passionate protests was the use of language typically associated with core biblical concerns, such as *fairness, justice, the marginalized* and *the voiceless*, that should have merited wider and more serious attention. Yet these concerns were lost behind the incessant media coverage of the very real violence at the event.

Much has been written on globalization in recent years, including influential books with provocative titles such as *The World Is Flat, When Corporations Rule the World, In Defense of Globalization* and *Why Globalization Works.*[2] Others bring in explicit Christian moral concerns, such as *God and Globalization, Globalization and the Kingdom of God* and *Globalization and the Good.* But what exactly is globalization? And why do business and corporate influences within it inspire such defiant opposition on one hand and passionate support on the other? Do the forces of globalization help or hinder the establishment of the necessary conditions for business to act as an agent of transformational service?

This chapter will introduce globalization and some of it's more controversial aspects, particularly those involving business-based influences. We will then develop a framework for approaching and understanding globalization. In particular, we will argue that globalization should be approached as an unprecedented opportunity to positively influence and transform lives, especially those of the poor. At the same time, however, we will argue that some aspects of globalization itself need to be transformed in order to properly reflect God's designs.

While the terms *globalization* and its more recent variant *globalizing* have become commonplace, they describe complex, often evolving and tension-filled phenomenon, and are thus not given to easy or clean definitions. However, a cautious but workable way to understand globalization is

---

[1]See Naomi Klein, *Fences and Windows: Dispatches from the Front Lines of the Globalization Debate* (New York: Picador, 2002).

[2]Thomas L. Friedman, *The World Is Flat* (New York: Farrar, Straus & Giroux, 2006); David Korten, *When Corporations Rule the World* (San Francisco: Berrett-Koehler, 2001); Jagdish Bagwati, *In Defense of Globalization* (New York: Oxford University Press, 2005); Martin Wolf, *Why Globalization Works* (New Haven, Conn.: Yale University Press, 2004).

to see it as an integration of people, cultures, economics, technology and governments.[3] While none of this is particularly new (some would argue the Roman Empire is an example of an earlier period of globalization), several aspects are unique today. For example, author and *New York Times* columnist Thomas Friedman notes the following:

> The globalization system, unlike the Cold War system, is not frozen, but a dynamic ongoing process. That's why I define globalization this way: it is the inexorable integration of markets, nation-states, and technologies to a degree never witnessed before—in a way that is enabling individuals, corporations, and nation-states to reach around the world farther, faster, deeper, and cheaper than ever before, and in a way that is enabling the world to reach individuals, corporations and nation-states farther, faster, deeper, cheaper than ever before. The process of globalization is also producing a powerful backlash from those brutalized or left behind by this new system.[4]

While Friedman's thesis has been criticized as overstating the case and some degree of reversal (deglobalization) has been caused by the global recession that began in 2008, visible signs of globalization are all around us.[5] To those of us who are old enough to notice the changes, clothing labels are among the most visible, bearing marks of origin, like Honduras, Cambodia, Sri Lanka, some African countries and increasingly rarely America. In some surprising developments, many Hondas and Toyotas are now made in the American Midwest, home of America's big historic auto manufacturers. IBM's (once a symbol and barometer of the health of American business) ThinkPad laptop brand is now owned by Lenovo, a Chinese company.

Cultural products such as music, entertainment and professional sports also alert us to the smaller world we inhabit. Big Macs can be ordered in places like Bangkok, and pad thai has become almost ubiquitous in many major cities in the West. Top American, Canadian and Latin American

---

[3]See Kevin Neuhouser, "In a Global World, Who Is My Neighbor?" Seattle Pacific University Weter Lecture, Seattle, Washington, March 1, 2002.

[4]Thomas L. Friedman, *The Lexus and the Olive Tree*, exp. ed. (New York: Anchor Books, 2000), pp. 8-9.

[5]See for example, Pankaj Ghemawat, "Why the World Isn't Flat," ForeignPolicy.com, March-April 2007 (subscription), www.foreignpolicy.com/articles/2007/02/14/why_the_world_isnt_flat; and Pankaj Ghemawat, "Businesses Beware: The World Is Not Flat," *Harvard Business School Working Knowledge,* October 15, 2007, http://hbswk.hbs.edu/item/5719.html.

soccer players can be found on the rosters of premiere level European teams, while Yao Ming (China) and a host of players from around the globe (including Europe, Africa, Australia and Latin America) play in the National Basketball Association (NBA). The (now "classic") rock band Journey is touring again after finding new lead vocalist Arnel Pineda (who sounds almost exactly like former lead singer, Steve Perry), a Hong Kong club singer originally from the Philippines, via YouTube. David Hassel-hoff (of *Knight Rider, Baywatch* and *America's Got Talent* fame) is a popular recording artist in Germany. Of course, as a testimony to the pace of change, any examples we can give today that have any shock value remaining will soon, if not already, produce a simple shrug.

Some of the major drivers of today's globalization include ease of travel, technology, media and government policies to liberalize trade (such as establishing trade agreements, relaxing border restrictions, setting up export zones and the use of common currencies). I (Kenman) had a glimpse of these forces interacting several years ago in preparing for a trip to China as part of a group of ten families who were traveling to a rural province to adopt children. Before embarking we were instructed by our domestic adoption agency to be culturally sensitive by bringing small items as gifts for translators and orphanage workers. Especially welcome would be items bearing landmarks or brands that would represent our home town. China has lots of NBA fans, so something with the Seattle Supersonics (now Oklahoma City Thunder) logo might be appreciated, we were told.

The fact that "foreigners" can now easily travel to China and are legally able to adopt children from this once closed communist country is a product of easy, relatively more affordable travel, relaxed border restrictions and international cooperation at the level of government. Technology and media have played certain roles: now people around the globe are aware of the need to adopt abandoned children, and people residing in rural parts of China are cognizant of places like Seattle and the NBA. Most surprising and ironic to those of us on the trip was that just about every item we bought in the United States to take with us as gifts was made in China! This fact and China's rapid ascension and integration into the world economy are indicative of governmental policy all over the globe to allow markets and trade to grow.

Corporations and Controversy

The foregoing factors (travel, technology, etc.) have been influential in shaping and driving contemporary globalization, yet arguably the most powerful force has been business interests, namely, those of large multinational corporations. Some of the most controversial issues (as seen in the Battle in Seattle) center on both the extent and desirability of this influence.

For large corporations and their investors, globalization represents unprecedented opportunities. For example, Narayana Murthy, the founder and CEO of Bangalore, India, software giant Infosys, aptly describes these opportunities when he states, "I define globalization as producing where it is most cost-effective, selling where it is most profitable, sourcing capital where it is cheapest, without worrying about national boundaries."[6]

Undoubtedly, globalization has permitted core business activities to be done with improved efficiency. Technology, raw materials and labor can be sourced, and finished or near finished goods can be produced almost anywhere in the world and then delivered through precise logistical planning systems. Capital can also be moved around the world and invested in places that achieve the greatest amount of return, while allowing for new ways to mitigate risk. New and sometimes enormous markets in which products and services can be sold have also been opened. In addition, virtual teams can take advantage of time zones and work literally around the clock on projects, shortening deadlines.

Critics, such as those who marched on Seattle's streets and who are dissatisfied with the current direction of globalization, believe that large multinational corporations have become so powerful they are unaccountable to governments.[7] Corporate influence on rule-making organizations such as the World Trade Organization on issues such as developing country debt and environmental standards comes at the expense of those who do not stand to benefit from "liberalized trade." For example, take U.S. workers in manufacturing industries and those living in developing countries who have little or nothing to sell to world

---

[6]Narayana Murthy, "Commanding Heights," PBS.org, February 5, 2001, www.pbs.org/wgbh/commandingheights/shared/minitext/int_narayanamurthy.html.

[7]See Naomi Klein, *No Logo: No Space, No Choice, No Jobs* (New York: Picador, 2002), and *Fences and Windows;* Korten, *When Corporations Rule the World;* Joel Bakan, *The Corporation* (New York: Free Press, 2004); Noreena Hertz, *The Silent Takeover: Global Capitalism and the Death of Democracy* (New York: Harper Business, 2003).

markets. Moreover, critics argue the corporate quest for efficiency (and thereby, greater profitability) leads to greater injustice, environmental degradation and the destruction of local cultures, traditions and thereby community life.[8]

Bringing in explicitly Christian concerns, Timothy Gorringe argues that modern global corporations (among other institutions) represent the "principalities and powers" mentioned in Ephesians 6:12, and sees them as promoting imperialism.[9] Based on an interpretation of Luther's theology, Cynthia Moe-Lobeda likewise argues that globalization is a force that should be resisted by Christians.[10]

In contrast, those who are more favorable toward globalization's current shape argue that the power of corporations is routinely overstated.[11] Governments can and do routinely pass regulations that govern the conduct of corporations, and markets have built-in measures of accountability. Moreover, globalization not only serves business interests but provides unprecedented economic opportunity (and thereby social and political empowerment) for the financially poor through economic growth and the creation of new wealth. Writing from a Christian theological perspective, Brian Griffiths argues that globalization based on market economics is consistent with Christian ideals because

> wealth creation is a direct implication of the creation mandate. The existence of markets in which people can buy and sell goods and services freely, and in which property rights are protected by the rule of law, strengthens personal freedom. This is something valuable in itself in that it allows individuals and families to develop and prosper, and creates a buffer against the control of economic life by the state. . . . In the context of globalization, increased trade and investment extend the benefits of markets to developing countries and in the process help reduce poverty.[12]

---

[8]See books listed in previous note.

[9]Timothy Gorringe, "The Principalities and Powers," in *Globalization and the Good*, ed. Peter Heslam (Grand Rapids: Eerdmans, 2004), pp. 79-91.

[10]Cynthia Moe-Lobeda, "Offering Resistance to Globalization: Insights from Luther," in *Globalization and the Good*, ed. Peter Heslam (Grand Rapids: Eerdmans, 2004), pp. 95-104.

[11]Philippe LeGrain, *Open World: The Truth About Globalization* (Chicago: Ivan R. Dee, 2004); Bagwati, *In Defense of Globalization*; and Wolf, *Why Globalization Works*.

[12]Brian Griffiths, "The Challenge of Capitalism: A Christian Perspective" in *Making Globalization Good*, ed. John H. Dunning (New York: Oxford University Press, 2003), pp. 165-66.

CORPORATIONS AND GLOBALIZATION

While corporations based all over the world, and especially in America, Asia and Europe, have helped shape contemporary globalization, one company in particular has come to symbolize the corporate role within it. Whether fair or not, Walmart has become a lightning rod for all that's deemed to be right and wrong with corporate influences in globalization.[13] In many ways the company's actions serve as a window into the bigger picture of globalization. According to Duke University professor Gary Graffeti, Walmart is a model for all businesses in all industries.[14] In fact, much has been written recently on the so-called "Walmart effect."[15]

One the largest companies in the world with $375 billion in sales for its 2008 fiscal year, Walmart, based in Bentonville, Arkansas, has capitalized on technology (particularly its inventory control system) and trade agreements (e.g., between the U.S. and China) to move to more global operations in its quest for greater profits. As chronicled in a PBS *Frontline* episode titled "Is Wal-Mart Good for America?" the company once used a "Buy American" strategy but abruptly abandoned it once it was no longer effective. In order to boost profit margins and fulfill its promise to bring low prices to customers, the company used its enormous purchasing power and began to aggressively squeeze its suppliers for cost concessions. In effect, this forced many suppliers to go offshore, especially to places like China, to manufacture products. In addition to sourcing, Walmart has also aggressively expanded from its humble southern U.S. beginnings to establishing a strong retail presence in other countries.

Walmart's mode of operation has become commonplace. According to critics these actions exemplify the tendency of globalization to create both domestic and global problems. On the domestic front the quest to lower production costs results in the elimination of well-paying jobs and replacing them with lower paying "Mcjobs." The loss of manufacturing jobs has been referred to as the "hollowing out" of a key American economic sector.[16]

---

[13]See, for example, Charles Fishman, "The Wal-Mart Effect and a Decent Society: Who Knew Shopping Was So Important?" *Academy of Management Perspectives* 20, no. 3 (2006); Charles Fishman, *The Wal-Mart Effect* (New York: Penguin, 2006); and "Is Wal-Mart Good for America?" *Frontline*, www.pbs.org/wgbh/pages/frontline/shows/walmart.

[14]Gary Graffeti, in "Is Wal-Mart Good for America?"

[15]See, for example, Fishman, "Wal-Mart Effect."

[16]See "The Great Hollowing-Out Myth," *The Economist*, February 19, 2004, www.economist.com/displaystory.cfm?story_id=2454530.

More recently, concerns have shifted to include white-collar professional jobs like computer programming and financial analysis, some of which have also been sent overseas.[17] Small businesses also purportedly suffer at the hands of giant retailers. The downward plight of older downtown shopping districts has often been tied to the opening of a nearby Walmart store. Family-run or locally owned businesses simply can't compete with retailing giants like Walmart on the basis of price or selection. In addition to job loss by shifting work overseas, astronomical increases in the U.S. trade deficit also takes place as more goods, particularly finished ones, have to be imported. While Walmart only plays a partial role, the U.S. balace of trade stood at roughly a $700 billion deficit for 2008 ($268 billion with China alone).[18]

Moving beyond Walmart, significant problems are created in the countries where the actual jobs are "sent." Because of intense price competition to win contracts by lowering costs, manufacturing and agricultural operations in developing countries are rife with sweatshop conditions. Workers put in long hours for extremely low wages and are subject to dangerous working conditions and possible mental and physical abuse. Many of these operations also suffer from lax environmental standards or enforcement.

In emerging markets or developing countries where goods and services are newly advertised and sold by powerful Western corporations, critics point to cultural insensitivity and Western hegemony. Coca-Cola, McDonald's and MTV, which have become globally ubiquitous, are often cited as examples of an American cultural takeover, (e.g., "Coca-colonization" or "McDonaldization"). More specific examples that have garnered negative attention for their audacity or cultural insensitivity include a Starbucks store in China's six-hundred-year-old Forbidden City (now closed amidst controversy) and Taco Bell's attempt to sell its "Mexican" food south of the U.S. border.

---

[17]Former Walmart Chief Operating Officer and current board member Donald Soderquist states that since Walmart does not manufacture anything, it would not serve the company well to drive suppliers out of business. In fact, the incentives actually work the opposite way. Walmart has every reason to treat suppliers fairly since Walmart is dependent on them for the goods they sell (see Albert Erisman and Kenman Wong, "Wal-Mart Way Produces Accolades, Criticism, Growth," an interview of Donald G. Soderquist, *Ethix* 58 [2008], http://ethix.org/2008/04/01/wal-mart-way-produces-accolades-criticism-growth).

[18]United States Balance of Trade, "Trading Economics," www.tradingeconomics.com/Economics/Balance-of-Trade.aspx?Symbol=USD, and United States Census Bureau, Foreign Trade Statistics, www.census.gov/foreign-trade/balance/c5700.html#2008.

Eliciting even more concern is the prospect for powerful cultural changes that take place. Younger people in particular tend to be more influenced by advertising and more easily lose their distinctive traditions and values. In so doing they are susceptible to becoming homogenized consumers who chase the same individualistic and materialistic dreams as wealthy Westerners. This shift in values harms their spiritual, physical and mental health, and can lead to communal and intergenerational strife.[19] Tom Sine observes:

> The world's youth are targeted for a very simple reason—they are more amenable to the values of the global shopping mall than their parents' generation. While adults often still prefer culturally specific customs, young people, according to economist Joseph Quinlan, "prefer Coke to tea, Nike to sandals, Chicken McNuggets to rice, [and] credit cards to cash." McWorld's marketers are not just interested in selling products to the global youth. They are intent on changing their values so they will all want to buy the same products. Whether we recognize it or not, people of faith are in a worldwide contest for the hearts and minds of the next generation.[20]

The adoption of consumer-oriented lifestyles brings another negative externality, namely, more waste and pollution as status seeking and disposability are embraced. It has been often proffered that if only half of the families in China (the world's most populous country) or India emulated a Western lifestyle by owning two cars, three televisions and disposed of many household items for reasons of fashion and acceptance rather than utility, the amount of damage to the earth would be unthinkable. Coupled with the pollution from the rapid growth of developing infrastructure (buildings and roads) and production and manufacturing facilities, wasteful consumerism contributes to a double impact in places like China (as seen and breathed during the 2008 Summer Olympics in Beijing) when it comes to environmental (and thereby human) health.[21]

In sharp contrast, those who are more favorable toward the current direc-

---

[19]For further discussion of this, see Tim Kasser, *The High Price of Materialism* (Cambridge, Mass.: MIT Press, 2002); and Rodney Clapp, ed., *The Consuming Passion: Christianity and the Consumer Culture* (Downers Grove, Ill.: InterVarsity Press, 1998).

[20]Tom Sine, "Branded for Life," *Sojourners*, September-October, 2000. Available at www.sojo .net/index.cfm?action=magazine.article&issue=soj0009&article=000912.

[21]For further discussion on this point, see Thomas L. Friedman, *Hot, Flat and Crowded* (New York: Straus & Giroux, 2008), esp. chaps. 3, 7.

tion of contemporary globalization see things in a much different light. Liberalized trade that is largely free from government interference, they argue, allows capitalism to do its work of "creative destruction" in the most efficient manner possible.[22] Some amount of pain (such as layoffs), they acknowledge, is necessary if markets are allowed to do away with old, inefficient industries and create new ones. Focusing on measures such as the trade deficit, some argue, is also misguided because trade permits economies, which no longer end at national borders, to flourish.[23] Moreover, market economies reflect some of God's designs as they allow for human freedom and private property, account for the realities of sin, and are much more resistant to the abuse of power when alternative systems such as socialism are considered.[24]

Supporters point out that globalization can be a tough sell to the general public because those who suffer at its hands are much more visible than the beneficiaries. Pollution and sweatshops abroad and shackled factories at home make for visually and emotionally persuasive images, while those who gain from the effects of globalization remain largely hidden. Former Clinton Administration Treasury Secretary and Harvard University president (and Obama economic adviser) Lawrence Summers notes:

> It certainly was difficult to sell NAFTA [North American Free Trade Agreement] because it's always difficult to sell open markets. There's a basic cost of open markets, [such as] somebody losing a job, [which is] particular or very obvious, [but] the benefits are much less clear. Who said on Christmas Day, "Gosh, thanks, without open markets I would have been only able to buy half as many toys for my kid"? Or whoever says, "You know, I'm not that great a worker, but they really had no choice but to promote me given the surge in export demand"? On the other hand, every job loss that can be remotely connected to international trade, people do. So this problem of invisible beneficiaries and very visible losers is one that bedevils the political economy of trade.[25]

---

[22]Joseph Schumpeter popularized this phrase to describe this economic phenomenon in *Capitalism, Socialism and Democracy* (1942; reprint, New York: Harper Perennial, 2008).

[23]Jenny Bates, "Putting the U.S. Trade Deficit into Perspective," Progressive Policy Institute Fact Sheet, February 1, 2000, www.ppionline.org/ppi_ci.cfm?knlgAreaID=108&subsecID=900009&contentID=609.

[24]Vicktoria Somogyi, "Lord Brian Griffiths on Globalization," *Zenit*, November 13, 2006, www.zenit.org/article-18173?l=English.

[25]Lawrence Summers, "Commanding Heights," PBS.org, April 24, 2001, www.pbs.org/wgbh/commandingheights/shared/minitextlo/int_lawrencesummers.html.

People living in places like Southeast Asia, China and India are also offered as prime examples of how the world's poor are lifted out of poverty much more effectively and quickly by the working of markets (and liberalized trade) than by government or donor aid programs. According to Jahangir Aziz of the International Monetary Fund, China has added 120 million people in new employment and pulled around 300 million people out of poverty since embarking on market-based economic reforms over roughly the last thirty years.[26]

While not defending or denying labor and environmental abuses when they do occur, proponents of globalization primarily see "factories" that offer economic opportunity rather than mass "sweatshops." For countries like China, labor has been a key export or, in the language of economic theory, the country's basis of "comparative advantage." While many of the newly created factory jobs (with relatively low wages) are not ideal from a Western viewpoint, they are very attractive compared to the alternatives. For example, many young people who have chosen to move to major industrial areas from the countryside would have to eek out a subsistence living on a family farm in the absence of factory work. Furthermore, a manufacturing/industrial stage has been historically common, if not necessary, in developing a country's economy.

In a provocative article published in the *New York Times Magazine* titled "Two Cheers for Sweatshops" (a play on the title of Irving Kristol's book *Two Cheers for Capitalism*), authors Nicholas Kristof and Sheryl WuDunn recount the differences in how factory (sweatshop) jobs are viewed in wealthy versus developing countries. While many Westerners see them as tragic, many locals embrace factory jobs as opportunity. The authors also recount their amazement at the changes that have taken place in the Pearl Delta region of China in only a decade or so. Increasing wages and glimpses of a middle class had begun to emerge during regular visits to the region.[27] Evidence of rising wage profiles and the creation of professional- and technical-class jobs in places like China and India have

---

[26]Wanda Tseng (moderator), T. N. Srinivasan, Minxin Pet, Jahangir Aziz, "China and India: Expanding Roles in the World Economy," International Monetary Fund, December 14, 2006, www.imf.org/external/NP/EXR/BForums/2006/121406.htm.

[27]Nicholas Kristof and Sheryl WuDunn, "Two Cheers for Sweatshops," *New York Times Magazine*, September 24, 2000. Available at www.nytimes.com/library/magazine/home/20000924mag-sweatshops.html.

been well documented.[28] In some cases, wages have risen so quickly that some observers wonder if low wages will actually be lost as a basis for comparative advantage.

Some farmers and small craftspeople have also benefited from globalization. Using technology to access weather forecasts and real-time world market prices, some farmers have been empowered to make smarter planting decisions and/or to avoid underselling their crops. Others are growing new crops and/or selling to new markets. For example, coffee exports from Southeast Asia and Africa have grown dramatically, and produce such as grapes grown in places like Chile and Mexico can be found in grocery stores, particularly during "off seasons" for domestic fruit. Retail markets have also been created for "fair trade" crafts, providing new retail channels to sell goods made by indigenous craftspeople.[29]

Proponents of globalization point to other domestic benefits. As customers, for example, a much broader variety of products and services are available. As noted earlier in the remark by Lawrence Summers, costs for many products have also been lowered or would be even higher if not for the savings derived from global sourcing. A study from the National Bureau of Economic Research found that Walmart's lower prices has an effect on reducing the rate of inflation.[30] The study noted that Walmart typically sells food for 15 percent to 25 percent less than competing supermarkets, a fact not accounted for in government consumer price index calculations. Accounting for this fact would reduce the published inflation rate by as much as 0.42 percentage points or 15 percent per year.[31]

Lower prices especially benefit the domestic poor, a demographic on which Walmart especially concentrates. While critics focus on the harmful effects of Walmart on small towns and its workers, Harvard Business School professor Pankaj Ghemawat is quick to point out that if poor *con-*

---

[28]"How Rising Wages Are Changing the Game in China," *Business Week*, March 27, 2006. Available at www.businessweek.com/magazine/content/06_13/b3977049.htm.

[29]Siddharthe Srivastava, "Could Rising Wages Diminish India's Outsourcing Competitive Edge?" *Siliconeer*, January 21, 2005, http://newsamericamedia.org/news/view_article .html?article_id=167d1c86c1d28e7607c942fd9891938e.

[30]Jerry Hausman and Ephraim Leibtag, "CPI Bias from Supercenters: Does BLS Know that Wal-Mart Exists?" National Bureau of Economic Research working paper 10712, August 2004.

[31]Bruce Bartlett, "Is Wal-Mart Good for America?" National Center for Policy Analysis, November 22, 2004. Available at http://townhall.com/columnists/BruceBartlett/2004/11/19/ is_wal-mart_good_for_america/page/full.

sumers are brought into the picture, some distributional justice concerns should be addressed. Ghemawat notes that Walmart operates primarily in the poorest states, and within these states it focuses on the poorest districts and poorest consumers. Thus the poor would "pay more for food and non-food items that—after housing—is their second largest household expense."[32]

In addition to lower prices customers also benefit from added convenience. Call centers located in places like India and the Philippines, while sometimes frustrating in terms of quality of service provided, do in fact permit us to inquire about credit card billing or technical problems outside of normal office hours. At a more personal level we can even practice offshore outsourcing by hiring our own overseas-based assistants to book appointments, make travel arrangements, type correspondence, transcribe recordings and handle some e-mail on our behalf.

Investors also benefit by having access to new opportunities (e.g., companies and economies of emerging markets), and through the ability to spread portfolio risk across a wider spectrum of holdings. For example, if the domestic economy (and thereby companies within it) is suffering, investors can mitigate risk by also putting their money in companies in other parts of the world that are doing better.

In addressing the particularly sticky issue of moving American jobs overseas, some proponents of liberalized trade argue that the offshore outsourcing phenomenon, particularly with respect to white collar jobs, has been well overstated in terms of numbers.[33] Others argue that offshore outsourcing is really a long-term win-win proposition, as benefits from savings on labor costs and increased incomes in other countries eventually accrue to the U.S. economy.[34] More specifically, some argue that while trade eliminates some jobs, it creates others.[35] The net effect, however, is not a function of international trade but of the number of people in the

---

[32]Pankaj Ghemawat, "Business, Society, and the Wal-Mart Effect," *Academy of Management Perspectives* 20, no. 3 (2006): 42.

[33]Jacob Funk Kirkegaard, "White-Collar Outsourcing: Myth Vs. Reality," *Globalist,* April 15, 2008, http://petersoninstitute.org/publications/opeds/oped.cfm?ResearchID=916.

[34]See "Offshoring: Is It a Win-Win Game?" McKinsey Global Institute, 2003; and "IT Outsourcing and the U.S. Economy," *IHS Global Insight,* 2004, www.ihsglobalinsight.com/MultiClientStudy/MultiClientStudyDetail846.htm.

[35]Douglas Irwin, "Does Free Trade Kill Good American Jobs?" *American Enterprise,* June 2004, pp. 31-33.

labor force. Using employment data, it would be more accurate to state that jobs (whether white or blue collar) *shift* from less efficient sectors to more efficient ones, rather than disappear. Neither, they argue, does trade replace higher paying jobs with lower paying ones. In contrast, lower paying jobs tend to get eliminated.[36]

With respect to the impact of corporations on local cultures and traditions, Philippe LeGrain argues that culture is much more than the sum of what people eat, drink or watch on television, and is more powerful than critics allege.[37] Indeed, products have to be tailored (glocalized) to fit each culture if they are to be appealing to consumers. For example, McDonald's sells lamb, beer and noodles in some locales. Likewise, Coca-Cola is formulated to be sweeter to fit Latin American tastes. Even Walmart stores that operate in places like China sell many food products that a Westerner would scarcely recognize, much less purchase. Instead of cultural hegemony (Western dominance), LeGrain believes that globalization should be more positively described as "cultural exchange," because even a cursory look at cuisine, books, music and clothing reveal that Westerners are also deeply influenced by other cultures.

GLOBALIZATION AND CHRISTIAN VALUES

Developing a fair and informed evaluation of globalization is a challenging task. Such an evaluation is dependent on factual items such as whether well-paying jobs are lost, the rampancy of abuses in factories and the root causes of cultural change. These issues are not easy to settle. Moreover, the facts may well change with time and circumstances. Underlying the facts, and often shaping their interpretation, however, are important values that are often unstated but must be examined. Recall from chapter two that a key part of God's mission Christ came to proclaim, as characterized by the full meaning of *shalom* and the *kingdom*, is a deep concern for human flourishing and transformation across multiple dimensions: spiritual, physical, emotional, social. Moreover, justice for

---

[36]Ibid., p. 33.

[37]LeGrain, *Open World*, pp. 293-319. See also Philippe LeGrain, "In Defense of Globalization: Why Cultural Exchange Is Still an Overwhelming Force for Good," *The International Economy*, summer 2003.

the poor, vulnerable and voiceless are of special concern to God.

In applying these ideals to globalization there is nothing in Scripture that would indicate these concerns should end at national or ethnic boundaries. We are simply commanded to love our neighbors. However, the interdependencies created by globalization have caused the neighborhood to expand in size and scope. In the Old Testament tradition sojourners were to be treated like the native born under the law (Lev 19:34). Jesus arrived on the scene to clarify that God's mercy should be extended to all. The kingdom properly seen is inclusive. Thus our neighborhood, and thereby our neighbors, has become global.

Several other components of shalom are worth developing in light of globalization. Many Old Testament laws that were intended to guide the communal life of ancient Israel were to insure economic justice. For example, the Jubilee year (in which all debts were to be forgiven and all land returned to its original owners) ensured that if someone were to lose the means to attain a sufficient living, they would receive an opportunity to start over. While the Jubilee year cannot be practiced in a literal sense in our modern economy, the principles of mercy and opportunity can and should be.

Moreover, the laws also ensured some measure of distributional justice. For example, gleaning laws and the third-year tithe insured that the poor had a sufficient means to survive. To be certain, there is no indication in Scripture that an equal distribution of wealth is required to insure justice. Forcibly creating conditions of equal wealth would violate human dignity by curbing freedom too greatly. Moreover, differences in choices, effort, talents and other circumstances can play significant roles in creating situations in which wealth is unequally held.[38] However, the presence of exploitation or increasing wealth concentrated in the hands of a few should certainly raise questions as to whether the shape of community life exists according to divine patterns.

The Bible also recognizes that wealth is not an end all. Rather, economic well-being is critical to other forms of empowerment and participation in community life. As Stephen Mott and Ronald Sider note, getting

---

[38]Stephen C. Mott and Ronald J. Sider, "Economic Justice: A Biblical Paradigm," in *Toward a Just and Caring Society: Christian Responses to Poverty in America* (Grand Rapids: Baker, 1999), pp. 15-45.

locked out of economic opportunity also excludes people from full participation in community life.[39]

With this framework in mind, we can examine some of the arguments (and their underlying values) used to criticize and defend the present direction of globalization. In so doing we can also cautiously affirm some of the gains brought about by globalization, while rejecting some of its inherent logic, and arguing that it must be reshaped if it is to bring about shalom.

Some of the critics of globalization focus much too narrowly on American interests, such as job loss. While losing one's livelihood can create understandable frustrations and tangible losses, focusing primarily on the protection of "our" jobs goes against a biblical outlook. Our point here is not that American interests should be neglected but that Christian love of neighbor properly construed translates into a global-citizenship perspective that includes active concern for those who live beyond our borders. More specifically, the fact that people in developing countries have increasing employment opportunities with prospects for rising wage profiles should be seen in a positive light. Focusing too much on our own well-being violates God's designs and can sometimes even lead to xenophobic attitudes such as "they're stealing our jobs." In fact, practicing love of neighbor converts "they" into "we." Thus the title of a PBS *Frontline* episode titled "Is Wal-Mart Good for America?" is much too narrow. Properly focused, it might be retitled (and thereby redirected) as "Is Walmart Good for Our Neighbors Across the Globe?" On a similar note theologian Eugene Lemcio asks, "Why isn't the American dream ever spoken of in terms of justice, equality, freedom and responsibility? Does the very definition of who we are as a people and nation have to boil down to things and owning them—however necessary and desirable?"[40]

Practicing love of neighbor on a more global scale would lead us to affirm and celebrate the very real and tangible economic benefits, especially for the poor and disenfranchised, brought about by globalization. The creative forces of the market (particularly trade and technology) have made significant contributions to the real economic growth and the creation of

---

[39]Ibid., p. 23.
[40]Eugene Lemcio, letter to the editor, *New York Times*, Oct. 17, 2008. Available at http://query.nytimes.com/gst/fullpage.html?res=9E05E1DF153EF93BA25753C1A96E9C8B63&sec=&spon=&pagewanted=2.

wealth around the world. To be certain, economic wealth is not sufficient as a measure of overall human well-being, but in its absence it is difficult to envision how improvements in physical health, education and social empowerment can be brought about.

While *wealth* conjures up images of "fat cats" (perhaps rightly) as prime beneficiaries, both the domestic and global poor have also gained, sometimes dramatically, as the previously cited three hundred million lifted out of poverty in China alone would indicate. Jeffrey Sachs writes in his acclaimed book *The End of Poverty:*

> Since 1978, China has been the world's most successful economy, growing at an average per capita rate of almost 8 percent per year. At that rate, the average income per person has doubled every nine years, and thus had increased almost eight-fold by 2003 compared with 1978. The reduction of extreme poverty in the country has been dramatic. . . . In 1981, 64 percent of the population lived on an income below a dollar a day. By 2001, the number was reduced to 17 percent. The engines of growth are still running strong, with per capita growth currently only slightly slower than a few years ago.[41]

When applied to a population of well over a billion people (one-fifth of the entire human population), these percentages are staggering. It is also important to affirm that the only proven way to lift people out of economic poverty is to make the entire pie bigger by creating new financial resources. Currently, the only known economic system that accomplishes this is market-based capitalism, though how unfettered (free of government influence) this needs to be is debatable. R. Glenn Hubbard and William Duggan argue that a thriving business sector and sound regulations are prerequisites for reducing poverty in developing countries.[42] Simply redistributing existing wealth by resizing is severely limited in efficacy, notwithstanding the significant moral, political and social problems radical reallocation would create. Thus reforms that would replace or too greatly hamper the market's ability to create jobs and a vibrant private sector would effectively deny hundreds of millions and perhaps billions of people the chance to effectively escape poverty.

---

[41]Jeffrey Sachs, *The End of Poverty: Economic Possibilities for Our Time* (New York: Penguin, 2005), p. 155.

[42]R. Glenn Hubbard and William Duggan, *The Aid Trap: Hard Truths About Ending Poverty* (New York: Columbia University Press, 2009).

Other inroads and connections made permissible by globalization have also been life-giving to the poor and should likewise be affirmed. Technology and media have allowed us to be more aware of natural disasters than ever before (e.g., Asian tsunami). And financial assistance and other forms of relief (e.g., clean water) can sometimes be gathered and distributed more quickly and efficiently using well-established commercial channels. Perhaps ironically we are also much more aware of human rights issues, such as labor abuses in sweatshops, and of environmental degradation, raising the stakes on corporate accountability and citizenship.

Bold and imaginative plans to alleviate poverty and to solve other social problems have also been developed and enacted. Organizations such as Kiva (founded by Christians, though not run as a Christian organization) allow us to connect with the world's poor by telling the stories of micro-entrepreneurs and their needs for capital to start or expand their businesses. We (even distant, wealthy Americans) are then enabled through technology to loan these entrepreneurs money (through an intermediary) to expand their businesses and hopefully pull themselves out of poverty. Kiva funded close to one hundred million dollars to microentrepreneurs in its first four years of existence, an amazing fact considering loans are made in small twenty-five-dollar increments. Without technology and the ability to move capital around the globe freely and quickly, these types of efforts would not exist.

The type and frequency of cultural and economic exchange made possible by globalization also plays a role in peacemaking and civility. The fact that we can escape "the tyranny of geography," as LeGrain puts it, and connect with people worldwide and experience their cultures helps to build bridges, whether by travel or use of technology.[43] Using our computers, for example, we can experience other cultures, see art in museums and listen to music even though we may never physically get to their places of origin. We can connect with fellow music fans, those interested in solving global poverty or environmental issues, photographers, art aficionados and travel buffs (or whatever our interests may be) from around the world.

And countries or people that engage in trade with one another have greater incentives to maintain peaceful relationships rather than become entangled

---

[43]LeGrain, *Open World* and "In Defense of Globalization."

in armed conflict. For example, Thomas Friedman points out humorously in *The World Is Flat* that no two countries that are part of a major supply chain such as Dell Computer's have ever fought a war against each other.[44]

Development is also a much better tool to fight against terrorism than military force, as affirmed by the likes of retired military generals Colin Powell (the former Secretary of State) and Pete Pace (former chairman of the Joint Chiefs of Staff).[45] When disenfranchised people experience improvements in their lives, they are less vulnerable to be recruited by angry groups bent on destructive means to secure a locus of power.

For all of the positive gains of globalization (and there are many genuine ones), however, some aspects of it should be central targets of efforts at transformation. More specifically, some supporters reduce globalization to its material, economic aspects alone. For example, Murthy's definition (see p. 142), while given in the context of business, reduces globalization to sourcing and selling. Likewise, people in developing nations are often referred to as "emerging *markets*." Reducing globalization and people to their economic dimensions does not reflect the totality of who God has created them to be, which is necessary to love our neighbors and bring them shalom.

Some of the language used to define globalization and measure human well-being proceed purely on the basis of secular grounds and categories. "Unmasking" words such as *efficient, more, cheaper, faster* (emerging) and *markets* reveal much about the logic of globalization and how parts of it run counter to Christian ideas.

The quest for *efficient* and *cheaper* can and does lead to human exploitation and greater injustice. While it is wrong to view all or even most factories as sweatshops, the abuse of poor, uneducated, young and often female workers at the hands of unscrupulous factory managers happens. Factory conditions have likely improved through the years as negative publicity has forced greater accountability and inspection and auditing systems have been put into place. But though growing in number, audits and inspections are very limited. It has also been well documented that some companies preannounce inspections before they occur, allowing unscrupulous factory managers to clean up their act before inspectors arrive.

---

[44]Friedman, *World Is Flat*, p. 421.
[45]See Albert Erisman and David Gautschi, "General Peter Pace: The Truth as I Know It," *Ethix* 61 (2008), http://ethix.org/2008/10/01/the-truth-as-I-know-it/.

Some factory managers intimidate and fire workers who tell the truth to inspectors. Government officials of some developing countries overlook labor abuses in true sweatshops and don't enforce laws for fear of raising costs for businesses and thereby chase jobs away.[46] It would also not be far-fetched for corporations in search of lower costs to source or manufacture in places with lower environmental standards.

More (goods) in both quantity and variety, made possible by *cheaper*, does not necessarily represent the biblical vision of an "abundant life." Ironically, material abundance, so often sold as "the American dream," can lead to waste, environmental degradation and psychological stress, not to mention spiritual malady.[47] Expanding sales into new markets may well mean paving the road to the spread of the gospel of consumerism. A careful look will reveal that while globalization might represent cultural exchange and not hegemony (as LeGrain argues), interactions are mostly based on shallow categories of *consumption* (e.g., food, music, clothing) rather than meaningful connections that serve others and foster true community.

More as measured by wealth creation and growth in a country's Gross Domestic Product (GPD) can also be a distorted measure of progress. GDP is, of course, an aggregate measure and not a distributive one. So, while a country or region's overall wealth may be increased, nothing is said of how that income is shared or spread. If only a few people benefit and others are actually harmed, GDP would still increase if the amount of gain is greater than the losses. To date, not all countries have enjoyed gains from globalization, particularly countries with little to sell on the basis of "comparative advantage" in the marketplace. Nor have many individuals been net winners in the global economy. While globalization might not be properly blamed, since poverty has many causes, growing income gaps should make us pause to take note. Some studies indicate increasing inequality within developing countries.[48] Is the size of the gap growing? Are the rich getting richer at the expense of the poor? Do trade policies favor

---

[46]Philip Pan, "Worked Til They Drop," *Washington Post*, May 12, 2002, www.hartford-hwp .com/archives/55/709.html.

[47]See Kasser, *High Price of Materialism.*

[48]See Ann Harrison, ed., *Globalization and Poverty* (Chicago: University of Chicago Press, 2007). Chapters 3 (by William Easterly) and 4 (by Branko Milanovic and Lyn Squire) provide evidence that increasing openness to trade is associated with greater inequality in developing countries.

corporations at the direct expense of the voiceless? Is the world actually getting any "flatter" in the sense of justice? If so, biblical standards of justice would be violated. Brian Griffiths says:

> The kind of global capitalism that a Christian will wish to see develop is one which encourages responsibility, fairness, and widespread ownership. . . . A Christian perspective will place a strong emphasis on economic justice. . . . In a fallen world, there will be exploitation, corruption and injustice. Those with power will bend the rules in their favor. The Christian must be prepared to stand up and confront injustice, and work to change the rules, structures, and ethos in order to create a more just society. The Christian understanding of justice will embrace wealth creation as much as wealth redistribution.[49]

Measures such as gains in household income (or other proxy measures of well-being), adjusted for purchasing power, at the bottom half of the economic ladder provide better measures of actual progress in economic development. However, it is important to recall that wealth (whether in the aggregate or at individual levels) is only one measure of human well-being or flourishing. Economic gains may well form the basis for better health care, improved nutrition and education, and perhaps political empowerment, but attention must be paid to social, psychological and spiritual dimensions as well. So, families may have increased income but at the same time may experience the negative effects of the empty pursuit of consumerism, newly introduced class struggles or conflicts over modernization versus tradition. A robust definition of *development* will consider these and other factors in trying to improve overall human well-being. Reducing people to material factors may also play a role in abusing workers—that is, "we pay them better, therefore . . ."

Faster may describe the speed of *disruption* that occurs in a global economy. Thomas Friedman captures the disruptive forces of globalization well in his use of several apt metaphors to contrast globalization with the Cold War era.

> In the Cold War we reached for the "hot line" between the White House

---

[49]Brian Griffiths, "The Challenge of Global Capitalism: A Christian Perspective," in *Making Globalization Good: The Moral Challenges of Global Capitalism*, ed. John H. Dunning (New York: Oxford University Press, 2004), p. 166.

and the Kremlin—a symbol that we were all divided but at least someone, the two superpowers, were in charge. In the era of globalization we reach for the Internet—a symbol that we are all connected but nobody is totally in charge. . . .

Indeed, if the Cold War were a sport, it would be sumo wrestling, says Johns Hopkins University foreign affairs professor Michael Mandelbaum. "It would be two big fat guys in a ring, with all sorts of posturing and rituals and stomping of feet, but actually very little contact, until the end of the match, when there is a brief moment of shoving and the loser gets pushed out of the ring, but nobody gets killed." By contrast, if globalization were a sport, it would be the 100-meter dash, over and over and over. And no matter how many times you win, you have to race again the next day. And if you lose by just one-hundredth of a second it can be as if you lost by an hour.[50]

These metaphors illustrate how uneasy people are with globalization, and this has been experienced in real life. As we have experienced several times now (Asian economic flu, technology bubble, subprime-related credit crunch), *faster* often describes the panic that ensues when interconnected economies start to falter, resulting in precipitous declines of corporate and personal wealth.

While companies gain from *cheaper* (sourcing) and from the opening of new global markets, employees often suffer from disruptions. Corporate executives are pressured to maximize quarterly earnings. Often this means more tenuous employment relationships as companies send jobs overseas or reduce workforce due to increased competition. Factories get shuttered. And the last decade has witnessed the outsourcing of white-collar work (such as computer programmers, financial analysis, etc.). Whether domestic jobs disappear or only shift by aggregate economic measures, they are certainly lost to wage earners, families and communities.

Around the globe, the lives of farmers and local producers are also disrupted at an unprecedented pace. Farmers may be hurt by trade bureaucrats' decisions in far away countries, such as policies to protect their own domestic agricultural interests, which effectively diminishes competition on a level playing field. In fact, the fair trade movement, best known for coffee but now encompassing a variety of other products such as chocolate,

---

[50]Friedman, *Lexus and the Olive Tree*, pp. 8, 12.

clothing and flowers, was a Christian movement started in Europe to mitigate the impact of the scope and pace of change on farmers in the developing world. As world coffee prices plummeted, farmers had to leave generations of family work. In theory these farmers should simply pack up and move their labor to more efficient economic sectors. These transitions do not take place so easily in reality, so farmers, their families and their workers are often left in dire situations. While "fair trade" has become a brand, with its own possible shortcomings, the driving force behind it was to counteract the disruptive forces of globalization.[51]

When connected to technology, the quest for *faster* can also make us worse off. Speed often negates work that is characterized by boundaries or a sabbath outlook that is marked by ceasing and rest. At the employee level the ability to work from anywhere often means an expectation to work from *everywhere*. It is becoming a standard expectation for employees to check e-mail regularly during off hours and to even tote laptops or other devices to their vacation destinations in order to stay in touch with the office.

While twenty-four-hour development teams shorten development cycles, they might also lead to disruptive working hours. It is becoming increasingly common for managers to work late into the evening or to go into work in the middle of the night for meetings in order to collaborate with team members who live on another part of the globe. Undoubtedly, some amount of work during nontraditional hours is necessary (and even desirable) in a global economy, but the line establishing a healthy boundary with work can get easily erased.

WHERE TO NOW?

Although the current period of deglobalization reminds us that it won't be without some bumps along the way, globalization is likely moving forward.[52] As we have seen, globalization has been a force for good *and* for ill. Parts of it should be embraced as an agent of transformation, while others should be resisted and treated as a recipient of change.

What is yet to be determined is its future direction and shape. Will core

---

[51]See Kerry Howley, "Absolution in Your Cup," *Reason*, March 2006, http://reason.com/archives/2006/03/01/absolution-in-your-cup.

[52]For a discussion of deglobalization, see "Turning Their Backs on the World," *Economist*, February 21, 2009, pp. 59-61.

human values, particularly those reflecting divine patterns, be overrun in the quest for greater efficiency and profit? Or will globalization move more in a direction that is characterized by the biblical vision of shalom? Is there a way to affirm the creative forces of the market while mitigating the very real harms caused by its destructive side?

Both detractors and supporters of the current shape of globalization agree that our collective actions will help answer these questions. Consistent with the subject of this book and the framework presented in chapter two, we must ask, What if businesspeople and organizations approached their work with a markedly different lens or worldview and turned the standard economic efficiency arguments on their head? Replacing criteria such as sourcing where it is cheapest, selling where it is most profitable and so on, globalization would be looked on as expanded opportunities to partner with God, serve others and help transform their lives in holistic, biblically consistent ways.

Instead of just a cost-cutting source, factories would become places to deliver people (more accurately, our global neighbors) from oppressive conditions by empowering them (economically, politically, socially and physically) through fair wages and by improving their income earning skills. Safe working conditions, enriching work that as much as possible is built around human needs, and building life skills and a spirit of community and camaraderie would be givens.

Likewise, emerging markets would no longer be reduced to impersonal places or niches to sell more good and services or invest our money. Instead, we would envision global neighbors who can be served and bettered in holistic ways by the products and services offered by our organizations. Of course, this takes us front and center to questions about the very nature and benefits of the products we manufacture and sell (what business are we in?). Do they better human life or are they simply frivolous and wasteful?

Undoubtedly, the ability to live up to this vision is challenging. The real world is a difficult place to operate and is hostile to what has been just described. Powerful forces like fierce global competition and quarterly earnings pressures that translate into cost-cutting do not voluntarily step aside so that Christian (or other concerned) businesspeople can change the world. But there are people (and organizations) that have prevailed despite the threat these types of forces make. To make positive changes requires much more than good intentions. Imagination, wisdom, courage, faithfulness and some degree of trial and error are among what is required if these ideals are to be implemented and put into operation. If our work shares in God's work, then the limits presented are surmountable.

To put the whole onus on businesspeople or corporations is a serious mistake. In our roles as employees, investors, customers and citizens we make many choices that also contribute to the shape of globalization. As employees, we must exercise as much choice as we have in determining the places we will work. If we see our work as a proper calling, we must as much as possible align that with the vision, values and practices of our employing organizations. No organization is perfect, so a part of our work is shaping them in a positive manner.

As consumers, we vote with our dollars. If we only shop based on price, businesses supplying our products and services will be driven to compete primarily on the basis of low cost. In turn, the quest for low cost is a primary starting block for the whole vicious cycle of injustice and exploitation that occurs in factories, on farms and in environmental degradation. If we purchase stuff made under oppressive conditions or with environmentally harmful materials or processes, businesses will continue to supply it. Conversely, if we want to see workers treated better and the environment tended to as if it were the Master's garden, then we must make these intentional considerations in our shopping patterns.

Likewise, investors also play a role in globalization. Many of us bemoan the instability of markets and poor long-term decisions made by executives under pressure to make quarterly earnings numbers. Yet we create the pressure by exclusively looking at the short-term financial picture (whether share price or quarterly statements) as investment criteria.

The biblical concept of stewardship is not limited to how we *spend* our money. It extends to how we earn and invest it as well. If we are to exercise good stewardship and influence the globe positively, we must broaden our view of investment and look at it on a longer-term and more holistic basis. This means being prepared, if necessary, to accept lower financial return in exchange for greater social return. This could mean investing in socially responsible companies (with strong human-rights and environmental records) or direct investment into multiple bottom-line businesses, such as microfinance institutions.

As citizens, we can vote and support initiatives that advance the good parts of globalization, namely, its creative ability (new wealth, etc.), while simultaneously supporting policies that mitigate harm from its destructive side. With respect to the latter, Christian love of neighbor would seem to imply support for fair representation of rule-making organizations, since many of the people affected do not have their interests represented and simply have an agenda forced on them. In addition, the support of safety nets, such as job retraining for those who are either left behind or suffer from disruption of one kind or another, should be supported.

Moreover, while corporations often fight for fewer regulations, markets need the visible hand of government to insure justice, honest dealings and fair economic opportunity and participation. As even former chair of the Federal Reserve Board Alan Greenspan, an avid fan of free, unfettered markets, has had to acknowledge with respect to the 2008 global economic crisis, self-interest alone does not adequately regulate markets.[53]

Globalization has been shaped by human hands, though sometimes hidden behind corporate interests. The future shape of globalization will be in part directed by the decisions and actions of business leaders. Whether globalization moves more in a harmful direction or in one that travels closer to God's vision for shalom will be decided in part by the work of his hands and feet—his human partners.

---

[53]Scott Lanman and Steve Matthews, "Greenspan Concedes to 'Flaw' in His Market Ideology," *Bloomberg*, October 23, 2008, www.bloomberg.com/apps/news?pid=newsarchive&sid=ah5qh 9Up4rIg.

ETHICS IN THE WORKPLACE

Every few years there seems to be a significant, seismic-scale crisis of ethics in business. Most recently the mortgage and banking meltdown has left banks, brokerage houses and investors reeling, and has sent the economy into serious recession.[1] In the early 2000s Enron, Worldcom, Arthur Andersen and Martha Stewart were associated with ethical scandals. In the late 2000s the names had changed to companies such as AIG, Countrywide (and other mortgage companies) and numerous other Wall Street financial firms. Actually the number of companies and individuals that have ethical clouds over them could be multiplied well beyond the names that have been prominent in the news. There is a widespread sense in the general public that the business community, particularly in the financial services sector, has lost its moral compass and that greed is the overriding principle governing how business is done.

But the excesses and scandals of the past few years have also spurred businesses to realize that ethics does matter and doing business in the right way morally makes a difference. In a special issue of *Business Week*

---

[1]The mortgage crisis of 2008-2009 actually has a variety of causes that contributed, from individual and corporate greed to government incentives that encouraged lenders to make subprime loans. For further discussion of the causes and cures of the crisis, see Robert Shiller, *The Subprime Solution: How Today's Global Financial Crisis Happened and What to Do About It* (New York: Princeton University Press, 2008); Mark Zandi, *Financial Shock: Global Panic and Government Bailouts—How We Got Here and What to Do About It* (New York: Financial Times Press, 2009); Kevin Phillips, *Bad Money: Reckless Finance, Failed Politics and the Global Crisis of American Capitalism* (New York: Penguin, 2008); and Thomas E. Woods Jr., *Meltdown: A Free Market Look at Why the Stock Market Collapsed, the Economy Tanked and Government Bailouts Will Make Things Worse* (Washington, D.C.: Regnery, 2009). For more information on the government's role in addressing the financial crisis, see Andrew Ross Sorkin, *Too Big to Fail: The Inside Story of How Washington and Wall Street Fought to Save the Financial System—and Themselves* (New York: Viking Books, 2009).

devoted to "25 Ideas for Post-Enron Setting," integrity was at the top of the list: "Trust, Fairness and Integrity matter, and they matter to the bottom line."[2]

In the operational world, an organization's mission, the business case for an activity, and a vision of business as a venue for service to God and others will undoubtedly come into conflict, presenting ethical challenges. What challenges do you face in your workplace? What strategies do you have for navigating the rough ethical waters in your company? What can organizations do to encourage ethical behavior?

See if you can find yourself in the ethical dilemmas these people face:

- Dave is in a bit of a tough spot with the construction company he's managing—he really doesn't know what to do with some of his employees. They are some of the best workers he could hope for, and they were really there for the company when it was founded. But they are in the country without proper documentation, and he's breaking the law every day he employs them. He also has to pay some of his workers in cash, and since some don't have legitimate social security numbers, he can't withhold taxes. But he doesn't feel right about putting them out on the streets—he understands their plight, they have families to support and have been loyal and hard-working. Where else would they go? And he didn't hire them; he inherited them.

- Kendra does business in parts of the world that are so different from here. She's involved in a deal in Asia where she knows she's going to be asked to pay a bribe to a government official to secure the deal. She knows the Bible says that a bribe corrupts the heart, but it's a way of life over there. She has some employees that couldn't get basic services like phone, electricity and mail without bribing a low-level civil servant. She knows it's against the law at home, but what about overseas? She wonders about some of the things her company does here to "build relationships." Like her company's luxury box at the Staples Center (a sports arena in Los Angeles) or the gifts that are often given to their best customers. She even wonders about the way she gives tips to servers for good service, especially since the acronym for tips is "to insure prompt service," suggesting that the tip is given prior to the service being ren-

---

[2]John A. Byrne, "After Enron: The Ideal Corporation," *Business Week*, August 26, 2002, p. 68.

dered, not after. Is there any difference between these common practices at home and what she is asked to do abroad?

- In Bill's work as an auto mechanic, if people don't trust him, he has great difficulty doing business. But it is so easy to suggest "preventive maintenance" for people's cars as their mechanic. They don't really need this work now—but they will later, and he needs the revenue now. People know so little about their cars and trust him to take care of them and their cars, but sometimes there is a significant temptation to sell them work that he knows they could get by without.

- Linda is an administrative assistant and faces ethical issues almost every day. They are sometimes as simple as lying for her boss—telling people he's not in when he actually is, or that he's in a meeting, when that meeting is with her. She knows he just doesn't want to talk to the person, but he makes her lie for him to get him out of it. She also sees how he treats people in the company—he's rude and arrogant; it's his way or the highway. It's hard for her to just stand by and watch him abuse the people around him.

- Tracy is on the accounting staff of her company. She receives constant pressure to make the numbers appear as good as possible. No one is asking her to break the law outright, and the law has gotten so much tougher since the Sarbanes-Oxley Act (2002) was passed. But at times she knows that they are presenting a misleading picture to investors, and if she doesn't go along, she will see her career prospects suffer. But she wonders what the company's investors would think if they could see what goes into their financial statements.

- Dale is in sales for a company that makes surveillance equipment for a variety of different uses. His supervisor asked him to bid on an installation for a man who has his elderly mother living with him and a round-the-clock caregiver for her. He travels a lot and is away more than he would like to be, and he wants to keep tabs on the caregiver to be sure she's not neglecting his mom or stealing from her. He wants the company to install hidden cameras around the house and even in the caregiver's bedroom. Dale is really uneasy about the invasion of privacy, but his boss insists he bid for that job, since revenue is down this particular quarter.

Think about the ethical issues you face at your work. What challenges to your principles do you encounter? What are you reticent to tell others, especially those closest to you? How do you deal with these quandaries when confronted by them? In this chapter we want you to be able to identify ethical issues and challenges when you see them, and to be able to think about them from a Christian worldview. It goes without saying that acting with integrity is a critical component of serving God in the workplace.

Work is dramatically affected by sin, producing alienation, drudgery and the potential for workers to be abused. But sin has made an even deeper impact on the world of work, by bringing the prospect of moral temptation into the workplace. Greed and a variety of other vices permeate the workplace because these vices have deep roots in us—fallen human beings. We should never be surprised at possibilities for ethical failure. Nor should we be surprised at how far people can fall into the morass of compromise. Social science confirms biblical teaching that human beings have an unlimited capacity for self-deception and denial about their ethical behavior. It is not uncommon for us to lament the general moral decline in the workplace while at the same time failing to live morally upright lives at work.

COMPARTMENTALIZATION

One common strategy for dealing with ethical challenges in the workplace is to create two separate worlds to operate in—our life in the workplace and our private life. Each sphere then has its own set of rules and guidelines that we follow. That is, we have one set of moral rules for the workplace, and a different and presumably higher set of rules for private life. We realize that the workplace is a very competitive place that requires us to set aside some of our values and virtues, such as love, compassion and sometimes even fairness. We insist that those values are fine for private life, but the business environment is such that we must play by a different set of rules in order to succeed.

We see colleagues who are involved in some very questionable business practices and we admit that the compartmentalizing of life is not that unusual. Perhaps a lot of people accept what Albert Carr wrote years ago: "A sudden submission to Christian ethics would produce the greatest economic upheaval in history."[3] He means that a person who practiced Christian ethics consistently in the workplace would not be competitive. It's been reported that Ray Kroc, founder of McDonald's, who claimed to be a Christian, said: "My priorities are God first, family second and McDonald's hamburgers third. And when I go to work on Monday morning, that order reverses." Though we can't be sure exactly what he meant by this, he's commonly interpreted to mean that he had two sets of priorities, one for the workplace and the other for private life, and a corresponding set of rules for each. Carr put it like this, "My point is that in their office lives they cease to be private citizens; they become game players who must be guided by a somewhat different set of ethical standards."[4]

Current research suggests that this practice of compartmentalization is a critical component in the acceptance of perpetuation of corruption within an organization. Organizations that have a strong emphasis on socialization of employees into the operating norms of the group (called creating a "social cocoon")[5] often create conditions compartmentalization can flourish in. Vikas Anand, Blake Ashforth and Mahendra Joshi put it this way in their research:

> When the individuals enter the workplace, they quickly and almost automatically slip into their work roles, along with the local norms and rationalizing beliefs. . . . When they exit the workplace, they slip into their other roles such as parent and good neighbor, along with the norms and beliefs of those roles. It's not that individuals forget their "other" selves; it's that they tend to defer to whatever identity is most salient. A manager engaged in price fixing is not thinking about her role as a mother and church member.[6]

---

[3]Albert Z. Carr, "Is Business Bluffing Ethical?" *Harvard Business Review*, January-February 1968, cited in Scott B. Rae and Kenman L. Wong, *Beyond Integrity: A Judeo-Christian Approach to Business Ethics*, 2nd ed. (Grand Rapids: Zondervan, 2004), p. 28.
[4]Ibid., p. 26.
[5]A. L. Greil and D. R. Rudy, "Social Cocoons: Encapsulation and Identity Transformation Organizations," *Sociological Inquiry* 54, no. 3 (1984): 260-78.
[6]Vikas Anand, Blake E. Ashforth and Mahendra Joshi, "Business as Usual: The Acceptance of Perpetuation of Corruption in Organizations," *Academy of Management Executive* 18, no. 3 (2004): 16. See also Blake E. Ashforth, *Role Transitions in Organizational Life: An Identity-Based Perspective* (Mahwah, N.J.: Erlbaum, 2001); R. A. Barrett, *Culture and Conduct: An Excursus in Anthropology* (Belmont, Calif.: Wadsworth, 1984); and Linda K. Trevino and Katharine A. Nelson, *Managing Business Ethics: Straight Talk About How to Do It Right* (Hoboken, N.J.: John Wiley, 2007), pp. 180-84.

This compartmentalization is evident in the cases of some very high profile executives who have gone to prison, yet are widely considered to be people of integrity in their private lives. For example, Kenneth Lay, the former CEO of Enron who was found guilty of six counts of conspiracy and fraud, but who died before his sentencing, was a self-proclaimed Christian (Southern Baptist), and during his tenure at Enron he worked tirelessly in a variety of charitable causes in the Houston area and was well-known for his philanthropy to these causes.[7] In addition, Bernie Ebbers, the CEO of WorldCom, who is currently serving a prison sentence, is also a self-proclaimed Christian who taught Bible studies in his church in Mississippi during his tenure with the company.

Some people, such as Carr, justify the need for compartmentalization by arguing that business is a game, much like poker, in which rules about lying and deception are a bit different. In fact, poker is premised on the ability to deceive opponents, and the ability to win depends on a person's ability to bluff and otherwise deceive fellow players. Poker still has rules, but they are a bit different than the rules for private life, which insist on truth telling, honesty and forthrightness. If we were playing poker, and I successfully bluffed you and won the hand, you couldn't accuse me of lying to you. You accept that deception is part of the game because that's the way the game is played. And you could say that you haven't really been deceived at all. This is what Carr means when he says that we become game players when we enter the workplace. He would likely cite the example of a used car lot, in which bluffing is common and virtually everyone knows how the game is played when they buy a used car. Or take the case of shopping overseas: the price is not set but subject to negotiation. These are examples of cases in which most everyone knows the rules, which are a bit different from the rules of private life.

But the poker analogy is not quite accurate when it comes to business. In reality, in order to build trust most people expect some degree of honesty and forthrightness in business dealings. This is especially important in the majority of businesses that depend on repeat customers, and is emphasized much more in the post-Enron environment. In most business

---

[7]Trevino and Nelson, *Managing Business Ethics*, pp. 181-82. For further reading on the culture that Lay perpetuated at Enron, see Bethany McLean and Peter Elkind, *The Smartest Guys in the Room: The Amazing Rise and Scandalous Fall of Enron* (New York: Portfolio, 2003).

situations, if there is a different set of rules that people are playing by, lots of people are not aware of them. It's one thing to have bluffing when everyone knows what is happening, but quite another to have a different set of rules when most people are unaware that a game is being played. We certainly would not want the used car lot to be the standard by which we measure ethics in the workplace. Further, poker is played voluntarily and for fun. A poker player can walk away from the poker table at any time. But the workplace is not like that. It's not a voluntary game, and many people who are adversely affected are not at the table by choice.

From a Christian perspective, compartmentalizing our life is full of difficulties. For one thing, it's debatable whether someone could maintain a dichotomy like this in life for that long. In fact, psychologists tell us that it is a formula for emotional pain caused by dissonance. But the Bible is very clear that we are to live *all* our lives under the lordship of Christ, that he is the boss over every aspect of our lives. No part of our lives is to be exempt from his scrutiny and direction. Following Christ is not something that we reserve for the weekend—it is a full-time vocation. Compartmentalizing our lives is incompatible with a life committed to Christ. If our work is indeed an altar, then we can't separate it from our Christian worldview. Our work can hardly be transformational service if it is untouched by the values and virtues of our private life and faith. If our work is an altar, there should be no difference between our workplace morality and the moral standards for our private life.[8]

GOOD ETHICS AND GOOD BUSINESS

Hidden in the previous statements of Albert Carr is the assumption that having integrity in the workplace is not good business, that is, it is costly to one's bottom line. But most people have the intuitive sense that that's not true, that doing the right thing in the workplace will pay off somehow. As management professor Ken Blanchard and renowned pastor Norman Vincent Peale put it on the front cover of their book *The Power of Ethical Management*, "Integrity pays. You don't have to cheat to win."[9] Consider

---

[8]For further discussion on this notion of compartmentalization from a Christian worldview see Alexander Hill, *Just Business: Christian Ethics for the Marketplace*, 2nd ed. (Downers Grove, Ill.: InterVarsity Press, 2008).

[9]See Kenneth Blanchard and Norman Vincent Peale, *The Power of Ethical Management* (New York: William Morrow, 1988).

the connection between good ethics and good business.

From a Christian worldview good ethics is always good business. This is because from God's perspective what constitutes good business is much broader than a company's bottom line. As we established in chapter two, good business, from a biblical perspective, includes both how we do business and what kind of business we are in. The company that makes a lot of money using immoral means or providing an immoral product or service would not be viewed by God as successful, regardless of the profitability of the company. Clearly, if our work is an altar, good ethics is nonnegotiable. We should also realize that just because a company has strong ethics does not necessarily mean that it will be profitable. It could have integrity but be incompetent in running a business or have a substandard product or service.

But in the general public, when people talk about the connection between good ethics and good business, what they mean by good business is profitability. Let's explore the connection between ethics and profitability more closely. In the short term good ethics are usually costly. That's why ethical challenges are often called temptations, because they involve costs for doing the right thing. Think about it this way—if doing the right thing were always profitable, everyone would always do it, and conversations on ethics would be totally unnecessary! The reality is that there is often a conflict between a person's principles and his or her self-interest. That's what makes ethical issues such dilemmas.

The Bible is full of references to the prosperity of the wicked. As we mentioned in chapter four, the psalmists regularly lament that the wicked are profitable, in most cases, on account of their wickedness (Ps 73:1-9). Some of the most profitable industries today, like pornography and the illegal drug trade, are those that could be accurately classified as wicked. It is also true that righteous people prosper too (Prov 13:21), but in the Bible there is no necessary connection between righteousness and prosperity.

In the long term, things may be different—there is a closer connection between integrity and a financial advantage (but still not a perfect one). The reason for this is that integrity builds trust, and trustworthiness is a critical component in building a successful business over time. Some people will go out of their way and sometimes even pay higher prices to do business with people they trust. And more important, they frequently go to great lengths to *avoid* doing business with people they don't trust. This is even truer when the service being provided involves a high level of trust in the provider, when it's something that the average person knows little about, like car repair, plumbing, investments, medicine and law. It is also especially true of businesses that are dependent on repeat customers.

One of the great myths of the business world is that greed is the engine of our economic system. Adam Smith, the ideological founder of capitalism, never said that "greed is good." He held that enlightened self-interest (not the same thing as greed) is the engine of capitalism, and that the free market would never work unless the individual participants had the moral values necessary to restrain their self-interest. For Smith, those values came from what he called the social passions, namely, justice and compassion, which reflected a moral consensus that could be seen as a holdover of Judeo-Christian morality. Greed run amok will alienate most of the parties that are necessary to build a lasting business, such as suppliers, employees, customers and partners (see chap. 3).

The reality is that trust is the engine of our economic system. Without trust, business relationships don't happen and the costs of doing business increase astronomically. Think about all the daily transactions that are premised on trust. Literally millions of them occur daily. Every time someone buys something on credit, trust is assumed. Every time we go to work, we trust that we will get paid. The reason that e-commerce has taken off in the past few years is that more people trust that their personal and financial information will not be misused. Think about how expensive it is to do business in cultures where interpersonal trust is low. It is not an accident that countries and cultures where this is the case have great difficulty attracting investment.

I (Scott) got a vivid lesson in this when I met Tedla. He was one of my graduate students in philosophy who came to Talbot School of Theology from Ethiopia. A few days after he arrived on campus, I had the opportunity to take him out to lunch. We went to a local restaurant down the street from the school and had a delightful time getting to know each other better. When it came time to pay for the meal, I handed our server my credit card. Tedla had never seen a credit card before and was unfamiliar with paying for goods or services on credit. When the server brought the bill back, I signed it, and we got up to leave. I'm not sure Tedla quite understood that I had just paid for the meal. In fact, I think he was wondering if his ethics professor had just stolen our lunch! He explained to me that in his country, credit transactions like this were very rare. In fact, he told me that sometimes buyers and sellers of commodities have a routine in which the buyer holds on to the money and the seller holds on to the product, and they both release their grip at the same time, thereby making the exchange. I explained that the restaurant trusts that my credit card company will pay the bill. Further, my credit card company trusts that I will pay my bill when it comes in the mail. Of course, if I don't pay the bill, they won't extend me credit any longer. But that transaction in the restaurant was premised on trust, and without it a good deal of the business that is transacted every day either would not happen or would be more costly and cumbersome to transact.

Good business actually requires not just trust but some other important virtues. Hard work, diligence, thrift, initiative, creativity, promise keeping and truthfulness are just a few other virtues that are at the root of successful individuals and companies. As we pointed out in chapter three, business actually encourages these virtues, and for long-run success they are generally considered very helpful character traits for which employers are always on the lookout. Of course, the converse is also true. Business can encourage greed too. In fact, the prospect of enormous payoffs in the past few years has made the temptation to cut corners ethically very difficult to resist. But people who act unethically usually have difficulty staying in business and prospering in the long run. The temptation is to get in, make our money however we can, and then get out. In the past decade in the dot-com boom, this pattern was something to which people aspired. It's perhaps not an accident that the vast majority of those companies are no longer in business today. Further, much of the mortgage crisis was fueled by greed, in which making subprime loans with little documentation was seen as relatively risk free. Such a short-term outlook, looking for a quick gain without much consideration for the long-run creation of value, turned out to be a very costly way of seeing the world.[10]

---

[10]See Jim Collins and Jerry I. Porras, *Built to Last: Successful Habits of Visionary Companies* (New York: HarperCollins, 2002). See also Jim Collins, *Good to Great: Why Some Companies Make the Leap and Others Don't* (New York: HarperCollins, 2001).

The bestselling research of Jim Collins and Jerry Porras points out that this long-term creation of value is a critical component of "visionary companies." They argue that the emphasis on profit maximization in these companies is usually subordinate to the companies' service to customers and the community, and more generally to living out the mission of the organization. These companies emphasize the significance of profit within the context of the ideals that the company holds and the mission that defines it.[11] They put it this way:

> Contrary to business school doctrine, we did not find "maximizing shareholder wealth" or "profit maximization" as the dominant driving force or primary objective through the history of most of the visionary companies. They have tended to pursue a cluster of objectives, of which making money is only one—and not necessarily the primary one.[12]

They repeatedly point out that the most successful companies they studied make service to their customers the primary goal, and they expect to be profitable if they accomplish that well. We would suggest that this emphasis on the long-run creation of value for customers and the community is another way of articulating what we call transformational service.

So we can say that in the long run good ethics is generally good business because it builds the level of trust necessary for keeping both customers and employees. But that may not always be true. Even in the long run there may be profitable companies that are engaged in unethical behavior. They can get away with it because of how powerful that company is in their industry or how good their product or service is. For example, it would be difficult to see how the market could punish a company like Microsoft if they were involved in unethical behavior. Its software runs the vast majority of the world's computers. Until recently, Microsoft was simply too powerful for the market to inflict adequate punishment for its alleged misdeeds. Too many people and organizations were dependent on their products to go anywhere else with their business. In fact, had the Justice Department not stepped in with its antitrust action against the company, it is quite unlikely that there would have been any market incen-

---

[11]Collins and Porras, *Built to Last*, p. 50.
[12]Ibid., p. 55. See also the examples of Hewlett-Packard and Motorola in this regard, ibid., pp. 56-57, 83.

tives for them to change their alleged improper behavior. But companies that can act unethically and get away with it over the long run are the exception rather than the rule. Even Microsoft now has rising competition in the market for computer operating systems. In the majority of cases, good ethics is an important component of being profitable.

A good example of ethics making the most financial sense is the case of Altrec.com. Started by CEO Mike Morford in 1999, during the heyday of the dot-com boom, Altrec is a Pacific Northwest-based online retailer of outdoor gear. When over a dozen of its competitors went under during the quickly ensuing down cycle, Altrec was able to survive and eventually grow. Early in the company's life, a potential hire stole Altrec's business plan, raised capital and started a copycat competing business. Not wanting to turn his attention away from customers, Morford "turned the other cheek." In part, Morford credits his Christian-based commitment to servant leadership and integrity, which kept him from pursuing a lawsuit. A short time later the competitor went under and another large firm took ownership of the assets. In a turn of Old Testament–style justice, the large firm eventually contracted with Altrec to run the former competitor's website.[13]

So we would suggest that good ethics is an important component of good business in the long run and an important part of creating long-term value for both customers and investors. But that doesn't mean that the connection between ethics and profitability is a sufficient reason for ethical behavior in the marketplace. From a Christian perspective, ethics is important because doing what's right is intrinsically valuable whether it's profitable or not. Even those in the business community often see it this way. For example, in a pointed article in the *Harvard Business Review* titled "Why Be Honest If Honesty Doesn't Pay?" Amir Bhide and Howard Stevenson find that businesspeople are often honest because it's right, not because it pays.[14]

ETHICS AND THE LAW

Many companies have compliance programs, especially companies that

---

[13]Peter Santucci, "King of the Mountain," *Washington CEO*, January 2002, pp. 11-13.
[14]Amir Bhide and Howard H. Stevenson, "Why Be Honest If Honesty Doesn't Pay?" *Harvard Business Review*, September-October 1990, pp. 120-29.

are subject to lots of regulation. But that's different than an emphasis on ethics. Compliance programs are aimed at getting employees to obey the law and industry-specific regulatory standards. But ethics goes beyond mere compliance. Obeying the law is the moral minimum. It is the moral floor, not the ceiling. Most ethical issues have to do with how far above and beyond the law we are obligated to go. We haven't done anything morally praiseworthy by simply obeying the law.

Recently I (Scott) spoke to a group of compliance officers of a statewide banking association and tried to convince them that ethics and compliance are not the same thing. I told the person who invited me what I was going to try to do, and she looked at me as though I had dropped in from another planet! The idea that ethics and compliance with the law were not synonymous had never occurred to her. Judging by the nods around the room, what finally helped persuade both her and the audience was when I recounted for them a conversation I had had with a compliance officer of an organization I consult with periodically. She too believed that there was not much difference between ethics and a compliance program. In a rare moment of candor she told me that her primary job responsibility was to be sure that the organization's top leadership did not go to jail. That is, she was to ensure that they did not run afoul of the law, either intentionally or inadvertently (possible because the laws change so frequently in health care). I replied that I hoped that the bar for ethics was higher than avoiding jail! I said that simply ending the year without indictments being handed down was not a particularly significant accomplishment.

Ethics has to do with values, not the law. It is concerned with the values that define and drive an organization. A company's values actually determine and structure what a company stands for. That's why the label "CEO" ought to mean "chief *ethics* officer." Of course, much of the law has moral values that undergird it. But on a daily basis people do unethical things that are not illegal. The law by itself is not enough to insure that the marketplace is fair and that people do the right thing.

Ethics and Organizations

We've already discussed the idea that our economic system is not built on greed but on trust. The numerous transactions that occur daily that are based on trust strongly suggest that trust is critical to a properly functioning economy. Further, cultures in which corruption is high have traditionally had difficulty attracting investment from outside the country because of the uncertainties created by an environment where trust is low. This also suggests that trust is important for a healthy economy. Without trust, transaction costs significantly increase, sometimes to the point where companies stop doing business in some parts of the world. In some cultures it's not necessarily that trust is low but that trust outside family members is low—that trust with outsiders is low. That too influences how a culture develops prosperity.[15]

But think about what happens on a smaller scale—within an organization in which trust is not strong. Good ethics is critical to establishing trust with employees inside an organization. If management cannot trust the employees and do not have strong relationships of trust, the costs incurred by that organization are significantly higher than if trust were high. If there is a low level of trust in an organization, think about the kinds of costly oversight mechanisms that must be put in place. For example, if we cannot trust people to use their computers properly, it adds to the company's information technology costs to have monitoring software installed and to have someone oversee computer use. To be sure, some layers of accountability are important, but more structure is needed if people cannot be trusted.

Sometimes lack of trust pervades an industry, requiring costly government regulation. In the aftermath of the accounting scandals of the past few years, Congress passed the Sarbanes-Oxley Act to insure greater disclosure and more corporate accountability. Though many of its provisions are both necessary and helpful, there is no doubt that complying with the law is now much more burdensome and expensive for public companies.

Lack of trust has other costs too that are more difficult to quantify in terms of dollar figures. When trust is low, that has an effect on the morale of employees. People who work hard in these companies may find themselves less committed to their work, less receptive to new ideas and less willing to follow the organization's leadership and go the extra mile in their work. Organizations with questionable ethical practices and corresponding levels of trust tend to have more turnover and less stability. Em-

---

[15]For further reading on this provocative thesis, see Francis Fukuyama, *Trust: The Social Virtues and the Creation of Prosperity* (New York: Free Press, 1995).

ployees need to have a good intuitive sense about their organization if they are to be committed to it and thus be as productive as they can. When trust is low, that good intuitive sense turns to cynicism, making them less willing to sacrifice for the good of the company.

To be more specific on how this works in an organization, some would say that the deck is stacked against someone who wants to have integrity and go against the grain to do what is right.[16] We will suggest later on that this is not always the case. But it is probably the norm unless organizations take intentional and appropriate steps to "restack the deck." The question worth taking up here is, How does being in an organization tend to make it more difficult for someone to do the right thing?[17]

Probably the easiest factor to identify is that in most organizations we get along by going along. Most companies go to great lengths to socialize employees into doing things the company's way. Much of this is very valuable because it builds group cohesion and insures that the company communicates its values to new employees. Though much of the socialization is formal, a good deal of it is communicated informally (through stories, examples set by leadership, etc.), and in some cases it is intended to be off the record. Socialization involves a company's efforts to orient employees into "the way things are done around here," and the goal is to build a unified team.[18]

This emphasis on being a team player that is the goal of much of the socialization process can stack the deck against someone who wants to dissent from the consensus of the team. We can become dissuaded from following our consciences even if we are convinced the team is heading in a direction that we consider unethical. When dissenters feel marginalized or become ostracized from the organization and it's decision-making processes, this can be evidence of what is known as "groupthink." Sometimes

---

[16]H. R. Smith and Archie B. Carroll, "Organizational Ethics: A Stacked Deck," *Journal of Business Ethics* 3, no. 2 (1984): 95-100. For more on the role of the organization in ethical decision making, see Linda K. Trevino, "Ethical Decision Making in Organizations: A Person-Situation Interactionist Model," *Academy of Management Review* 11, no. 3 (1986): 601-17. Trevino argues that ethical decision making combines individual moral development and sensitivity with situational and organizational factors. Both are influential in the process of moral decision making.

[17]For more discussion on the nature of the organizations in which managers and executives must make moral decisions, see Robert Jackall, *Moral Mazes: The World of Corporate Managers* (New York: Oxford University Press, 1988).

[18]Trevino and Nelson, *Managing Business Ethics*, pp. 259-61.

leaders will surround themselves with people who either will not or cannot challenge them by asking hard questions—that is, with "yes men." This enables groupthink to proceed smoothly and makes it more difficult for people to go against the tide and do what they think is right.[19]

Not only are new employees socialized into the norms of the organization, they can also be socialized into existing unethical practices. In fact, for those practices to continue it is essential that newcomers be subject to these socializing pressures and thereby be initiated into these practices. Anand, Ashforth and Joshi point out that newcomers can be co-opted into corrupt behavior both by the rewards for the unethical practices (which can be substantial in the short term and can include both financial compensation and job security) and the threat of being marginalized or fired.[20]

A second factor that can stack the deck against ethical behavior is the "frog in the kettle" syndrome. This is the "incremental immorality" factor. You may be familiar with the frog in the boiling water experiment: when put in a kettle of boiling water a frog quickly recognizes the danger and jumps out. But when the frog is placed in room temperature water and the water temperature is gradually increased, the frog will not notice the incremental changes and soon find itself in a kettle of boiling water. Organizational ethics works in much the same way. In many companies plagued by scandal, employees consistently express surprise about how they got to the place where they were breaking the law. They took it one small step at a time, and the steps were so small that they did not notice where they were ultimately headed or how close they were to getting there. In organizations where corruption is endemic, this is a part of an intentional strategy to bring people into unethical and in some cases illegal behavior.[21] Employees are introduced to the corrupt practices incrementally by being asked to make small compromises that create an initial sense of discomfort, but in many cases not enough to cause the employee to go against the consensus that the behavior is acceptable.

---

[19]For further discussion on this phenomenon of being ostracized from one's organization for failure to go along, see ibid., pp. 194-95, and Linda Klebe Trevino and Bart Victor, "Peer Reporting of Unethical Behavior: A Social Context Perspective," *Academy of Management Journal* 353 (1992): 38-64.

[20]Anand, Ashforth and Joshi, "Business as Usual," p. 14.

[21]Ibid., pp. 15-16. See also Gerald Mars, *Cheats at Work: An Anthropology of Workplace Crime* (Aldershot, U.K.: Dartmouth Press, 1994).

A third factor is the oft-repeated phrase "everyone else is doing it." Research in social psychology has established that humans are social in nature. We take cues for how we should behave from what people around us are doing. Moreover, we want to be liked by others, so we have a tendency to give in to pressures even when we know doing so violates some of our treasured values. For example, an accountant may perform tasks that inflate earnings because other members of his or her workgroup are doing it too or because it is common practice in the industry. Padding expense reports is considered acceptable because it is common practice in the company. Organizations help enforce the "everyone is doing it" way of thinking, and it is not unusual for people who think that the way everyone is doing it is wrong to be marginalized. When people game the system or take advantage of a loophole in the law or part of the law not being enforced, they often justify it with the notion that "everyone else is doing it."

A fourth factor that tends to stack the deck against ethics is the notion that "it's not that simple." This is often accompanied by the reply of the management that "you don't have the big picture." It is true that in some cases what might appear morally wrong is actually acceptable when seen in the light of all the available facts. Some employees may not be privy to certain information that would make a material difference in how they assess their ethical decisions. But in many cases we don't need the big picture to see that something is morally wrong or even illegal, and the appeal to it being more complex is often used to deflect criticism and marginalize a person trying to exercise moral courage. Sometimes employees will be told to stick to their areas and leave the moral driving to his or her superiors. They are to do what they are told and leave their concerns to those above them. When we do this, we should know that the "I was just obeying orders" defense has never been a great success, from the Nuremberg trials to the present day.

These pressures that tend to stack the deck against employees who want to exercise moral courage and resist the organizational consensus also require a set of rationalizations that accompany these in order to enable employees to resolve the tension they initially experience when first participating in unethical practices.[22] They are often used because when making

---

[22]These common rationalizations are summarized in Anand, Ashforth and Joshi, "Business as Usual," pp. 10-14. See also Blake E. Ashforth and Vikas Anand, "The Normalization of Cor-

moral decisions employees frequently do not have the luxury of time for considered reflection about what they are facing. These rationalizations include a denial (I had no choice) or diffusion of responsibility (It's not my responsibility),[23] a minimizing of the harm (No one got hurt, or It's a victimless crime), or a minimizing or depersonalizing of the victim in cases where there is harm (They deserved it, or They should have known better). In addition, unethical actions can be rationalized by pointing out others who are doing far worse things—the rationalization of selective comparison. Often the mindset of participants in unethical behavior justifies it by a belief that due to their success or position, they are simply not subject to the rules.[24]

Despite the pressures on employees and the rationalizations available to them to justify unethical behavior, organizations don't have to make it more difficult for people to have integrity and follow their conscience. Leaders can restack the deck and create an atmosphere in which integrity is valued, doing what is right is recognized and groupthink is avoided. But they must do it intentionally—it requires calculated leadership to do so. We may be in a leadership position in our company or organization, or we may have a specific sphere of influence over which we can make a difference. We need to think about how we could have a redemptive influence on our workplace by being an agent of change, helping produce a workplace that's conducive to ethics.

The first step is to determine what kind of ethical culture exists in our organization. This is done through what is known as an "ethics audit," in which leaders determine how the deck is stacked when it comes to ethical behavior and expectations. Business ethicist Linda Trevino suggests a series of questions that will help leaders understand the ethical environment in the organization. She suggests the following as a sample set of questions:

1. How are the leaders of the organization perceived in terms of integrity?

---

ruption in Organizations," in *Research in Organizational Behavior*, ed. Roderick M. Kramer and Barry Staw (Amsterdam: Elsevier, 2003), 25:1-52.

[23]Trevino and Nelson, *Managing Business Ethics*, pp. 202-5. For further reading on how this diffusion of responsibility can work, see M. Scott Peck, *People of the Lie: The Hope for Healing Human Evil* (New York: Touchstone, 1983).

[24]This view of being above the rules is well documented in Barbara Ley Toffler's book on the demise of the accounting giant Arthur Andersen in *Final Accounting: Ambition, Greed and the Fall of Arthur Andersen* (New York: Broadway Books, 2003).

2. How is ethics modeled by the leaders in the organization?

3. Are employees encouraged to question authority when asked to do something they consider wrong?

4. Does the organization have a formal code of ethics that employees know about? How is it regarded and reinforced?

5. What confidential channels exist for employees who have moral or legal concerns?

6. Does ethical or legal misconduct get disciplined? How does that happen?

7. Is integrity emphasized to newly hired employees?

8. Are managers trained in ethical decision making?

9. Does the organization have a body that is charged with considering ethical issues?

10. Who are the organization's heroes? What values to they represent?

11. What informal ethical messages are given to new employees?

12. What are the unwritten ethical rules? Are they consistent with the formal code of ethics?[25]

These auditing questions are a beginning; of course others may be added that are specific to the type of business the organization engages in. Once the leadership has a better understanding of the ethical climate that exists, they can begin the process of changing the culture if necessary. In some cases such an ethics audit is the result of a sentencing guideline issued by the court if the company has run afoul of the law. In those cases, what Trevino calls an "ethical culture change intervention" may be necessary.[26]

Five consistently "aligned" components are necessary to restack the deck so that it becomes more conducive to ethical behavior.[27] Each com-

---

[25]These questions are taken from Trevino and Nelson, *Managing Business Ethics*, pp. 297-98. For further discussion on the notion of an ethics audit, see Domingo Garcia-Marza, "Theoretical Approaches to Ethics Auditing," *Journal of Business Ethics* 57, no. 3 (2005): 209-19; and Michael Metzger, Dan R. Dalton and John W. Hill, "The Organization of Ethics and the Ethics of Organizations: The Case for Expanded Organizational Ethics Audits," *Business Ethics Quarterly* 3, no. 1 (1993): 27-43.

[26]Trevino and Nelson, *Managing Business Ethics*, pp. 298-300.

[27]The literature on the subject of creating and maintaining an environment conducive to ethical behavior is both voluminous and multidisciplinary. A sample includes Patrick Murphy, "Cre-

ponent needs to be aligned not only with each other but with the framework set out in chapter two, which provides the contours of an overarching ethic for business. The first is to have *a companywide credo*. A credo is a broad values-aspiration statement that should be tied to deeply rooted moral principles and to the company's overall mission and purpose (provided the latter reflects an appropriate goal). The second is to have *a code of ethical behavior* in which unethical conduct and positive ethical behavior is clearly spelled out in behavioral terms.

I (Scott) was asked to help develop the first of these two components for a small construction company. Because they were a very decentralized group with most of the thirty to forty employees out in the field most of the time, they didn't have to check in that often, and it was difficult to keep track of work patterns. The president of the company expressed concern about the loose accountability and had a great desire to clarify for her employees what she thought was unethical. I suggested to her that if a companywide code of ethics were perceived as coming from the top down, it would be less successful than if it were built from the ground up. That way everyone got to contribute and have a sense of ownership in the code, seeing it as something they were all agreeing to. This is not to suggest that ethics is a matter of group consensus or that the group determined what counted as ethical behavior. Rather, the exercise was designed to articulate the moral norms and underlying principles that were already intuitive for most of the people in the room.

We got the entire group in a room for a half-day session, and we began an exercise that led to a rough draft of the company's code of ethics. I asked them to list all of the practices of the industry that they thought constituted unethical behavior, and to rank them on a one-to-ten scale (one for things that were not that big of a deal and ten for things that were blatantly illegal). I then asked them to identify the moral value or principle

ating and Encouraging Ethical Corporate Structures," *Sloan Management Review* 30 (1989): 81-87; Lynn Sharp Paine, "Managing for Organizational Integrity," *Harvard Business Review*, April 1994; Arleen Thomas and Lynn Gibson, "Management Is Responsible Too," *Journal of Accountancy* 195, no. 3 (2003): 53-55; Dawn S. Carlson and Pamela L. Perrewe, "Institutionalization of Organizational Ethics Through Transformational Leadership," *Journal of Business Ethics* 14 (1995): 829-38; Luis Rodriguez-Dominguez and Isabel Garcia-Sanchez, "Corporate Governance and Codes of Ethics," *Journal of Business Ethics* 90, no. 2 (2009): 187-202; and Saul W. Gellerman, "Managing Ethics from the Top Down," *Sloan Management Review* 30, no. 2 (1989): 73-79.

that was being violated with each example of unethical behavior. This formed a key part of the basis for the organization's credo of core values.

At the end of the brainstorming session I was pleased and surprised to discover that virtually everyone agreed on the set of unethical behaviors, though there was some debate over how serious they thought they were. This session formed the raw material for a rough draft of their code of ethics. It also helped identify the values that they held in common as a group. There was a high degree of consensus on those values. I set out to draft the code, putting in one or two items that the president wanted included that didn't come up specifically in the group discussion. We then met for another half day, where we presented the draft back to the group to be sure that it represented what they had expressed in our earlier session. As expected, they made some changes—I had misunderstood a few items—but it moved along well, and at the end of the day people felt a sense of ownership, recognizing that "this is something we all agreed to." I then wrote up a final draft that was organized around the company's obligations to their various constituencies—namely, employees, suppliers, contractors and partners. We instituted it, and the company scheduled an annual ethics education session and allotted a time during employee orientation devoted to education on the code of ethics. In some organizations employees must sign off on the code in conjunction with their hiring, and some require that they reeducate themselves and sign off on the code on an annual basis.

To keep the code of ethics from becoming just another piece of paper on the wall or in the policy manual, *ethics must be modeled from the top.*[28] This is the third component that is nonnegotiable. The company's leadership serves as the guardians of the company's vision, values and ethics. In addition, leadership is responsible for shaping the organization's culture in ways that are conducive to ethical behavior, including hiring men and women with properly functioning moral compasses.[29] A person can work very hard at putting together a company mission statement, a statement of core values and a code of ethics, but if the leadership does not model those elements, those documents have little significance. People listen more

---

[28]Trevino and Nelson, *Managing Business Ethics*, pp. 261-70.

[29]For further reading on how to construct interviews for determining the integrity of the applicant, see Donna R. Pawlowski and John Hollwitz, "Work Values, Cognitive Strategies and Applicant Reactions in a Structured Pre-Employment Interview for Ethical Integrity," *Journal of Business Communication* 37, no. 1 (2000): 58-76.

carefully to what leaders do than to what they say. If the leaders do not adhere to the values and behaviors that are in print, they might as well not be on the wall.

An organization's traditions are kept alive through the stories that are told. Often, these narratives illustrate those things that are important to the company and capture its mission and values. These stories are often formally recounted at various training and educational sessions. But their real power is in the way they are told informally. A fourth component for companies with an environment conducive to ethical behavior are *narratives about people who had the courage to do the right thing*. The organization both recognizes and holds up as models people who have acted in ways that are consistent with the company's overall mission and credo.[30]

A final component of restacking the deck is to *reexamine performance measurement and reward systems* (both formal and tacit). "You get what you measure and reward" has now become familiar industry jargon, but it is true. If we say we value ethical behavior but reward "top performers" (as measured by dollar volume or output alone) without attention to how these results are achieved, we are sending a mixed message to our employees. Other employees will see the behaviors that are really viewed with favor and mimic them. Achieving ethical behavior requires appropriate metrics (e.g., customer service) and ensuing rewards.

ETHICS AND CHARACTER

Though it is true that there is much more to organizational ethics than hiring ethical people, there is no substitute for personal character and integrity. Personal integrity often serves as the first (sensitivity to the fact that something is wrong) and the last line (the courage to take a stand when all other safeguards have failed) of defense. If someone's moral compass is broken, no amount of organizational effort can compensate for that. But companies can help educate their employees about integrity in their specific work arena, and should recognize that they have a vested interest in building an environment where trust and ethics are taken seriously. For a Christian who views work as an altar, it is critical that such a workplace is conducive to ethics and integrity. Of course, for many employees there

---

[30]Trevino and Nelson, *Managing Business Ethics*, pp. 285-89.

are limits on what kind of formal impact they can have. But if our work is our place of service to God, we have to contribute to making our work environment a place where ethics is taken seriously.

One component of personal ethics that is common to many ethical scandals is the notion that someone is above the rules. One of the key dangers of both groupthink and leaders surrounding themselves with yes men is that there is no one in the system they are accountable to. From a Christian worldview no one is above accountability to the norms of ethics and to the laws of the land. Particularly if our work is an altar, a place of service to God, we ultimately answer to God. No one is entitled to arrogantly put him- or herself above having to answer for their actions.

From a Christian perspective character is of critical importance. In the Bible ethics is much more than simply obeying God's commands. Ethics also is about the cultivation of virtue or character traits that reflect the character of Christ. Paul suggests that the fruit of the Spirit is an essential element of spiritual growth. The traits that he describes are a good start on the important Christian virtues: "The fruit of the Spirit is love, joy, peace, patience, kindness, goodness, faithfulness, gentleness and self-control" (Gal 5:22-23). Jesus insists that character is developed from the inside out, and that what comes out of a person (his or her behavior) reflects what is inside (his or her character [Mk 7:17-23]).

The Bible reflects an ancient view of ethics that is very different from the current perspective. The Bible has much in common with the ancient philosophers who believed that ethics is not fundamentally about decisions and dilemmas but about being a good person and living a good life. Success as a person was measured by what kind of person we are, not by what we achieved or accumulated. It was first and foremost about being a person of character. Aristotle connected happiness with virtue and believed that a person could not be happy without a commitment to being virtuous. Similarly, Epicurus pointedly said, "It is not possible to live pleasantly without living prudently, honorably and justly." The prophet Micah anticipated this, saying,

He [God] has showed you, O man, what is good.
    And what does the LORD require of you?
To act justly and to love mercy
    and to walk humbly with your God. (Mic 6:8)

Jesus put it clearly when he asked his disciples, "What good is it for a man to gain the whole world, yet forfeit his soul?" (Mk 8:36). Though we would argue that it's more the exception than the rule, it is entirely possible to be at the top of our profession and be at the bottom in terms of character. Take the person who has wealth and success (in the narrowly defined sense of business), but has earned it through less than honorable means, or has alienated his or her family and has no significant friendships to speak of due to years of treating people poorly in his or her business dealings. Though that person may be a success in the narrow sense of business, his or her life falls well short from a broader definition and with respect to other dimensions of life.

ETHICAL DECISION MAKING

So what happens when we face an ethical dilemma? How do we go about thinking about it from within a Christian worldview? First, we gather the *facts*. We take stock of what we know and what we need to know in order to make this decision. Some ethical issues are resolved at this point and turn out to be communication problems, strategic issues or misunderstandings rather than ethical issues. Sometimes, clarifying the facts will make the issue pretty black and white and the decision easier. Second, identify the *ethical issue*—that is, who are the parties involved, what are their interests, and what are the values underlying them? That's the definition of an ethical issue—a conflict of two or more value-driven interests. That's usually why ethical issues are so tricky—they involve people's values and deepest held beliefs. Third, clarify the *values and virtues* that are involved. What moral principles are undergirding people's interests in this case? Specifically, what biblical principles and virtues should be brought to bear on the case at hand? That is, how are the broader values of God's kingdom reflected or not? This is the part of the decision-making model that distinguishes it from ordinary checklists and infuses it with biblical values and virtues. Fourth, what are the *alternatives?* Are there alternatives that satisfy most if not all of the values at stake? That's a win-win situation. We must be creative here and realize that sometimes the best solutions are the ones few people have thought of before. Fifth, *weigh the values*—that is, some values are more influential than others.[31] Jesus accused the religious

---

[31]For further discussion on weighing values and the theological framework in which it is set, see Scott B. Rae, *Moral Choices: An Introduction to Ethics*, 3rd ed. (Grand Rapids: Zondervan,

leaders of being diligent on Pharisaic traditions and neglecting the weightier values of the Mosaic laws (Mt 23:23). Sixth, consider the *consequences*. This is not to say that the consequences resolve the dilemma, but they should be considered. Usually following the principles produces the best outcome too—that is, consequences support the principles.

Of course this model is not like a software program that will automatically produce the right ethical decision. But it will help us to be sure we ask all the right questions and consider all the relevant factors. We'd encourage you to use a model like this not only for your own personal ethical issues, but it can be used to facilitate group discussion of issues facing organizations too.

CONCLUSION

Character plays an important role in ethics. We must be willing to make decisions that impact our self-interest in order to do what is right. Many ethical issues are actually temptations in which there is a conflict between our self-interest and a moral or biblical principle. Over the long run having integrity will make us better businesspeople, but more importantly, it will make us a better person. God requires integrity in the workplace not because it's profitable but because it's right and honors him. Since our work is our altar, our place of service to God, having integrity is not negotiable.

A revival of character and ethics in the workplace is tied to spiritual transformation and renewal.[32] From a Christian perspective ethics is grounded in God's character, expressed in his commands and enabled by his Spirit. Though of course there is common grace available to all, lasting character is ultimately produced by a sense of accountability to God and the internal work of God's Spirit, making someone to be more like Christ.

However, structures (organizations and economic systems) also curtail our choices, place us into "moral binds" or provide enabling environments to move in positive directions. Organizations need to take steps to unstack the deck and encourage ethical behavior. Better economic conditions around the globe would do much to relax some of the causes of the dilemmas in the scenarios that opened this chapter (e.g., undocumented work-

---

2009), pp. 50-51.

[32]For more discussion of this from a sociological perspective, see James D. Hunter, *The Death of Character* (New York: Basic Books, 2000).

ers, bribery). Perhaps longer-term orientations in markets would release accountants from feeling so much pressure to make the short-term picture look better than what it is. In addition to spiritual renewal on the individual level, serious attention must be paid to transforming business institutions and the global economic system so they too reflect all that God has intended them to be.

LEADERSHIP AND MANAGEMENT

SERVING EMPLOYEES

Until a few years ago Rich was a senior executive at a privately owned, medium-sized financial services company. He had been with this firm for about two decades and was highly satisfied with both his work and the culture of the organization. About five years ago his firm was purchased by a holding company with multiple lines of business. Since the new owners took over, the culture of the organization became much harder driving and focused on making the quarterly numbers.

Over time Rich grew weary of the new ownership's management policies. While the pay increased rapidly, so did turnover in his department. Rich also had to spend more of his time intervening on issues of frustration and relational conflict on the part of employees who remained. New hires seemed to be driven primarily by money and were less interested in team work and serving the best interests of clients.

Three years ago Rich made a courageous and risky decision to launch out on his own; he started a business while promising a small group of investors, and the leadership team he initially hired, that he would treat employees much better. His firm, he hoped, would focus on developing employees and on creating an organizational culture that would make people want to come to work in the morning to achieve something meaningful, not just to earn a paycheck.

Until recently his start-up company had been growing and employed about fifty people. The business had been doing well financially until a downturn in the economy. Now, with resources in shorter supply and increasing customer demands, Rich finds himself dealing with lots of challenges and with some self-doubt about his ability to lead in a way that matches his ideals. He has come to appreciate why so many books have been written about effective management and leadership.[1] While he would love to favor his employees in most major decisions, he has to balance their interests with those of investors, suppliers and customers.

Workers are commonly viewed as resources that serve an organization's interests. In many cases work is seen as an economic exchange between the employer and the employee, something along the lines of "a fair day's work for a fair day's pay." At worst workers are treated as mere objects. For example, the older but still influential school of "Scientific Management" (pioneered by Fredrick Winslow Taylor's famous time-and-motion studies) effectively dehumanizes employees and reduces them to their productive capacity.

In contrast, Rich has spent lots of time and effort in coming up with ways his organization can also serve its employees. He has aimed to create a context in which people develop and approach their work with great passion and purpose. Recently, however, these goals have seemed like remote luxuries given the fact that he and his senior leadership team have had to reduce a number of positions due to an economic downturn. Rich has lost much sleep thinking about how his organization can serve while simultaneously laying off some employees, most of whom he knows well and respects. Other tensions are troubling him too. In day to day management he realizes that some people need to be pushed to achieve work goals. Occasionally he has to resort to coercion and threats to get people moving or the mission of the entire organization suffers.

Rich has spent time pondering the biblical description of the upside-down attributes of the kingdom of God (e.g., the focus on meekness in the Beatitudes) and how they might be applied to leading a company that operates in a highly competitive environment. He fears that employees, suppliers and competitors may misread those types of traits as weaknesses and try to take advantage of him.

---

[1]See, for example, Stephen A. Covey, *Principle-Centered Leadership* (New York: Fireside Books, 1992); Warren Bennis, *On Becoming a Leader* (New York: Perseus Books, 1989), and *Leaders: Strategies for Taking Charge* (1989; reprint, New York: HarperCollins, 2003); John C. Maxwell, *The 21 Irrefutable Laws of Leadership* (Nashville: Thomas Nelson, 1998); Peter F. Drucker, *The Effective Executive* (1967; reprint, Classic Drucker Collection, 2007); Max De Pree, *Leadership Is an Art* (New York: Doubleday, 1989); James MacGregor Burns, *Leadership* (New York: Harper & Row, 1978).

Moving into high level formal leadership roles can create a variety of tensions. The level of ambition that is often required to attain such positions can come into conflict with the mandate to serve others. Furthermore, leaders are responsible for entire organizations, and this obligation may directly collide with duties to serve the needs of individual employees. Tensions like these are the central focus of this chapter. In particular, we will explore how biblical teaching informs the practices of leadership and employee relations in business.

To be certain, executives are not the only leaders in an organization. A middle manager, with twenty to thirty people reporting to him or her, a supervisor of a small department, or a peer who is influential in a flat work group all exercise leadership. Regardless of your position, if you influence people, the principles explored in this chapter apply to you (or may apply to you in the future).

In addition to biblical teaching there are clear, practical reasons why sound leadership and its effect on employee relationships is so important. It has been keenly observed that in a knowledge-based economy, an organization's most important assets (its employees) leave the building every night.[2] Thus, the whole person must be engaged if employees are to be invested in their work.

Throughout this book we have argued that work should ideally be viewed as a calling (more accurately, as *one* of our particular callings), business should be practiced as a form of service to God and neighbor, and we must guard against falling into vices such as overidentification with work, greed and overambition. In order for this to occur, however, organizations and their leaders must do their part. To simply place the burden on employees to change their attitudes is far from sufficient and abdicates the role of leaders. An enabling context or a community where employees can live out their callings, grow as people and maintain a proper perspective on work must be intentionally developed and nurtured. This, we argue, begins with good leadership.

LEADERSHIP IN THE BIBLE

Though the Bible is not a textbook on leadership theory, it contains both

---

[2]See Marc Gunther, *Faith & Fortune* (New York: Crown Business, 2004), pp. 35-36.

narrative and direct teaching material that addresses the subject. The Bible does not present a developed theory of leadership, though it does directly address the subject, especially as it pertains to the church and the kingdom. The Bible's teaching has elements in common with some of the key aspects of leadership that have emerged through current research and empirical study on the subject.

One common distinction made is the difference between transactional and transformational leadership. *Transactional leaders* are sometimes said to be mere managers. They act as brokers and accomplish the objectives of the organization by deal-making within the more "traditional exchange relationship between leader and follower." Typically, they set up structures and rewards, clarify requirements and encourage conformity to organizational values.[3] By contrast, *transformational leaders* inspire change and high levels of accomplishment. They often challenge the status quo and change their organization's mission and culture. They also create deep personal loyalty on the part of followers and work to motivate employees to serve broader purposes and goals.[4]

Martin Luther King is an example of transformational leadership in society. Through his inspiration and vision for a colorblind society, he not only changed the racial landscape of the country but also dramatically changed the lives and perspectives of his followers so that their goals and the goals of the movement became more closely identified.[5]

Bernard Bass emphasizes that transformational leaders unite their followers by showing them "individual consideration, intellectual stimulation, inspirational motivation and charisma."[6] The notion of transformational leadership was first coined by the political scientist James MacGregor Burns, and was focused on political and military leaders who both initiated and persevered to implement changes that "meant basic

---

[3]Though not an advocate of transactional leadership, this style is described in Bernard M. Bass, "From Transactional to Transformational Leadership: Learning to Share the Vision," *Organizational Dynamics* 18 (1990): 19-31; Bass, *Leadership and Performance Beyond Expectations* (New York: Free Press, 1985).

[4]For a concise summary of the differences between transactional and transformational leaders, see Bruno Dyck and Mitchell Neubert, *Management: Current Practices and New Directions* (Boston: Houghton Mifflin Harcourt, 2010), pp. 447-48. See also James MacGregor Burns, *Leadership* (New York: Harper Perennial, 1978), p. 4.

[5]For numerous other examples of transformational leadership see James MacGregor Burns, *Transforming Leadership* (New York: Grove Press, 2003).

[6]Bass, "From Transactional to Transformational Leadership," p. 24.

alterations in entire systems—revolutions that replace one structure of power with another."[7]

Bass calls this a higher order of change, as opposed to changes in degree or first order change.[8] This requires a leader to empower those he or she leads to become leaders themselves. Burns emphasizes leaders who "champion and inspire followers" through a variety of factors, personal charisma and vision among them.[9] Bass and Avolio spell these out further by suggesting that transformation leaders act as role models for their followers in order to produce trust and respect. In addition, they encourage creativity and risk taking from followers, and act as mentors to those they lead.[10] Dangers in the transformational leadership model include the potential that these types of leaders might pursue their own self-interest, and that the emphasis on inspirational leadership could make the followers vulnerable to manipulation or dependency.[11]

A slightly different emphasis in leadership studies has focused on *servant leadership*.[12] Here the stress is less on the inspiration and charisma of the leaders and more how the leader serves his or her followers. Servant leaders emphasize "service before self, listening as a means of affirmation, creating trust and nourishing followers to become whole."[13] Servant leaders consis-

---

[7]Burns, *Transforming Leadership*, p. 24.

[8]Bass, *Leadership and Performance Beyond Expectations*, p. 4.

[9]Burns, *Transformational Leadership*, p. 27. It should be noted that Burns was skeptical of an overemphasis on charisma because of its potential to become a form of tyranny. He described transformational leadership not as "enslaving followers but liberating and empowering them" (ibid.).

[10]B. M. Bass and B. J. Avolio, "Transformational Leadership and Organizational Culture," *International Journal of Public Administration* 17 (1994): 541-52.

[11]For more on these potential dangers of transformational leadership, see C. Johnson, *Meeting the Ethical Challenges of Leadership* (Thousand Oaks, Calif.: Sage, 2001); and Joanne Ciulla, *Ethics: The Heart of Leadership* (Westport, Conn.: Quorum, 1998).

[12]The notion of servant leadership that began in the teaching of Jesus was popularized in the leadership discussion by Robert K. Greenleaf, *Servant Leadership: A Journey into the Nature of Legitimate Power and Greatness*, 25th anniv. ed. (1977; reprint, New York: Paulist Press, 2002). See also Robert K. Greenleaf, Larry C. Spears, *The Power of Servant-Leadership* (San Francisco: Berrett Koehler, 1998); James C. Hunter, *The Servant: A Simple Story About the True Essence of Leadership* (Roseville, Calif.: Prima, 1998); James A. Autry, *The Servant Leader* (New York: Three Rivers, 2001); J. W. Graham, "Servant Leadership in Organizations," *Leadership Quarterly* 2 (1991): 105-19; S. Sendjaya and J. C. Sarros, "Servant Leadership: Its Origin, Development and Application in Organizations," *Journal of Leadership and Organizational Studies* 9 (2002): 57-64; B. N. Smith, R. V. Montagno and T. N. Kuzmenko, "Transformational and Servant Leadership: Content and Contextual Comparisons," *Journal of Leadership and Organizational Studies* 10 (2004): 257-83.

[13]This summary appears in R. Daft, *Leadership: Theory and Practice* (Fort Worth: Dryden, 1999).

tently give priority to the service of the needs of others, encourage group and participatory decision making, and model self-awareness, humility and altruism. A major criticism of servant leadership is that it can be weak, naive, and neglect the performance of the organization.

To be certain, servant leadership appears in the Bible more in seed form than as a fully developed theory. Though we will propose below that the Bible advocates something akin to the servant approach, there also seems to be substantial overlap with transformational leadership. Both of these theories advocate leaders operating out of deeply held values, have an emphasis on care for and consideration of the follower, and see effective leaders as promoting a higher level of motivation, performance and morality.[14]

The Bible speaks to leadership in a variety of literary genres. For example, there is much rich material on leadership in the narrative sections of the Scriptures. The Bible is full of stories of both good and bad leaders. Noah stood his ground against ridicule in order to build the ark and survive the flood. Abraham took tremendous steps of faith to follow God's direction as the father of the nation Israel. Joseph was extremely wise and competent as an administrator and insisted on being morally pure in resisting sexual temptation. Moses stood against a far more powerful nation and trusted in God's ability to deliver him and the Israelites. Deborah was one of the judges of Israel who led the nation to military victories. Esther stood courageously against high-ranking government officials and protected her people from genocide. Daniel trusted God in the midst of adversity, proved himself highly competent in government and administration, and established a reputation over many years of consistent service.

It is also worth noting that most of these great leaders had glaring personal flaws. Noah was "drunk and naked in his tent" (the latter being a euphemism for something sexually shameful) after the flood.[15] Abraham twice attempted to pass his wife off as his sister in order to save himself. Moses was a condemned murderer. David was an adulterer and tried to cover it up by an egregious abuse of his power as king when he ordered the woman's husband to the front lines of battle.

---

[14]John H. Humphrys, "Contextual Implications for Transformational and Servant Leadership: A Historical Investigation," *Management Decision* 43 (2005): 1415.

[15]For further reading on this section of Genesis, see Allen P. Ross, *Creation and Blessing* (Grand Rapids: Baker, 1998); Gordon J. Wenham, *Genesis 1-15* (Waco, Tex.: Word, 1988); and Bruce K. Waltke, *Genesis: A Commentary* (Grand Rapids: Zondervan, 2001).

The story of great leaders in the Bible is not so much about their leadership qualities but how they were used by God in the service of a greater mission in spite of their weaknesses. God is the hero of these stories, not the particular leader. For example, the real story of the life of Abraham is God's faithfulness to Abraham, not his great leadership qualities. The story of Joseph is the story of God sovereignly placing a faithful person in positions of influence, though Joseph did exercise effective leadership in his position as prime minister of Egypt. The real story of the exodus is not Moses' leadership but God's dramatic rescue of Israel. Likewise, the real story of the rebuilding of Jerusalem is not Nehemiah's leadership but God's faithfulness to his people in enabling them to overcome obstacles. We suspect that if we could talk to these great leaders, they would emphasize that the real story is about God, not them. They would probably tell us that they didn't aspire to leadership—that God chose them against their desire. That is not to say that they were not great leaders with qualities to emulate, but when we use their examples of leadership, it is important to remember who the real leader was in these stories—God.

The Bible does directly address the subject of leadership in Paul's letters to Timothy. Paul is instructing his young protégé about how to lead in the church. To be sure, Paul is not addressing corporate leadership, but many of the principles he gives to Timothy apply to leadership roles in general.

First Timothy 3 lays out criteria for leadership in the church. Paul assumes that Timothy will delegate responsibility and share leadership with those who are qualified. The criteria for elders/overseers listed in 1 Timothy 3:1-10 are all criteria of character—things like being temperate, self-controlled, respectable, of good reputation, hospitable, gentle and able to manage his finances and family well. Character is central when it comes to leadership, though certain areas of competence are also important. Leaders must be able to communicate and must have been tested, presumably by adversity. The passage also emphasizes how well people manage their homes. What occurs in private life is critical to qualifications for leadership.[16] How people handle money and family reveals a great deal about how they will deal with larger areas of responsibility. The home is a micro-

---

[16]For an illuminating case study and commentary on the relationship between a leader's private life and his or her ability to lead, see Suzy Wetlaufer, "A Question of Character," *Harvard Business Review* 77 (1999): 30-34.

cosm for leadership and how consistently people live out their faith.

Paul emphasizes to Timothy that the aspiration to leadership is a good thing: "If anyone sets his heart on being an overseer, he desires a noble task" (1 Tim 3:1). There is nothing problematic per se with aspiring to leadership, though a person can have a variety of poor reasons or motivations for having such a goal. People can be motivated by arrogance, greed, control, insecurity, narcissism, power or prestige to seek a position of leadership. Or they can be motivated by a sense of calling. To be realistic, motives for seeking such a position are likely mixed. But assuming motives that are not improper, people should be encouraged to aim for leadership if they are gifted accordingly. At the top of a list of appropriate reasons is the desire to discover a suitable place in the organization to utilize the complement of one's gifts, skills and talents in a niche in which a person can most significantly advance God's work in the world. To put it another way, it's not the aspiration to a position that matters most; it's the aspiration to maximize our gifts and talents that is key in the service of God and others.

Perhaps the central passage in the entire Bible that addresses leadership is taken from Jesus' discussion with his disciples about greatness in the kingdom. In Matthew 20:25-28, Jesus responds to a request for leadership and recognition when the kingdom comes. Jesus turned the disciples' view of this upside down when he insisted:

> You know that the rulers of the Gentiles lord it over them, and their high officials exercise authority over them. Not so with you. Instead, whoever wants to become great among you must first become your servant, and whoever wants to be first must first become your slave—just as the Son of Man did not come to be served, but to serve, and to give his life as a ransom for many.

For Jesus, leadership and greatness are tied up with a person's willingness to be a servant. Jesus powerfully modeled this by not only his earthly life but also his willingness to give himself completely by his death on the cross. This stood in sharp contrast to the way leadership was exercised in the ancient world. Rulers at that time governed ruthlessly and capriciously, and people lived in fear of their leaders. Leaders misused their power for personal gain regularly and habitually—probably the most common way for a person to obtain wealth in the ancient world. Jesus used the terms *exercise authority* and *lord it over them* interchangeably, suggesting that the abuse of power was the norm in the ancient world. In other words, leadership in the ancient world was badly tainted.

There certainly are parallels with the exercise of power today, both in business and in government. We don't have to think very hard to come up with examples of how frequently power is abused. Power is frequently a function of one's position. In these cases, authority can be "lorded over" someone. This phrase is used to refer to the abuse of position-based power. By virtue of the position of the one in authority, he or she is able to bend another person's will to do what the authority wants them to do. Leadership is followed not because people want to but because they have to. It's leadership by coercion, not by character or mutual respect. It's the person who demands respect rather than earns it.

Power is often abused in today's workplace to exercise self-promotion, often at the expense of others or a greater purpose or mission. In many organizations an inordinate amount of time and energy is spent securing and maintaining a person's position of power. Often this can come at the expense of his or her organization—as is the case when a leader extends control over a domain or works to derail promising projects because doing so serves to weaken a rival.

This kind of abuse of power is often associated with highly charismatic leaders and reflects the dark side of leadership. While they can be inspirational and command a significant following, charismatic leaders are often also highly ego driven, if not outright narcissistic.[17] Charismatic leaders have a high degree of self-confidence and strong convictions.[18] However, they can also be "overly sensitive to criticism, poor listeners, lacking in empathy, have a distaste for mentoring, and display an intense desire to compete."[19] In some extreme contexts this kind of leadership can create a cult-like setting in which dissent is marginalized and a dangerous confor-

---

[17]M. Maccoby, "Narcissistic Leaders: The Incredible Pros, the Inevitable Cons," *Harvard Business Review* 78 (2000): 69-77.

[18]R. DeVries et al., "On Charisma and Need for Leadership," *European Journal of Work and Organizational Psychology* 8 (1999): 109-26.

[19]Dennis Tourish and Naheed Vatcha, "Charismatic Leadership and Corporate Cultism at Enron: The Elimination of Dissent, the Promotion of Conformity and Organizational Collapse," *Leadership* 1 (2005): 459.

mity results from an insular view of the organization. Some of the most serious liabilities of the charismatic leader occur when the demands of an outsized ego force the leader to "project purely personal needs and beliefs onto those of constituents."[20] These abuses of power can eventually alienate employees, prevent needed change from occurring and, if not checked, lead to the collapse of the organization. Today there is a profound sense of disillusionment with the notion of highly charismatic, celebrity-type leaders, given the well-publicized excesses of some and the organizational damage that they have caused.[21]

In contrast to the abuses of power and narcissistic self-promotion, Jesus advocated servanthood as the key to greatness in his kingdom. In other words, we become great in the kingdom by serving others, not by seeking the spotlight for ourself. We reach the top in God's economy by being willing to serve at the bottom. We lead by serving others not by promoting our own interests. We lead by *developing* people and helping them fulfill their callings, not by using or manipulating people or treating them well solely for the sake of what they can do for us. This is a redemptive form of leadership, leadership that reflects the values of the kingdom and treats people with the dignity they deserve by virtue of being made in God's image.

To be more specific, the right kind of exercise of power in the workplace empowers confidence, not subservience, in the people we lead.[22] Often, leaders tear down a person's confidence in order to make them more compliant and easier to lead. A leader who serves nurtures self-assurance instead of inadequacy. It may be that some of the best leaders actually have the least compliant followers, because they have encouraged their confidence and given them the freedom to dissent from the prevailing opinion.[23] Similarly, leaders who serve encourage employee growth and devel-

[20]Jay A. Conger, "The Dark Side of Leadership," *Organizational Dynamics*, autumn 1990: 45. See also Jay A. Conger, *The Charismatic Leader: Behind the Mystique of Exceptional Leadership* (San Francisco: Jossey-Bass, 1989).

[21]H. Mintzberg, "Leader to Leader," *Harvard Business Review*, spring 1999, p. 12; R. Hogan et al., "The Dark Side of Charisma," in *Measures of Leadership*, ed. Kenneth E. Clark and Miriam B. Clark (West Orange, N.J.: Leadership Library of America, 1990), pp. 343-54; Beverly Alimo-Metcalfe and John Alban-Metcalfe, "Leadership: Time for a New Direction?" *Leadership* 1 (2005): 54. Interestingly, these call for servanthood as a nonnegotiable trait of a newly emerging model of leadership.

[22]We are indebted for the material in this section to Richard J. Foster's discussion of power in *The Challenge of the Disciplined Life* (New York: HarperCollins, 1985), pp. 201-11.

[23]Keith Grint, *The Arts of Leadership* (New York: Oxford University Press, 2000), p. 420. Grint

opment, not inferiority. Their goal is for the people who work with them to grow in their skills and competence, not to highlight their inadequacies and thereby elevate themselves at someone else's expense. They view leadership as *developing* people, not using them. The right kind of exercise of power inspires trust, not mere conformity. Power that produces conformity is based on factors like position, charisma or coercion, but power that inspires is built on a relationship of trust and mutual respect. The right kind of power is exercised by leaders who care about relationships. They typically describe those who report to them as those who work *with* them, not those who work *for* them. These kinds of leaders enhance communication and trust instead of stifling it. They contribute to an environment of a team working together instead of producing isolation.

The pioneering work of Robert Levering and his associates (who generate *Fortune*'s annual "The Best Companies to Work For" list) confirms the value of mutual respect and trust. While these types of lists conjure up images of companies with generous and creative benefits, such as video games in the office, free meals and extensive vacation time, a deeper look reveals that something else is at work. As Levering says, "The primary defining characteristic of a great place to work is the level of trust between management and employees, not specific policies and practices."[24]

The kind of leadership that the Bible describes puts a high premium on the humility of the leader. In contrast to the leadership that is based on charisma, leaders who serve their organizations and their employees well are characterized by a realistic view of themselves and a focus on the well-being of others. Current management research has highlighted the importance of humility and has warranted including it in the essential traits for successful leadership. Andrew Morris and his colleagues conclude:

> Humility in leadership serves several potential functions. First, humility may influence leaders to behave in a manner that is primarily other-enhancing rather than self-enhancing. Second, possession of humility may

---

suggests that the reason for the correlation between successful leaders and the least compliant followers is that "when leaders err—and they always do—the leader with compliant followers will fail," because debate has been stifled and there are fewer resources for producing change and necessary corrections (ibid.).

[24]Robert Levering, *A Great Place to Work: What Makes Some Employers So Good (and Most So Bad)* (San Francisco: Great Place to Work Institute, 2000), p. 3.

shield the CEO from needing to receive public adulation and may cause him or her to shun such attempts.[25]

A further benefit of humility is that it actually may contribute to a company's competitive advantage by fostering what some scholars call "organizational learning and organizational resilience." That is, leaders that exhibit genuine humility find that they are less rigid in their categories, more open to learning from a variety of sources, including employees and other subordinates, and thus model this kind of openness to new information and changing course when necessary. Humility, with its realistic assessment of oneself, enables leaders to evaluate without exaggeration and to "distinguish between self-confidence/self-esteem and over-confidence, narcissism and stubbornness."[26]

The importance of humility in leadership is a focal point of the research of management consultant Jim Collins. In his follow-up work on visionary companies and what enabled them to make the transition from "good to great," what he calls "Level 5 leadership" emerges as a constant. He describes Level 5 leadership as the paradoxical blend of "extreme personal humility and intense personal will."[27] Collins describes these Level 5 leaders as having a "compelling modesty," in which ambition is channeled to the company not the leader him- or herself, public praise is avoided and credit is given to others rather than to the leader (and often attributed simply to "good luck").[28] Collins noted surprise at how rarely these types of leaders talked about themselves. By contrast, Collins points out that the majority of his comparison companies, which did not make the leap from good to great, are characterized by a leader with an outsized ego that either held the company back or contributed to its downfall.[29]

One of the reasons for the latter is that leaders without humility often

---

[25]J. Andrew Morris, Celeste Brotheridge and John C. Urbanski, "Bringing Humility to Leadership: Antecedents and Consequences of Leader Humility," *Human Relations* 58 (2005): 1325.

[26]Dusya Vera and Antonio Rodriguez-Lopez, "Humility as a Source of Competitive Advantage," *Organizational Dynamics* 33 (2005): 398.

[27]Jim Collins, "Level 5 Leadership: The Triumph of Humility and Fierce Resolve," *Harvard Business Review* 79 (2001): 68. This article is a shorter version of the book *Good to Great: Why Some Companies Make the Leap . . . and Others Don't* (New York: Harper Business, 2001).

[28]Collins, "Level 5 Leadership," p. 75.

[29]Ibid., p. 71. Collins also points out that Level 5 leaders are characterized by a fierce resolve to build the organization, not their own position or prestige. Humility and resolve are thus a duality but not contradictory.

have difficulty planning and executing their succession. As a result their organizations suffer decline after their departure. Level 5 leaders are ambitious, but they channel their ambition to the organization and not to themselves. The leaders of Collins's great companies accomplished their succession successfully, but the comparison leaders struggled to do this. Collins says, "Level 4 leaders often fail to set up the company for enduring success. After all, what better testament to your own personal greatness than that the place falls apart after you leave?"[30]

This phenomenon is further borne out in the research of Bryan Poulin and associates in their distinction between personalized and socialized leadership. What they call socialized leadership combines the notions of servant style with Collins's emphasis on humility; personalized leaders, on the other hand, mirror the dark side of charismatic leadership mentioned earlier (they "act in self-interest, exploit others, reject those who do not comply with their agenda").[31] Poulin points out that humility is a crucial component of socialized leadership which is essential to executing succession strategies effectively.[32]

Servant style leadership assumes some critical theological ideas about the employees who are under a person's leadership. It assumes that the people who report to a leader are made in God's image and thus have intrinsic dignity, not simply replaceable cogs in a company's machinery. Regardless of their competence, they have the right to be treated with respect and are not to be demeaned by their leaders. This is why the concept of leadership as *developing* people beyond just what they can accomplishment for the company's business is so important.

The Bible addresses the treatment of employees, but it should be noted that in the ancient world employees were frequently slaves or servants, who were considered property and could be used or abused at their master's

---

[30]Ibid., p. 72.

[31]Bryan J. Poulin, Michael Z. Hackman and Carmen Barbarasa-Mihai, "Leadership and Succession: The challenge to Succeed and the Vortex of Failure," *Leadership* 3 (2007): 302, 315. On the distinction between personalized and socialized leadership, see J. M. Howell, "Two Faces of Charisma: Socialized and Personalized Leadership in Organization," in *Charismatic Leadership: The Elusive Factor in Organizations*, ed. J. A Conger and R. N. Kanungo (San Francisco: Jossey-Bass, 1988), pp. 213-36; J. M. Howell and B. Shamir, "The Role of Followers in the Charismatic Leadership Process: Relationships and Their Consequences," *Academy of Management Review* 30 (2005): 96-112; R. J. House and J. M. Howell, "Personality and Charismatic Leadership," *Leadership Quarterly* 3 (1992): 81-108.

[32]Poulin, Hackman, and Barbarasa-Mihai, "Leadership and Succession," pp. 319-20.

whim. The Bible dramatically elevated the status of slaves to that of something like a household employee, with rights and dignity.[33] They were to be treated with a level of care akin to family members or trustees over the owner's estate who could go free and were required to be freed every seventh year (Deut 15:12-18). Significantly, when servants were freed, the master was required by Old Testament law to supply them with sufficient capital to support themselves (Deut 15:13-15). When in service, servants were to be treated with justice and fairness, a radical departure from the normal treatment of slaves (Eph 6:9; Col 4:1). Servants were responsible for faithful service to their masters, which many have taken as parallel to employees giving a full day's work to their employers (Eph 6:5-8; Col 3:22-25). Underscoring their fundamental dignity is the crucial theological notion that "in Christ" all status distinctions between servants and masters are irrelevant, similar to gender and ethnic distinctions (Gal 3:28). The book of Philemon illustrates this well, as Paul appeals to Philemon to receive his runaway slave Onesimus back and to treat him like a brother (Philem 16).

The Bible also briefly addresses "workers," who were in a somewhat different category than slaves; they appear to be something akin to contract labor. The Bible mandates that they also be treated with fairness, reflecting the proverbial statement that "a worker deserves his wages" (Lk 10:7; 1 Tim 5:18). That is, employees are to be paid fairly and in a timely fashion because their economic survival so frequently depends on it. Similarly, those who work hard are entitled to share in the fruit of their labor, either through fair pay or a share in the profits (2 Tim 2:6).

If you recall our earlier discussion of work in the ancient world (see chap. 1), you'll remember that we pointed out a sharp contrast in the way work was perceived in biblical times. There was very little discussion of "meaningful work" or work that contributed to a person's self-esteem or sense of purpose in life. People in the ancient world worked primarily to survive, not to have their work be personally meaningful. People in the ancient world didn't typically think of their work in those terms, since daily subsistence was the goal for the majority of working people. Mean-

---

[33]For further discussion on the social ethics of the Bible and slavery, see William Webb, *Slaves, Women and Homosexuals: Exploring the Hermeneutics of Cultural Analysis* (Downers Grove, Ill.: InterVarsity Press, 2001).

ingful work was an added bonus, given the way that economic life worked in the ancient world. However, economic life today is not the zero sum situation like it so often was in biblical times. Given both the productivity and variety of work that market capitalism has made available, it is more the norm today to speak of work having an important effect and contributing to a person's growth and development. It seems to us that an important extension of the idea that employees are made in God's image, with fundamental dignity, is that a good leader should create an environment where the work is seen as important, enriching and purposeful. In the section that follows we try to spell out more specifically what that involves. Work that is boring, mindlessly repetitive or fundamentally stultifying can have a deadening effect on a person's spirit, which is not consistent with seeing people as made in God's image. Of course, this must be balanced by the need for efficiency and getting the necessary work done. In addition, one of the painful reminders of the brokenness of this world is that at times all work, and even the best jobs, can feel mundane and seem pointless.

Applying the Concept of Servant Leadership

Working out the ideal of servant leadership in the competitive world of business raises significant challenges. In the chapter's introduction, Rich, an executive, is struggling to figure out exactly what it means to lead in this way. He fears that if he comes across as a humble servant in his company, his constituents would mistake the trait for weakness.[34] He is also trying to reconcile laying off some employees with his obligation to serve them.

Though servant leadership is a key concept, we should recognize that employees have reciprocal duties and are not recipients of charity. Although periodically companies may take on certain employees as an act of benevolence, it is not the norm. Employees are bound by mutual obligations to the company, and when they do not live up to them, leaders are not being unjust or unfair in holding them accountable and firing them if necessary. Of course, servant leaders will work with employees at risk and attempt to redeem the relationship. But if the employee must be let go, the leader will give a truthful reason for termination, provide input to the

---

[34]This criticism occurs in Norman Bowie, "Business Ethics, Philosophy and the Next Twenty-Five Years," *Business Ethics Quarterly* 10 (2000): 7-20.

employee so that a pattern does not repeat itself with the next employer, and treat the person with dignity throughout the entire process.

What Rich is wrestling with are *competing obligations*. He is responsible to serve a variety of stakeholders, including the company's investors. He must balance the obligation to serve the organization with the responsibility to serve his employees.[35]

Imagine if Rich had retained employees out of a desire to serve them. This might be helpful in the short term by enabling them to stay employed, but it would not be serving them in the long run. Keeping staff when they are not doing their work properly, when they are a poor fit for the position or there is not enough work to justify their employment, does not serve to enhance their dignity. Remember, people need to accomplish something significant and in a way that fits their gifts. Serving them best may involve letting them go so they can find a more suitable place to develop and contribute. Furthermore, if Rich had kept the employees he had laid off, he would not have been serving the entire organization well, particularly if failure to cut costs resulted in the company laying off more people later. To be certain, how Rich goes about deciding who gets released and the process he uses in cutting their positions is critically important. He can serve them by safeguarding their dignity and by providing assistance (e.g., severance pay and networking help) in their transition to another job.

Servant leadership seeks to develop people to reach their potential. Max De Pree, former CEO of Herman Miller, calls leadership an art and defines the art of leadership as "liberating people to do what is required of them in the most effective and humane way possible."[36] He sees the company's employees as those who are investing their lives in the company, thus creating another category of ownership—those with ownership of the company's mission. For many years De Pree sought to make that ownership more tangible through a broad employee stock-ownership program. To take this a step further De Pree actually encouraged his managers to view the men and women who report to them as analogous to volunteers. He says,

---

[35]For further discussion of this important point, see Max De Pree, *Leadership Jazz* (New York: Dell, 1992), pp. 19-20.
[36]Max De Pree, *Leadership Is an Art* (New York: Doubleday, 1989), pp. xix, 1.

Because of the variety of gifts and skills that people bring to the workplace, the need for good people and their willingness to move, we should treat the great majority of people as volunteers. They don't have to stay in one place. They don't have to work for one company or one leader.[37]

De Pree's point is that effective leaders avoid the more hierarchical, coercive forms of leadership (the more transactional form of leadership) in favor of serving and seeking to help their employees maximize their potential.

Effective servant leaders recognize that they are building communities in the business of developing people. Of course, they are also in the business of the specific products and services that generate their revenue. Robert Greenleaf, widely recognized as the ideological founder of the modern notion of servant leadership, pointedly asked managers and leaders, "What are you in business for?" He answered his own question:

> *I am in the business of developing people*—people who are stronger, healthier, more autonomous, more self-reliant, more competent [and we would add, who are fulfilling their callings]. Incidentally, we also make and sell at a profit things that people want to buy so we can pay for all this.[38]

In view of our discussion in chapter two, we would not see the product or service of the business as incidental to developing people. Business for the common good begins with the product or service that is the company's business. But part of the community that is transformed includes the employees, and good leaders see themselves as being in the people-developing business.

Jim Sinegal, CEO of Costco, practices this kind of servant leadership in the way he treats his employees.[39] Costco is well known in the retailing industry for paying their employees well, including the benefit packages (particularly health care), both of which are well above the industry aver-

---

[37]De Pree, *Leadership Jazz*, p. 22.

[38]Robert K. Greenleaf, *On Becoming a Servant-Leader* (San Francisco: Jossey Bass, 1996), p. 122.

[39]This is summarized from Maxwell, *21 Irrefutable Laws of Leadership*, pp. 47-50. For further discussion of Costco, Jim Sinegal and his style of leadership, see Albert Erisman and David Gill, "A Long Term Business Perspective in a Short Term World: A Conversation with Jim Sinegal," *Ethix* (March-April 2003): 6-9, 16, reprinted in Scott B. Rae and Kenman L. Wong, *Beyond Integrity: A Judeo-Christian Approach to Business Ethics*, 2nd ed. (Grand Rapids: Zondervan, 2004), pp. 146-51.

age and over 40 percent higher than the closest competitor. As a result Costco has a high degree of employee loyalty and the lowest turnover rate in retailing, a typically high turnover industry. In response to criticism he has received from Wall Street analysts that he treats his employees too well (at the expense of shareholders), Sinegal says that good treatment of his people is also good business in the long term. Serving his employees in the process of retailing involves treating them with dignity and showing that they are cared for. Other companies display this same philosophy in a different manner. Omni Duct, led by a visionary president, Bob Brumleu, pays all health care insurance premiums for all employees and their families and provides the money every fall for school supplies for all their school-age children. He doesn't have to do this but considers it a part of taking care of his employees, which in turn creates company loyalty that is the envy of the industry.[40]

Beyond benefits and pay, management professors Bruno Dyck and Mitchell Neubert describe *multistream* (as opposed to mainstream) leaders "who are driven by a desire to foster community and a variety of other forms of well being." Consistent with Christian principles such as service and humility, they describe leaders who display styles characterized by enabling (sharing information related to a job and its context), equipping (creating an environment for continuous learning), engaging (encouraging affiliation and enhancing the intrinsic meaningfulness of work) and empowering (honoring the inherent power and potential in others and freeing them to be responsible).[41]

Effective servant leaders see their employees as people, not simply as employees hired to get a job done. The oft-cited lament of Henry Ford "Why is it that I always get the whole person, when all I want is just a pair of hands?"[42] is a sharp contrast to servant leadership, in which people are not used but developed and coached to reach their potential and fulfill their callings, while at the same time doing what is required of them. Leaders who serve their employees see them as more than economic units

---

[40]This practice is described in Celeste Navalos, "Sharing Their Success," *Orange County Register*, September 5, 2009, p. D3. I (Scott) learned of this company paying all medical insurance for employees and families through personal conversation with Brumleu.

[41]Dyck and Neubert, *Management*, pp. 461, 463-67.

[42]Henry Ford, cited in C. William Pollard, "Mission as Organizing Principle," *Leader to Leader Journal* 16 (2000): 3.

or simply contributors to production, but as people with hopes, aspirations and, often, a sense of calling. Specific job tasks and responsibilities should then be designed accordingly, and an organizational culture that respects and nurtures a sabbath outlook, and places work in proper perspective (see chap. 3) should be developed. Clearly other institutions also cultivate people to reach their potential, but business plays a key role in investing in people and nurturing their growth in the process of doing their work.

To put it another way, employees want to do something that matters, beyond simply bringing home a paycheck. Effective leaders create an environment in which a complex balance is achieved where employees can buy in to the mission of the company and see their work as a difference-making calling, but not to the extent that work consumes them or becomes their identity. Good business involves service that transforms the community and the individual (see chap. 2). That is, business exists to serve the community, contribute to human flourishing and care for creation. As Bill Pollard, former CEO of ServiceMaster, says, "People want to contribute to a cause, not just earn a living."[43] Serving one's employees involves creating and maintaining an environment in which the company's mission is clear and that people have a sense that what they do matters, not only to the company but to the community and to themselves.

Pollard tells the story of Shirley, one of the housekeepers for their hospital janitorial services division. To an outsider her position might look like a dead-end job with no purpose other than an economic transaction. But at ServiceMaster these positions have significance, and it is part of the manager's responsibilities to articulate and reinforce that purpose. Pollard says Shirley is still motivated to come to work after fifteen years of doing the same thing.

---

[43]Pollard, "Mission as Organizing Principle," p. 3. This concept is also developed in Pollard's longer treatment, *The Soul of the Firm* (New York: Harper Business, 2000), pp. 45-47. See also Warren Bennis, *Why Leaders Can't Lead* (San Francisco: Jossey Bass, 1989), p. 23. He points out that one of the critical tasks of leadership is to create an environment in which people feel significant, where work is challenging and stimulating, where learning is valued, and where there is community. We would add to this the notion that the leader should create a context in which the individuals can fulfill their calling. However, it should be noted that one of the potential dangers of seeing work as a calling in this way is the overidentification with work (see chap. 3). In addition, if the cause is overinflated and attached to a highly charismatic leader, there is the danger of reinforcing a cult-like environment, which can produce a stifling of dissent and a dangerous conformity. See Tourish and Vatcha, "Charismatic Leadership and Corporate Cultism at Enron," p. 462.

Shirley sees her work as extending to the welfare of the patient and as an integral part of a team that helps sick people get well. She has a cause that involves the health and welfare of others. When Shirley first started, no doubt she was merely looking for just a job. But she brought to her work an unlocked potential and a desire to accomplish something significant. As I talked with Shirley about her job, she said, "If we don't clean with a quality effort, we can't keep the doctors and nurses in business. We can't serve the patients. *This place would be closed if we didn't have housekeeping.*" Shirley was confirming the reality of our mission.[44]

Shirley had a clear sense of purpose for her work, which kept her coming back to work motivated for many years, a purpose that her company had helped to instill. Shirley's story is particularly poignant because if managers can do their part to give mopping floors a greater sense of purpose, its not too difficult to imagine the meaning that can be given to other types of work.

Here's another important aspect to consider regarding employees who are working in these kinds of environments. They can usually answer some important questions that help make this sense of purpose more specific. The following are some questions to ask any employee about the work environment their leaders are creating:

• Does what I do count?

• Does what I do make a difference to anybody?

• Why should I come here? (The correct answer presumes that it's for more than a paycheck.)

• Can I be somebody here?

• Does coming here add any richness to my life?

• Would I show this place to my family?[45]

People want work that matters and provides an opportunity for contributing to the community, thereby giving them a chance to be committed to something that gives them an opportunity to grow, develop and be appreciated.[46]

---

[44]Pollard, "Mission as Organizing Principle," p. 3. This story is retold in more detail in Pollard's *Soul of the Firm*, pp. 46-47.
[45]These questions are taken from De Pree, *Leadership Is an Art*, pp. 110-11.
[46]Ibid., p. 21.

CONCLUSION

How leaders treat employees matters greatly. In studies that attempt to examine the primary influences on job satisfaction, the quality of relationship with one's supervisor and core job characteristics such as task significance and autonomy are reported to be as important, if not more so, than pay and compensation.[47] Moreover, some research links job satisfaction with overall life satisfaction.[48] Thus, how employees are treated at work affects their overall well-being. If you are a leader (or will be one in the future), how would you like to be remembered? What type of work experience do you want to create? At the end of their time with your organization, do you want your employees to look back at their time with you and your organization, department or work group as just a place they collected a check? Or would you rather have them see themselves as having been valued members of a community where they were significant contributors to meaningful goals, a compelling mission, and where they were cared for as people, lived out a calling and developed their skills and abilities?

---

[47]Y. Fried and G. R. Ferris, "The Validity of the Job Characteristics Model: A Review and Meta-analysis," *Personnel Psychology* 40, no. 2 (1987): 287-322.

[48]J. S. Rain, I. M. Lane and D. D. Steiner, "A Current Look at the Job Satisfaction/Life Satisfaction Relationship: Review and Future Considerations," *Human Relations* 44 (1991): 287-307.

Marketing

Serving Customers

A former child psychologist who once specialized in working with autism patients, Dr. Clotaire Rapaille now serves as a consultant to large corporations, including many of the Fortune 500, and purportedly half of the top one hundred. Procter & Gamble, Nestlé, Boeing and General Motors are among the large, well-established companies that appear on Rapaille's client list. Rapaille's work involves helping companies design and sell products that make an emotional connection to consumers through mining the depths of the human psyche to unlock cultural codes. Marketing that is "on code" greatly improves the odds of a product being successful in the marketplace.

In order to successfully decode elements of culture and thereby discover the emotional motivators behind purchases, Rapaille conducts unusual focus-group-like meetings he calls "imprinting sessions." Groups of thirty participants are taken through a process in which they are eventually asked for associations that come from a deep, unconscious level. Rapaille then uses these associations to develop a key to unlocking a culture's code, which in turn is used to develop and market products. Believing that the key to understanding consumer behavior lies at the unconscious imprint or "reptilian" level of the brain where meaning and emotions lie, Rapaille states, "my theory is very simple: The reptilian always wins. I don't care what you're going to tell me intellectually. I don't care. Give me the reptilian. Why? Because the reptilian always wins."[1] Using his focus group dis-

[1]Clotaire Rapaille, interview in "The Persuaders," *PBS Frontline*, November 2004 <www.pbs.org/wgbh/pages/frontline/shows/persuaders/interviews/rapaille.html>.

covery process, Rapaille helped Nestlé develop a market for coffee products in Japan, a traditionally tea drinking country. Rapaille says:

> They needed to give the product meaning in this culture. They needed to
> create an imprint for coffee for the Japanese. Armed with this information,
> Nestlé devised a new strategy. Rather than selling instant coffee to a coun-
> try dedicated to tea, they created desserts for children infused with the
> flavor of coffee but without the caffeine. The younger generation embraced
> these desserts. Their first imprint of coffee was a very positive one, one they
> would carry throughout their lives. Through this, Nestlé gained a mean-
> ingful foothold in the Japanese market. . . . Understanding the process of
> imprinting—and how it related directly to Nestlé's marketing efforts—
> unlocked a door to the Japanese culture for them and turned around a
> floundering business venture.[2]

Rapaille's work has a manipulative feel to it. Capitalism is arguably
predicated on rational consumers making informed choices in the marketplace. Tapping the unconscious (versus the conscious or rational) seems to
transgress the bounds of meeting needs and takes us deep into the manipulative territory of creating them. Making imprints on children and
changing centuries-old practices in order to cultivate consumers seems
also seems invasive and culturally insensitive. In sharp contrast, however,
some argue that work like Rapaille's is simply marketing research at its
best. Ultimately, marketing mirrors social and cultural values. Serving
customers means offering products they want, even if their feelings can't
be articulated on a conscious level. And, with respect to the entire field of
marketing, it might be reasonably asked, What can be so wrong with a
profession devoted to giving consumers what they want, where they want
it, and at a price they wish to pay?

Because of controversial work like Dr. Rapaille's, marketing may be
the most challenging part of business to revision as an extension of God's
work in the world. At a cursory glance marketing, often called the art and
science of selling us things we don't really need, seems to actually undermine human well-being. One commentator has even referred to one part
of marketing, advertising, as "covetousness engineering."[3] An installment

---

[2]Clotaire Rapaille, *The Culture Code* (New York: Random House, 2006), p. 9.
[3]David Gill, *Doing Right: Practicing Ethical Principles* (Downers Grove, Ill.: InterVarsity Press,
2004), p. 319.

of Scott Adam's *Dilbert* comic strip has "the Boss" stating, "We can't compete on price. We can't compete on quality features and service. That leaves fraud, which I'd like you to call marketing."[4] In this chapter the field of marketing will be examined to inquire about its compatibility with an overall vision of business for the common good. While we will argue that it can play an indispensable role in human flourishing, we will also discuss some practices that need to be changed if marketing is to be more in alignment with a Christian vision for business. We will then describe the possible shape of marketing as informed by a Christian vision and conclude with an example of one organization (and its charismatic leader) that practices it in ways that demonstrate high standards of concern for customers.

How Marketing Enables Human Flourishing

While provocative, the type of work performed by Rapaille represents only a very narrow segment of marketing. Although some might argue that most marketing is manipulative or deceptive, its scope is not limited to research, particularly the controversial variety that focuses on subterranean motives. Neither is it synonymous with advertising, marketing's most common association and visible form. In actuality, marketing is composed of a wide range of activities, including research to understand customer needs (though perhaps more accurately described as "wants"), designing products and services, branding, packaging, pricing, sales and placement/distribution.

In light of this broader scope, marketing can and does contribute to human flourishing. If we accept the ideas that material sufficiency is one of God's intentions for people,[5] and that market-based economies are an important tool to create wealth, marketing (though not in all of its present forms) is necessary and, if (this is a big if) done according to proper values, helpful.

At the consumer level, marketing can help us make more informed decisions and allow us to provide input into how products and services are designed. All of us have found a convenient time and place to see a movie, become aware of an opportunity for charitable giving or located a product or service that contributed to our well-being at a discounted price. And the

---

[4]Scott Adams, *Dilbert*, United Media, September 13, 2007.
[5]See the discussion of God's intention for physical abundance in chapter 4.

role of marketing should be credited. Marketing is also at least partially responsible when we have enjoyed a new or improved version of a product, were alerted that our favorite musical group was coming to town to play a gig, or satisfactorily purchased something different than what we had intended because of an important feature we were previously unaware of.

From an organizational and societal perspective, marketing can also provide many benefits. For any company to fulfill a more holistic mission (i.e., serving customers, employees and the broader community), products and services must be effectively designed and efficiently placed into the hands of users. Assume for a moment that a company that tries to uphold a Christian approach to business in all its dealings had a technological breakthrough for a potentially game-changing product. The company has made significant progress toward developing a medical screening device that could improve the lives of millions of people at a dramatically lower cost than current technology. Moreover, the company wants to manufacture the devices in places that are in dire need of economic development through job creation.

At this point the company has only a product concept on its hands. In order to turn the idea into a useful product and get it into the hands of people who need it, create jobs in communities that need them and return a fair profit to investors, the company needs to make many more decisions. The product's design still needs refinement, its pricing structure must be determined, potential users must be made aware of its existence and value added features, and efficient distribution channels need to be established. None of this is possible without the full scope of activities that fall under the umbrella of marketing.

From a macroperspective, marketing plays a critical role in facilitating exchange and, thereby, overall wealth creation. Exchange involves two or more parties who voluntarily come together as buyers and sellers with the goal of completing a transaction in which they are all better off than when they began. This form of exchange, when considered on a systemic level, is relatively new historically and is much more peaceful and civil than alternative means of acquiring goods and services, namely by physical force or decree. In order for exchange to happen with any measure of efficiency, however, buyers and sellers must be made aware of at least three things: each other; what the other party has to offer, whether goods, services or money; and where they should meet each other. Marketing provides this information efficiently and plays a critical role in facilitating ongoing relationships.

While by no means supporting all marketing practices, Gary Karns points out that there is basic alignment of the purpose served by exchange and marketing within a Christian worldview, noting:

> The need for exchange is inherent in the interdependent, communal nature of humankind which is itself a reflection of God's communal nature. . . . Exchange and marketing are the avenues for participating creatively with God in work that provides for each other's needs. . . . It is a deep expression of the sharing of our unique gifts.[6]

In a provocative and thoughtful essay titled "Marketing as a Christian Vocation: Called to Reconciliation," David Hagenbuch points out that the American Marketing Association defines marketing as "an organizational function and set of processes for creating, communicating, and delivering, value to and for managing customer relationships in ways that benefit the organization and its stakeholders."[7] He argues that if practiced according to these fundamental tenets, marketing is a legitimate vocation because it facilitates mutually beneficial exchange and thereby supports reconciliation by bringing people together in positive ways.

Hagenbuch further argues that many practices we find objectionable may be conducted under the auspices of marketing but actually fall outside of its fundamental tenets or normative (what it "should" be) definition. For instance, selling products that consumers do not need or the use of deception in advertising facilitate exchanges that favor sellers disproportionately and thereby promote estrangement over reconciliation. Such practices, he argues, are not mutually beneficial and are therefore not consistent with a Christian understanding of vocation.

As its most visible form, advertising is a much-maligned part of marketing. Advertising draws regular criticism for its questionable content and for its power to manipulate us.

While being mindful of its potential abuses, advertising should be ac-

---

[6]Gary Karns, "A Theological Reflection on Exchange and Marketing," *Christian Scholar's Review*, fall 2008, p. 104.
[7]David Hagenbuch, "Marketing as a Christian Vocation: Called to Reconciliation," *Christian Scholar's Review*, fall 2008, p. 88.

knowledged for its important contributions. In addition to the critical information role of making people aware of the availability of a wide range of products and services, advertising also contributes to rising living standards by encouraging aspirations and thereby hard work. David Ogilvy's classic book *Confessions of an Advertising Man* attributes the following quote to Sir Winston Churchill: "Advertising nourishes the consuming power of men. It sets up before a man the goal of a better home, better clothing, better food for himself and his family. It spurs individual exertion and greater production."[8]

While some of Churchill's language appears to be at odds with Christian values, his words must be understood in their context. He was speaking in a different era in terms of advertising techniques, and during a time when there were lower levels of materialism. Undoubtedly the lines between proper aspirations and envy and conspicuous consumption can and do get easily crossed. However, setting our sights on reasonable levels of economic advancement can accrue to the benefit of others. Former U.S. president Franklin D. Roosevelt said,

> If I were starting life again, I am inclined to think that I would go into the advertising business in preference to almost any other. . . . [T]he general raising of standards of modern civilization among all groups of people during the past half century would have been impossible without the spreading of the knowledge of higher standards by means of advertising.[9]

One controversial aspect of advertising is its alleged ability to make us buy things we really don't want or need. With respect to this particular criticism, it is important to note that the advertising industry itself is circumspect and insecure about its own abilities to persuade consumers. In fact, a statement made by department-store pioneer John Wanamaker has become something of an industry wide aphorism: "I know I waste half the money I spend on advertising. The problem is I don't know which half."[10]

A look at simple statistics may help us see that the balance of power

---

[8]Winston Churchill, cited in David Ogilvy, *Confessions of an Advertising Man* (1963; reprint, New York: Ballantine, 1980), p. 133.

[9]Franklin D. Roosevelt, cited in John Hood, *Selling the Dream: Why Advertising Is Good Business* (Westport, Conn.: Greenwood, 2005), p. 4.

[10]John Wanamaker, cited in Randall Rothenberg, "The Advertising Century," *AdAge.com*, n.d., http://adage.com/century/rothenberg.html.

between consumers (especially adults) and advertisers may be more even than critics sometimes make the case to be. By some estimates, when all of their forms are counted, including television and radio commercials, logos, billboards, Internet banners and so on, we see between three hundred and fifteen hundred ads per day.[11] Over a year the numbers are simply staggering: 110,000 on the low end, or almost twenty for each waking hour.[12] Yet, how many of these ads do we actually notice? And given the comparatively low number of items we purchase in a given year, its quite clear that we actually respond to even fewer. While the larger question of its overall impact on human flourishing is still in play, given these statistics, it seems reasonable to conclude that advertising, at least when it comes to individual ads, may have far less power to manipulate or even persuade us into purchase decisions than critics assume.

On a practical level it is very difficult for a company to disregard consumer needs (or wants) by simply creating demand for a product through advertising and other forms of promotion. While we might argue that products like bottled water and designer clothing are examples of products for which demand was simply manufactured, the underlying consumer need (want) was already there. Bottled water fills a want for convenience, while designer clothing appeals to status. Economically successful products and services are designed with the end user in mind. Through marketing research consumers have input from the beginning stages, and most products are test marketed extensively to see if they fit what consumer's desire. In fact, many products, services and entire businesses fail each year due to insufficient attention to what customers truly want (e.g., product design or price). Of course, whether or not all needs and wants reflect appropriate values and should be met is a different and perhaps more important question (which we will consider a bit later).

Another potentially helpful part of marketing is *branding*. Branding has attracted its share of vocal detractors who decry large corporate brands for their superficiality, ubiquity and their homogenizing effect on the world's cultures. While some of these criticisms are valid, brands can and do func-

---

[11]John Phillip Jones, *Fables, Fashions and Facts about Advertising: A Study of 28 Enduring Myths* (Thousand Oaks, Calif.: Sage, 2004), cited by James Potter, *Media Literacy*, 3rd ed. (Thousand Oaks, Calif.: Sage), p. 133.
[12]Potter, *Media Literacy*, p. 133.

tion to make purchasing more efficient by establishing easily recognizable identities. For consumers brands function as symbols of quality. Consumers often do not have the time to make well-researched decisions into all of their purchases. As consumers come to associate a particular label with high quality or some other dimension of value, such as low price, brands function as heuristic devices to save time. Without the benefit of brands, imagine, for instance, the time that would be required to sort out all of the choices during a simple trip to the supermarket.

Brands also function to facilitate marketplace accountability. While some organizations use brands as substitutes for quality, many others are emphatic about protecting the reputation of their brands. In so doing, consumers benefit from better quality, value and service as a result. For example, many companies have very generous warranty or return policies to stand behind what they make or sell. An editorial in *The Economist* had the following take:

> [Brands] began as a form . . . of consumer protection. In pre-industrial days, people knew exactly what went into their meat pies and which butchers were trustworthy; once they moved to the cities, they no longer did. A brand provided a guarantee of reliability and quality. Its owner had a powerful incentive to ensure that each pie was as good as the previous one, because that would persuade people to come back for more. Just as distance created the need for brands in the 19th century, so in the age of globalization and the internet it reinforces their value. A book buyer might not entrust a company based in Seattle with his credit card number had experience not taught him to trust the Amazon brand . . . because consumer trust is the basis for all brand values, companies that own the brands have an immense incentive to work hard to retain that trust.[13]

How Marketing Works Against Human Flourishing

Along with the benefits of marketing are many costs and problems that also need to be explored. Arguably, all of the items we will discuss fall outside of marketing's normative definition. As noted earlier, there is a wide gap between marketing as practiced and what it is as an ideal. These areas can be categorized as encroachment, methodology/technique, and content.

---

[13]"Why Brands Are Good for You," *The Economist*, September 8, 2001, cited in Steve Hilton and Giles Gibbons, *Good Business: Your World Needs You* (New York: Texere, 2002), p. 128.

First, marketing seems to be encroaching on many areas of life, including the physical, social, psychological and spiritual. Marketing, especially commercial advertising and branding, has become an almost ever-present physical presence in our lives, and there seems to be no apparent sanctuary from it. Mark Crispin Miller argues that its creators want advertising (as a form of propaganda) "not simply to suffuse the atmosphere, but to become the atmosphere. It wants to become the air we breathe. It wants us not to be able to find a way outside of the world that it creates for us."[14]

The presence of advertising does feel increasingly ubiquitous. In addition to the usual mass media outlets, sides of buses, placements in movies and television shows, logos, and computer banners, advertisements can now be found almost anywhere there are captive eyes. For example, we can't even escape overt forms of advertising while using a public restroom (bulletin boards), filling up a car (video screens on gasoline pumps), playing golf (the bottoms of golf course hole cups) or while dining in some restaurants (advertising of *other* businesses in Cheesecake Factory menus). One high school teacher even sells ad space on student examinations to local businesses in order to help cover the printing costs, which his school district no longer pays.[15]

Marketing, especially through commercialized advertising, may also encroach on the spiritual values realm by reinforcing a consumerist worldview that leads to a myriad of problems, including social and ecological ones. While commercial advertising sells dreams and aspirations, James Potter argues that the most important product of advertising is really us.[16] Taken on the whole, commercial advertising transforms us, and not in positive ways, by making us more "shopping friendly."

While we tend to agree with those who argue that the persuasive power of *individual* ads may be limited, advertising in its aggregated form may be very powerful. More important, the more pertinent question is how it affects human flourishing. Just about every commercial advertisement carries unspoken "meta-messages" that encourage some sort of dissatisfaction

[14]Mark Crispin Miller, interview for "The Persuaders," *PBS Frontline*, November, 2004, www.pbs.org/wgbh/pages/frontline/shows/persuaders/interviews/miller.html.

[15]Linda Lou, "Funds Sliced, Teacher Sells Ads on Tests," *San Diego Union-Tribune*, November 22, 2008, www3.signonsandiego.com/stories/2008/nov/22/1mc22rbteach114024-funds-sliced-teacher-sells-ads-/?zIndex=15188.

[16]Potter, *Media Literacy*, p. 133.

and that our problems will be solved or our dreams achieved through the act of purchasing something.

Some who defend advertising note that it simply reflects culture, and for it to be effective it must do so. Advertising (and marketing) cannot get too far outside of what society already values or it will be ineffective. Thus it is really value neutral. Stephen Fox, author of *The Mirror Makers* says,

> The image in the advertising mirror has seldom revealed the best aspects of American life. But advertising must take human nature as it is found. We would all like to think that we act from admirable motives. The obdurate, damning fact is that most of us, most of the time, are moved by more selfish, practical considerations. Advertising inevitably tries to tap these stronger, darker stains.[17]

While Fox is correct that advertising undoubtedly reflects cultural values, at least partially, this does not negate its ability to simultaneously shape them. Marketing is a reflection of social values, but as Richard Pollay describes it, the image is more like one found in a distorted mirror.[18] Further, marketing research like Rapaille's may work because it "takes human nature as it is found" by appealing to our "reptilian" brain. However, this part of us may represent our basest impulses or what the apostle Paul refers to as our flesh, rather than our spirit or better parts of who we are (Gal 5:16).

Seeing and hearing the same message time and again very likely has a significant impact on us. Surveys indicate that the majority of Americans believe that our society would be better off if there was less emphasis on money and material things. Yet, sociologist Robert Wuthnow says, "the American public voices concern about the reign of materialism in our society while wandering the corridors of the mall."[19] As a country we certainly have household debt burdens to indicate that we shop well beyond our means. Is advertising all to blame? No. Does advertising play some role? Yes. If advertising had *no* effect (individually or aggregated) companies would not spend the current astronomical sums on it—an estimated

---

[17]Stephen Fox, *The Mirror Makers: A History of American Advertising and Its Creators* (New York: William Morrow, 1984), pp. 329-30, cited in Jerry Kirkpatrick, *In Defense of Advertising* (Claremont, Calif.: TKJ Books, 1994), p. 23.

[18]Richard W. Pollay, "The Distorted Mirror: Reflections on the Unintended Consequences of Advertising," *Journal of Marketing* 50, no. 2 (1986): 18-36.

[19]Robert Wuthnow, *God and Mammon in America* (New York: Free Press, 1994), p. 155.

$220 billion per year in the United States alone as of 2000.[20]

While a cursory definition of consumerism suggests a fixation with acquiring material goods, a deeper examination reveals that as a worldview it may well creep into other areas of life. Craig Gay notes, "Even more seriously, consumerism suggests a preoccupation with the immediate gratification of desire. It implies foolishness, superficiality and triviality, and the destruction of personal and social relationships by means of selfishness, individualism, possessiveness and covetousness."[21]

Evidence seems to exist all around us that people are increasingly approaching every relationship with a consumerist mindset of "what am I getting out of it?" and then, of course, never getting enough to be satisfied. Friendships, marriages, education, parenting and professional relationships are seen through a primary identity of consumerism versus citizenship, duty or obligation.[22] Christians seem even less apologetic, often describing their quest for what should be a place to worship, serve and participate in community as "church shopping." While marketing, as a partial reflection of existing social values, is not solely to blame for these ills, the sheer amount of commercialized advertising that pervades our culture surely does not help.

While branding does serve some useful purposes, it may also contribute to crossing spiritual and emotional boundaries. Brands in particular have enormous cultural power because over the last decade or two marketers have successfully moved them beyond mere markers of quality and have infused them with an identity that goes well beyond product functionality or quality. Brands now appeal to our emotions, have meaning and carry associations such as belonging, community and even transcendence. Naomi Klein captures the "big idea," "story" or "epiphany" behind some popular brands:

> Nike was the essence of sports, transcendence through sports. Starbucks was community, the idea of the "third place" that is not home and not work.

---

[20]Potter, *Media Literacy*, p. 133.

[21]Craig Gay, cited in Robert B. Krushwitz, "Consumerism," *Christian Reflection: A Series on Faith and Ethics* (Waco, Tex.: Center for Christian Ethics, 2003), p. 8.

[22]For further discussion of this issue, see Robert N. Bellah et al., *Habits of the Heart: Individualism and Commitment in American Life* (Berkeley: University of California Press, 1985), and on the notion of cultural costs of capitalism, see Craig M. Gay, "On Learning to Live with the Market Economy," *Christian Scholar's Review* 24, no. 2 (1994): 180-95.

Disney is family. Virgin is the sort of rebel working stiff, the rebel inside their suit. Benetton, of course, was marketing racial diversity and multiculturalism. The Body Shop was marketing environmentalism.[23]

Some marketing carries a message that we can purchase our way to things that were once gained through active participation in social institutions. Klein argues, "So what brands started selling was a kind of pseudo-spirituality—a sense of belonging, a community. So brands started filling a gap that citizens, not just consumers, used to get elsewhere, whether from religion, whether from a sense of belonging in their community."[24]

In addition to encroachment across important boundaries, some aspects of marketing employ questionable techniques and shift power away from consumers and into the hands of marketers, significantly altering the mutually beneficial part of the exchange equation that lies at the heart of the discipline. Rapaille's work comes to mind, as do techniques that target vulnerable groups.

Despite an industry-wide code with specific constraints, some advertisers capitalize on ignorance by targeting younger children. Others target consumers who may be elderly or less educated.[25] Spending on advertising to children has grown rapidly over the past two decades. Children represent an important target market because of their influence on family purchasing decisions. Furthermore, if they can be groomed as loyal customers early, children can be "branded for life" with respect to some products and services that have a long-term use span.

Numerous strategies are employed, including direct advertising, placing sponsored educational materials in schools, getting trendsetting cool kids to use products, branding computer games, and cross-promotion of merchandise with movies and television shows. One of the most memorable scenes from the documentary film *Affluenza* is footage of a marketing conference titled "Kid Power," in which a speaker is sharing strategies

---

[23]Naomi Klein, an interview on "The Persuaders," *Frontline*, November 9, 2004 <www.pbs.org/wgbh/pages/frontline/shows/persuaders/interviews/klein.html>.

[24]Ibid.

[25]See Martin Lindstrom, *Brand Child: Remarkable Insights into the Minds of Today's Global Kids and Their Relationship with Brands* (London: Kogan Page, 2003); James U. McNeal, *The Kid Market: Myths and Realities* (Ithaca, N.Y.: Paramount Market Publishing, 1999); and Gene Del Vecchio, *Creating Ever-Cool: A Marketing Guide to a Kid's Heart* (Gretna, La.: Pelican, 1997).

for "branding kids and owning them in that way," including the need to market to "aggressive play patterns" in young boys.[26]

In addition to persuading children to purchase, or nag their parents to purchase, products, the frequency of ads and their metamessage schools children as consumers and gives them a highly skewed sense of what is necessary to sustain a flourishing life. For example, unless parents are very careful the television show *Extreme Makeover: Home Edition* may sell an unwelcome worldview to the children who watch it. There are certainly genuinely redemptive aspects of each episode, including the celebration of heroism, viewers experiencing empathy and generosity, and communities coming together to help needy families. However, the show's other more subtle message is that a material object, in the form of very large home that is outfitted with an overabundance of branded (paid for by advertisers) gadgets, is *the* solution to serious problems.

Other advertisers attempt to "break through clutter" and fly under the well-tuned radars of consumers by engaging in various forms of "undercover marketing" that do not announce themselves as promotional activity. For example, someone asking us to take their picture with the latest cell phone on a busy downtown street may be a hired promoter of the device that is now in our hands. Likewise, hip patrons of a trendy club or bar may actually be paid advertisers of cigarettes or alcoholic beverages.[27] Other advertisers sponsor programming that blurs the lines between promotion and content. Stealth or "black" marketing is a strategy aimed toward reaching those of the upcoming generation who scrutinize traditional advertising and want to hear about things "virally" or through informal networks.

In addition to encroachment and technique issues, some marketing, particularly commercial advertising, may reinforce harmful values through its content. Some advertisements make their appeal or pitch to our most broken, base appetites. The most obvious ones are ads that serve to reinforce unhealthy ideas and values about beauty and sexuality. Some play on ethnic or gender stereotypes while others appeal to our deepest insecu-

---

[26]John de Graaf and Vivia Boe, prods., *Affluenza* (KCTS Seattle and Oregon Public Broadcasting, 1997).

[27]Rebecca Leung, "Undercover Marketing Uncovered," *60 Minutes*, October 23, 2003, www .cbsnews.com/stories/2004/07/22/60minutes/main631317.shtml. Also see Joel Bakan, *The Corporation* (New York: Free Press, 2005).

rities about fitting in socially or our need to be envied, and thereby contribute to conspicuous consumption.

Transformed Marketing

How might marketing be reenvisioned and reformed to participate in the
work of transformational service for the common good? First, a change in
entire outlook, particularly in purpose, is the requisite starting point. If we
see business as only or primarily about a quest for profit, we will likely see
marketing from a pragmatic orientation: it will be judged as good or effective based solely on the criteria of whether or not marketing helps us sell
more products or services (whether or not it "feeds the bulldog"). In contrast, if we take a broader perspective on business, we will see marketing
in a far different light. Marketing, and how it is done, should help stakeholders flourish in the holistic ways that God intends.

Once we have the right outlook and perspective, consistent with the
framework developed in chapter two, we must then evaluate our products
and services. If our products or services truly help others flourish by meeting their needs and enhancing their lives, we can begin the work of critically examining our marketing practices. If, on the other hand, we make
or sell frivolous or harmful products, we must back up. No amount of
change in our marketing will redeem our participation in making or providing objects of services that work against human flourishing.

In order to participate in the work of transformational service, marketing should be seen as the means by which exchange can be facilitated
through an organization's efforts to build authentic relationships with its
customers and community. While the language of "relationships" already
has frequent use in marketing, it is typically informed by a solely self-
serving orientation: treat customers well because we can then make a deep
emotional connection with them, and they in turn will buy more from us.
From a Christian perspective authentic relationships are built on dignity,
trust, mutual respect and true concern for others. In fact, representative
biblical language for how we are to treat others is expressed in terms such
as *covenant* or *love of neighbors*. Would we gladly trade places with those on
the other side of a transaction? In fact, one exemplary Christian business
leader takes the approach that customers should be treated as valued
friends. In so doing, his company's marketing activities express genuine

concern for customers through empowering them to make good decisions that will enhance their well-being. Of course, we can only approach marketing in this fashion if we have good reason to have faith in the quality and value of the products and services we have to offer.

In rethinking specific marketing practices, the American Marketing Association definition (2007 version) is a good starting point, especially the part that emphasizes: "value for customers, clients, partners, and society at large." Indeed, marketing as a whole should facilitate mutually beneficial exchange as indicated by value creation for numerous stakeholders. However, *value* must be defined in such a way that it does not solely rest "in the eye of the beholder." Otherwise, the American Marketing Association's definition ceases to have any real meaning. *Value* as defined from a Christian worldview serves the distinct purpose of encouraging holistic human flourishing.

By implication then, honesty is a given. Deception, manipulation or withholding information in order to place customers at a disadvantage does not show love of neighbor or contribute to reconciliation. As a practical matter we might add that in an age of increasingly available consumer data, businesses that trade on asymmetries of information may well find their business models swiftly headed toward obsolescence.

Attempts to appeal to higher, rather than to debased or unconscious, values should be made. For instance, there is a vast difference between promoting travel as a form of recreation (re-creation) or connecting with family and friends versus hedonism or creating envy and covetousness in others. Likewise, advertising alcoholic beverages like wine in the context of food is far different than promoting them in the context of irresponsible partying. Furthermore, beauty and healthy sexuality have their place as legitimate parts of God's creation and surely may be recognized as such, but they should not be promoted in unhealthy forms or elevated to the status of false idols.

Marketing as transformational service also respects healthy boundaries. The sheer volume of commercial speech is simply overbearing. Mark Crispin Miller believes that we are now at or near a point where so much clutter is created that advertising is asphyxiating itself.[28] Commercial-free

---

[28]Miller, "Persuaders" interview.

areas should not be a luxury afforded exclusively to super-wealthy people who can pay to escape the reach of marketing. Products and services cannot meet our legitimate needs for meaning or deep connection and should not be branded in such a way. While statistical analysis is helpful for research purposes, customers should not be objectified as this or that demographic.

Special care must be taken with respect to vulnerable audiences such as children. Children are much more impressionable than adults and cannot fully function as educated and informed consumers in the marketplace. Taking advantage of this fact for self-serving purposes surely does not help our young neighbors flourish. Moreover, targeting children to influence their parents' purchasing decisions causes very real strife in the home and schools them in the rival consumerist worldview at important developmental stages in their lives. No one should be used, especially young children.

Reconceiving broken parts of marketing so they promote shalom and flourishing is a challenging task. Doing so may well put a firm at a disadvantage. Yet trust and mutual respect are indispensable in the well-ordered functioning of any society or organization. With creativity and a significant and intentional effort, an organization can practice marketing in ways that build authentic relationships and that may not result in harm to the financial bottom line. The following is an example of one extraordinary and exemplary company (and its CEO) that is making such an attempt.

FLOW MOTORS

A thriving business based in Winston-Salem, North Carolina, is an outstanding example of a company that practices marketing as a means to build genuine relationships with its customers. This company is deeply committed to allowing Christian ideals to "inform, infuse, and reform" its entire set of values, culture and practices.[29] With respect to customers the company is highly committed to treating them as they would "guests in their home." This translates into taking a genuine attitude of looking after customer well-being; dealing fairly, honestly and in a transparent fashion; and keeping promises even when it is costly to do so. The company has won many awards for its practices, and loyal customers drive for hours, sometimes across state lines, just to make a purchase. While this sort of

[29]Albert Erisman, "Ethics at Flow Automotive: A Conversation with Don Flow," *Ethix*, March/April 2004, pp. 7-12.

reputation is not necessarily unique, it is not one that we would typically associate with the particular business the company is in, automobile sales.

Founded by current CEO and majority owner Don Flow, Flow Motors is a group of automobile dealerships that represent thirty-four franchises and nineteen manufacturers, and is located in both North Carolina and Virginia. As of late 2007 the company had sales of $650,000,000 and 900 employees. Don Flow has looked at the whole business, from top to bottom, and has tried to build it in as consistent a manner as possible, with Christian ideals. He has attempted this in an industry in which it is almost assumed that a business must operate at the ethical margins (at best) in order to succeed.

With mission and purpose as the starting point, Flow inverts traditional views of what business is about. The purpose of business, as he sees it, is "to enhance the flourishing of life" through promoting "shalom,"— truth, beauty, justice and plenty. With respect to the place of profit, Flow states:

> Wealth is never a first thing. It is always a second thing. When wealth becomes a first thing, it becomes an idol and moves from creating plenty to plundering lives. Wealth is created by creating value in this world. Wealth to a company or a person is like blood to the human body. No normal person gets up in the morning and says "I live for my blood." However, there is no person who can live without blood. The creation of wealth is a necessary condition for culture and people to flourish but it is not the reason for existence for either a healthy person (or organization).[30]

For Flow profit is a byproduct of providing superior service to customers. This sense of mission and purpose translates down throughout the organization. Flow is committed to enhancing the lives of customer by refusing to carry some lines of automobiles and by refusing to use advertising that objectifies people or focuses on an automobile as a social status enhancer.

Flow also attempts to make the shopping experience for an automobile (typically rated by consumers as the worst shopping experience) as fair, enjoyable and stress free as possible. In order to ensure transparency, Flow

---

[30]Don Flow, "Christianity: Informing, Infusing and Reforming Business," speech given at the Bridging Sunday and Monday Conference, Seattle Pacific University, Seattle, Washington, October 5, 2007.

Motors provides computer kiosks so that customers so can look up pricing information. At the vast majority of their stores (there are some exceptions at stores that carry high-priced vehicles in which consumers prefer to negotiate), Flow does not use the standard back-and-forth negotiation model used by most dealerships (which can and often does lead to deceptive practices). The company conducted an in-depth study of its profit on transactions and found that when using the typical negotiated sales model, those who had more education and who had a higher socioeconomic status paid less because they had more information or ability to negotiate. Don Flow believes that this violates the admonition found in the book of Proverbs to not take advantage of the vulnerable. So, Flow Motors uses a fixed-pricing model at most of its dealerships. Likewise, the company does not charge market rates of interest to customers with marginal credit, even if they are willing to pay more. According to Flow, maximizing profit in these instances would gain wealth through taking advantage of the plight of another.

The company also goes to extraordinary lengths to keep promises made even when it results in a net disadvantage to do so. If company mechanics don't fix a vehicle right, according to the estimate or on time, the company eats the difference and will also bring a service-loaned vehicle to the customer, so the customer will not be inconvenienced. The company also details the customer's car and changes its oil with no charge for the customer's trouble.

In order to demonstrate and encourage the seriousness of these commitments, Flow's training programs, metrics and employee promotion and reward systems all revolve around customer satisfaction. For instance, one simple test used in training programs involves challenging employees to recount at the dinner table with their family all of the conversations and interactions they had with customers:

> "Would you send your wife (I know this sounds chauvinistic [laughing]), your mother, or your daughter, unaccompanied, to buy a car?" "Without any coaching or counseling?" Then I ask, "Would you go home to the dinner table tonight and tell every person at your table exactly what you did and said today?" If you can't embrace that, then we're doing something wrong.[31]

In addition to customer relationships the company approaches its man-

---

[31]Don Flow, quoted in Erisman, "Ethics at Flow Automotive," p. 7.

agement philosophies and community engagement activities with similar levels of commitment and intentionality. The company is committed to a "whole person at work" philosophy and recognizes that every employee is unique and makes important contributions. Employees may also qualify for assistance on home purchases, and college scholarships are offered to their children. Flow gives generously to local community charities.

While the company enjoys high levels of profitability and employee and customer loyalty, its practices do not necessarily result in *more* profit than its competitors.[32] Keeping such high commitments does have its financial costs. Moreover, no business is perfect, a fact that Don Flow readily acknowledges. Automobiles pollute, and Flow Motors may well benefit from the type of national marketing campaigns conducted by manufacturers that play on social status. Yet the company still stands as one outstanding example of how marketing and customer relationships (and other aspects of business) should be done.

Although marketing may not often be seen in a positive light, it plays an irreplaceable role in encouraging human flourishing through providing information that facilitates exchange and thereby provides for material abundance. However, some marketing activities may increase material abundance at the expense of well-being in other areas of human life; namely, the spiritual, emotional, social and ecological. While damaging or unfair marketing methods like those that focus on unconscious motives may work well in achieving the objective of increasing sales, they are not consistent with a broader Christian vision for the ultimate purposes of business. Marketing should be practiced as a tool to build authentic and helpful relationships with customers in order to serve and empower them, and not undermine their ability to make thoughtful and responsible choices.

---

[32]Erisman, "Ethics at Flow Automotive."

9

STEWARDSHIP AND
SUSTAINABILITY

SERVING THE GARDEN AND OUR NEIGHBORS

For 100 years, the industry has been releasing carbon dioxide (CO_2) into the atmosphere. Carbon has been held underground in geological formations either as a gas, solid, or liquid. Through burning, we release it into the atmosphere. . . . It seems to me that from any basic sort of precautionary principle, you would want to reduce carbon in the atmosphere. The issue is, are we going to do anything about it or not? . . . [T]he track we are on could make this planet very inhospitable, and the people who are going to suffer most are the world's poor. . . . [W]e need to ask ourselves, "What are we doing to these people?"[1]

The preceding statement could well have come from a spokesperson for Greenpeace or the Environmental Defense Fund, but it may surprise you to learn that it was articulated by Clive Mather, a devout Christian who recently retired as the CEO of Shell Canada after a long career in the petroleum industry.

The source of this observation is not the only notable item about it. The merging of natural interests with human ones lies in sharp contrast to how the relationship between business and the environment is often framed: as a direct standoff. For example, the dispute over Pacific Northwest forestland that has served as habitat for the endangered northern spotted owl was often posed as "owls versus [logging] jobs." Likewise, domestic oil exploration and drilling is often framed in similar terms, "energy security versus saving the planet."

---

[1]Albert Erisman and Tom Cottrell, "Harmonizing Energy and the Environment: A Conversation with Clive Mather," *Ethix* 62 (2008).

This construct is of course partially based in fact. Natural interests do sometimes collide with human ones, especially in the more intermediate time horizon. Limited farmland creates a situation in which growing crops for corn-based fuels (ethanol) may serve to raise food prices. Likewise, "shop locally" initiatives (motivated, in part, to reduce carbon from long-distance transportation) may hurt farmers, particularly those in the developing world who are dependent on export markets.

The connecting forces of globalization, however, seem to be rapidly contributing to a much more complex understanding of this important relationship. Namely, there is a growing awareness of how integrally connected human interests are with natural ones, and how they are intertwined *now* and not in some benign distant future. In his bestselling book *Hot, Flat and Crowded*, Thomas Friedman expands on these concerns and stresses the importance of why environmental issues and human well-being (on multiple dimensions) need to be seen in terms of mutual, shared interests:

> The world also has a problem: It is getting *hot, flat and crowded*. That is, global warming, the stunning rise of the middle classes all over the world, and rapid population growth have converged in a way that could make our planet dangerously unstable. In particular, the convergence of hot, flat and crowded is tightening energy supplies, intensifying the extinction of plants and animals, deepening energy poverty, strengthening petro-dictatorship and accelerating climate change.[2]

If Friedman is correct, the current pattern of global economic development, particularly rapidly increasing use of nonrenewable fuels to support Western high-consumption lifestyles across the globe, harms human health, contributes to geopolitical turmoil and destroys nature. Moreover, the living conditions of economically impoverished people around the globe will be worsened as they compete for increasingly scarce (and thereby higher priced) resources needed to support basic living conditions, health care (such as electricity to run medical clinics and refrigerate medications), and to access the resources needed to escape their circumstances (access to technology).

---

[2]Thomas L. Friedman, *Hot, Flat and Crowded: Why We Need a Green Revolution and How It Can Renew America* (New York: Farrar, Straus & Giroux, 2008), p. 5.

Add to this list the burden we are leaving for future generations and it would be difficult to imagine outcomes that can be any more antithetical to the divine mission of human flourishing. Even those who maintain some degree of skepticism about global warming would be wise not to dismiss these concerns. Many of these consequences (e.g., threats to health, global instability, competition for scarce resources) are byproducts of continuous dependence on nonrenewable energy sources rather than on climate change.

In this chapter we will examine the place of environmental concerns within a Christian vision for business. In particular, we will examine biblical teaching on the environment in order to address questions such as, What place and priority should nature receive in business strategy and decisions? How consistent is the recent sustainability or greening movement with a vision of business as transformational service? To what extent does nature exist to serve our interests? And, as we move from biblical ideals into the real world of competitive pressures, what practical implications, challenges and limits may be present?

THE ENVIRONMENT AND A CHRISTIAN WORLDVIEW

Christianity has sometimes been criticized for being the ideological cause of environmental degradation. In what was long considered the conventional wisdom in environmental ethics, Lynn White Jr. published a 1967 article in which he held Christianity responsible for humankind's abuse of nature.[3] In it, he accused Christianity of reducing the natural world to the status of a natural object that could be controlled for the benefit of human beings without regard for the harmful impact of this misuse. He further indicted Christianity for its role in the origin of modern science and technology, which gave humankind mastery over nature and the potential to

---

[3]Lynn White Jr., "The Historical Roots of Our Ecological Crisis," *Science* 155 (1967): 1203-7. This is echoed by the historian Arnold Toynbee, who linked monotheistic religion in general with environmental abuse (see Toynbee's article "The Religious Background of the Present Environmental Crisis," in *Ecology and Religion in History*, ed. David and Eileen Spring [New York: Harper & Row, 1974]). For a more detailed response to these criticisms, see Steven Bouma-Prediger, *For the Beauty of the Earth: A Christian Vision of Creation Care* (Grand Rapids: Baker Academic, 2001), pp. 69-80; and Thomas Sieger Derr, "The Challenge of Biocentrism," in *Creation at Risk: Religion, Science and Environmentalism*, ed. Michael Cromartie (Grand Rapids; Eerdmans, 1995), pp. 85-104, which is reprinted in Scott B. Rae and Kenman L. Wong, *Beyond Integrity: A Judeo-Christian Approach to Business Ethics*, 2nd ed. (Grand Rapids: Zondervan, 2004), pp. 379-91.

exploit the environment while at the same time neglecting any responsibility for protecting the natural world. It is true that the church has a history of contributing to environmental problems, but whether or not the Bible justifies such action is an entirely different question (and White may have actually made that distinction himself).[4]

The majority of religious groups today advocate for environmental responsibility, and it is becoming increasingly rare for any major religious group to hold the view that White critiques. To be certain, some parts of the Christian tradition have come to environmental commitment more recently while others remain suspicious due to political associations. However, we could make the case that religion has contributed positively to environmental concern by observing that spiritual traditions of all kinds, Christianity included, emphasize limits on materialism and consumption, and thus provide necessary checks on the kinds of economic growth that threaten the environment.

Viewing the environment from within a Christian worldview begins at the beginning—in Genesis 1. Here God is portrayed as the sovereign Creator of all things, who spoke creation into existence and called all things good. In the Genesis account, the created world has intrinsic value by virtue of it being *the good creation of a good and all-powerful God*. The natural world is good because it's *his* creation. However, the creation is not itself an object of worship; the Genesis text clearly distinguishes between God the Creator and his creation. As a result of this basis for creation having value, a theocentric view of the environment—not anthropocentric (the environment exists solely for the benefit of human beings) or biocentric (all living things have value because they are living things)—seems to be the most appropriate.[5]

---

[4]Derr, cited in Rae and Wong, *Beyond Integrity*, p. 380.

[5]An example of biocentrism is found in the work of Paul Taylor, *Respect for Nature: A Theory of Environmental Ethics* (Princeton, N.J.: Princeton University Press, 1986). Biocentrism is often identified with a movement called "deep ecology," which maintains the intrinsic value of nonhuman organisms. See also Bill Devall and George Sessions, *Deep Ecology: Living as If Nature Mattered* (Salt Lake City: Peregrine Press, 1985); Alan Dregnson and Bill Devall, eds., *The Ecology of Wisdom: The Writings of Arne Naess* (Berkeley, Calif.: Counterpoint, 2008); and Frederick L. Bender, *The Culture of Extinction: Toward a Philosophy of Deep Ecology* (Amherst, N.Y.: Humanity Books, 2003). One of the primary criticisms of biocentrism is its inability to establish any kind of ranking of priority when the interests of human beings conflict with the interests of the natural world. That is, if all living things have biocentric equality, then it is difficult to resolve conflicts when competing interests collide. For further discussion of these

The Genesis account gives human beings dominion over creation, with the responsibility to be junior partners with God in extending his rule over creation. The entrance of sin into the world complicated this notion of dominion considerably, shifting the focus of dominion to that of alleviating and minimizing the effects of sin (see chap. 1). Along with the command for human beings to exercise dominion over the creation also came the obligation of stewardship. That is, human beings were charged with being trustees over creation, using the created world for their benefit but doing so responsibly, knowing that they answer to God.

The notion of dominion has been terribly misapplied over the centuries of church history, often serving as a justification for human beings to meet their own needs and pursue development without regard for environmental impact. That's why it's critical to acknowledge that in Genesis the call to exercise dominion *over* creation presumed stewardship *for* creation. Dominion does not imply that human beings were granted the right of domination over the environment. Though it is true that the Hebrew term for dominion literally means "to rule over," in the overall context of the Bible, ruling and serving always go together (Lk 22:24-26). This is reinforced by the call to human beings to tend the garden in Genesis 2:15, which called Adam and Eve to serve and protect that which they were given dominion over.[6] That is, human beings were given the natural world to use for their benefit, but they were also required to exercise careful responsibility, consistent with their role as a trustee over God's creation. Such a role suggests that human beings will be held to account by God for their stewardship over creation. In *Earth-wise* (a biblical response to environmental issues), Calvin DeWitt expands eloquently on this point:

> Genesis 2:15 conveys a marvelous teaching. Here, God expects Adam to serve the garden and to keep it. The Hebrew word for serve *('abad')* is translated as till, dress or work in most recent translations of the Bible. Adam and his descendants are expected to meet the needs of the garden so that it will persist and flourish. But how on earth can we serve creation? Shouldn't creation serve us instead? . . .

critiques, see Bouma-Prediger, *For the Beauty of the Earth*, pp. 129-32, and Derr, in Rae and Wong, *Beyond Integrity*, pp. 386-90.
[6]Bouma-Prediger, *For the Beauty of the Earth*, p. 74.

God also expects us as Adam's descendants to keep the garden. This word keep is sometimes translated tend, take care of, guard, and look after. The Hebrew word upon which these translations of *keep* are based is the word *shamar*. And shamar indicates a loving, caring, sustaining type of keeping. In our worship services, we often conclude with the Aaronic blessing from Numbers 6:24: "The Lord bless you and keep you." The keep here is the same Hebrew word used in Genesis 2:15: shamar. When we invoke God's blessing to keep us, we are not asking that God keep us in a kind of preserved, inactive, uninteresting state. Instead we are calling on God to keep us in all of our vitality, with all of our energy and beauty. The keeping we expect of God when we invoke the Aaronic blessing is one that nurtures all of our life-sustaining and life-fulfilling relationships with our family members, with our neighbors and our friends, with the land, air, and water, and with our God. We ask God to love us, to care for us, and to sustain us in relationship to our natural and human environment.[7]

Not only is God the sovereign creator, *he also tends to and cares for his creation* in an ongoing way. The biblical portrait of God is not the god of deism, who initially created the world and then remains uninvolved in his creation. God is intimately involved with his world, which he made as a home for his living beings. Psalm 104, a creation hymn, points out that the natural world is the home he has provided for his creatures (Ps 104:12, 17-18, 26; see also Job 39:6). It is also clear that God uses creation to provide the daily sustenance for his creatures, human beings included. The psalmist declares:

> He waters the mountains from his upper chambers,
>   the earth is satisfied by the fruit of his work.
> He makes grass grow for the cattle,
>   and plants for man to cultivate—
>   bringing forth food from the earth. (Ps 104:13-14)

For God to house and feed his creatures, both animal and human, the natural world is critical. The psalmist underscores how dependent all creatures are on God when he writes,

---

[7]Calvin B. DeWitt, *Earth-wise: A Biblical Response to Environmental Issues* (Grand Rapids: CRC Publications, 1994), pp. 40-41.

These all look to you
  to give them their food at the proper time.
When you give it to them,
  they gather it up;
when you open your hand,
they are satisfied with good things. (Ps 104:27-28)[8]

God's care for his creatures is also evident from the sabbath command requiring rest for animals (Ex 20:8-11; Deut 5:12-16), and penalties in the law for their mistreatment. In these commands God makes it clear that he expects human beings to emulate his care for creation and for his creatures. The command to keep the sabbatical year, thereby giving the land periodic rest, reinforces God's care for his creation and extends it to the land itself (Lev 25:1-7). This was considered so important that its repeated violation was a basis for the nation Israel being taken into exile (2 Chron 36:20-21).

God's care for the living things he has created is evident from an often-overlooked passage in the covenant he made with Noah following the flood. In Genesis 9 God actually makes the Noahic covenant not only with Noah and his family, but with all the living beings on earth. The covenant involved a promise never again to destroy the earth with a flood, and its significance in part has to do with how God's care for all living beings is reflected in his promise (Gen 9:8-16, summarized as "the everlasting covenant between God and all living creatures of every kind on the earth" [v. 16]).

God's creation has value for other reasons that Scripture underscores. For example, the wisdom literature is clear that *God has embedded his wisdom into the created order.* In Proverbs 8:22-34, wisdom is personified and is said to have been present with God while he was creating and is described as having been born to prior to creation. Wisdom was the craftsman at God's side (Prov 8:30) and was there when God marked out the world and its boundaries. What this suggests is that there is something about creation that exhibits God's wisdom, in the same way that the natu-

---

[8]It should be noted that in Psalm 104:20-22, the psalmist recognizes that part of the provision God makes for animals involves predators obtaining food by killing and consuming their prey. It seems that animals were not restricted to being vegetarians any more than human beings were.

ral world testifies to God's handiwork and glory (Ps 19; Job 38–41). These texts suggest that the creation is more than simply a tool to display God's attributes. Rather, these passages make it clear that the natural world has intrinsic value because it is one of the clearest mirrors of the magnificence of God.

God's creation has intrinsic value because *the natural world will be redeemed when Christ returns*. God's plan of redemption includes more than simply individual human beings. It also includes a proper ordering of society (Is 42:1-4) and a renewal of the created order. Romans 8:19-21 makes this promise:

> The creation waits in eager expectation for the sons of God to be revealed. For the creation was subjected to frustration, not by its own choice, but by the will of the one who subjected it, in hope that the creation itself will be liberated from its bondage to decay and brought into the glorious freedom of the children of God.

The text speaks of the natural world being freed from the curse of sin and thus the object of God's renewing work. What this passage makes clear is that the present creation will not be destroyed at the return of Christ but will be restored, analogous to a master painting that is need of restoration to its original beauty and artistry. Creation will be brought back to its original magnificence, which has been tarnished and compromised by the curse of sin. Thus care for creation today is consistent with and required by the long-term plan of God for the natural world, and is part of his plan for redeeming everything he created.

There have been some who, as a result of a misconstrued eschatology, have insisted that the created order will be destroyed at the return of Christ, and thus we need not be concerned with the environment. But such a view is not supported by the Bible. In fact, in Romans 8 the renewal of creation is analogous to the renewal of the body for the believer (Rom 8:23). No one can argue that the future resurrection body justifies abuse or neglect of the body today. In the Bible there is as much hope for the body as there is for the soul. In the same way, no one can maintain that the future renewal of the creation justifies current abuse or neglect of the environment today. In fact, proactive care of our bodies is a well-accepted Christian standard. Why should care for the creation deserve any less, especially when direct connections with human flourishing are brought into the picture?

Business and Creation Care

Business has a complex relationship with the environment. Wonderful inventions that help us flourish come from the meeting of natural resources, human creativity and economic incentives. Silicon chips necessary to power our computers come from sand, drugs to treat infectious diseases have been derived from rare compounds found in soil, and wind is increasingly being harnessed to power our dwellings. Of course, the other side of the relationship is not so tidy. Business activity affects the environment in multiple ways. The recent BP oil crisis in the Gulf of Mexico is one devastating example. In everyday operations, raw materials sourcing, production, transportation and packaging all affect the environment. Taken together, these processes have produced staggering amounts of pollution in our air, land and waterways. Moreover, harmful chemicals and additives are also often used in the quest to lower costs, quickly bring products to market and to increase shelf life. And a seemingly infinite number of cheap, disposable and overpackaged products are promoted for our consumption, but it's ironic that most of these products are really not disposable at all when we consider ecology.

Sadly, environmental considerations have been primarily viewed as constraints that need to be worked around. While a growing number of sincere efforts are being made, there has been so much public pressure (and perhaps brand value) to go green that some companies are simply posturing (greenwashing) by making false claims. Others are arguably purchasing their way toward a green identity by buying renewable energy credits (carbon offsets) in order to make the claim (possibly dubiously) that they have reduced emissions or are actually carbon neutral when there have been few if any actual reductions in their business processes.[9]

From the overview of biblical teaching on the environment several implications can be drawn. First, if business activity is characterized and contextualized by transformational service, it can be legitimately served by natural resources. Responsible use of the garden's resources is permissible

---

[9]Ben Elgin, "Another Inconvenient Truth," *Business Week*, March 26, 2007; Ben Elgin, "The Fuzzy Math of Eco-Accolades," *Business Week*, October 29, 2007.

to support the production of services and products that are driven by and result in the enhancement of human flourishing. However, consistent with broader biblical themes and specific teaching on our relationship with the environment, particularly Genesis 2:15, the relationship is reciprocal. Business too must be an active partner in serving the garden.

Protecting the garden is the first step, but a second implication takes the concept further. Tending and serving the garden, and the broader divine mission of transformation and reconciliation, imply that movement beyond making things less bad and into the positive territory of making things whole again is necessary. Although conditions cannot be made perfect on earth, serving the garden implies that our ultimate objective must be to make things right or transform and restore them to harmony as much as possible. By comparison, most environmental efforts to date have been after-the-fact (end-of-pipe) solutions aimed at slowing down the inevitable or minimizing harm (e.g., reducing "our footprint").

Restoration and transformation are undoubtedly lofty standards that seem to be place us in a conundrum. Based on our historical construct of natural and human interests existing in a standoff, the only path to restoration and harmony would appear to be zero growth initiatives or, even more extreme, a negative growth mandate, which would take us back to some sort of preindustrial state. Yet, as we have stated earlier, if people who are economically poor are to be liberated from their conditions, increasing the size of the financial pie is a necessity. And as a practical matter, economically impoverished people have direct incentives to act in ways that further threaten the environment (and harm all of us in the process). For example, a person living in a poor country with little or no income has good reasons to cut down trees (which are necessary to sustain life, support biodiversity and curb carbon) to be used either as firewood or to be sold as a product in a microenterprise.

Traditional methods of approaching and measuring economic growth have largely relegated environmental impact as an afterthought. In fact, Gross Domestic Product (GDP), the most widely used barometer of growth, fails to capture negative environmental impacts. For example, it has been often stated that an environmental crisis (e.g., the Exxon Valdez disaster in Alaska, BP disaster in the Gulf of Mexico) leads to a higher GDP since cleanup costs are counted *positively*. Furthermore, our current patterns of growth may actually hurt economically poor people in the long run by driving up the price of fuels and contributing to energy poverty. If economically impoverished people have to pay more for fuel, this effectively reduces any gains in income they may achieve.

Moving toward a solution to this puzzle and taking steps toward holistic flourishing requires a paradigmatic shift in how economic activity fits into larger natural systems. In other words, we need sustainable growth that is harmonious with nature rather than destructive of it. With modification the recent movement toward a triple bottom line (*economic, social* and *environmental* measures of success; sometimes referred to as *"people, profits and planet"*) offers a good starting point to envisioning the responsibilities of business.[10]

An even more robust way to frame environmental care has been proposed by William McDonough and Michael Braungart in *Cradle to Cradle: Remaking the Way We Make Things*. McDonough and Braungart point out that manufacturing from the industrial revolution forward has been an unplanned, contrary to nature, linear, cradle-to-grave process that was not designed to be part of a larger system. Products are manufactured to be placed quickly into the hands of consumers and then thrown into landfills or incinerated when their useful life comes to an end. At best, some products are recycled (more accurately, down-cycled). For example, carpeting can be made from recycled soda bottles, but the process of wrestling them into forms they were never designed to take requires as much energy, creates as much waste and may add more dangerous additives than starting from new.[11]

McDonough and Braungart call for a paradigm shift that moves beyond "sustainability" to a "partnership" that can enable "good growth" to occur. Instead of multiple *bottom* lines, they call for the environment to be one of the "top lines" that is used in business decisions and to shift to a "cradle to cradle" orientation that "begins in the designer's head instead of at the end of pipes."[12]

---

[10]See, for example, Andrew Savitz, with Karl Weber, *The Triple Bottom Line: How Today's Best-Run Companies are Achieving Economic, Social and Environmental Success* (San Francisco: Jossey-Bass, 2006).

[11]William McDonough and Michael Braungart, *Cradle to Cradle: Remaking the Way We Make Things* (New York: North Point, 2002), p. 4.

[12]Ibid., pp. 153-54, 168.

If humans are truly going to prosper, we will have to learn to imitate nature's highly effective cradle to cradle system of nutrient flow and metabolism, in which the very concept of waste does not exist. *To eliminate the concept of waste means to design things—products, packaging, and systems—from the very beginning on the understanding that waste does not exist. . . .* Products can be composed of either materials that biodegrade and become food for *biological cycles*, or of technical materials that stay in closed loop *technical* cycles, in which they continuously circulate as valuable nutrients for industry.[13]

Undoubtedly, these are very high (and likely unattainable) standards; progressing through all of these steps is very expensive, and some materials and reclamation methods do not yet exist. McDonough and Braungart, however, are realistic in that incremental changes may only be possible at this point. And they note that if businesses are to be involved, the shift to "eco-effective" design has to make economic sense too. Among the many corporate clients who have incorporated "cradle to cradle" design ideas is furniture maker Herman Miller. With founders and executives motivated by Christian values, Herman Miller has long been known for its proactive environmental practices. As we noted in chapter two, the company took a great risk in using a more environmentally friendly wood in it signature Eames Chair.

Today, the company takes even more comprehensive moves by stepping backward in the manufacturing process and practicing "design for the environment."[14] Executives at the company try to achieve holistic, integrated implementation of environmentally responsible concepts in its entire product development cycle. For example, with its Aeron and Mirra chairs, company personnel broke down the chemical composition of the designs, examined human health and environmental impacts, incorporated findings (and new materials) into design processes, and engaged its supply chain in acquiring better materials. Company products are now also being designed for eventual reclamation, so that discarded materials can be placed back into the product lifecycle with minimal waste and ecological impact.[15]

---

[13]Ibid., pp. 103-4.
[14]Marc Gunther, *Faith and Fortune* (New York: Crown Business, 2004), p. 170.
[15]William McDonough and Michael Braungart, "The Anatomy of Transformation: Herman Miller's Journey to Sustainability," *green@work*, March-April 2002.

Many other businesses have taken smaller steps, many of which fit within a profitable win-win framework. The hybrid engine of the highly popular Toyota Prius is an example of a design that captures what ordinarily would be waste (from braking and downhill driving) and converts it into energy. The car sells at a significantly higher price than similarly sized and outfitted vehicles (often with long customer waiting lists) and is well ahead of competitors when it comes to fuel efficiency.[16] Concerned about the impact of its packaging, Clif Bar (makers of nutritional food bars) was able to eliminate shrink wrap at a significant cost savings, and is investigating alternative packaging to its foil-lined paper wrapping.[17] Other businesses have increased energy efficiency in facilities, turned byproducts into new lines of business (e.g., old tires into playfield cushioning, old blue jeans into building insulation) and marketed environmentally friendly products at premium prices.

Is Green the New Gold?

Given these types of examples, popular sources of literature claim that environmental initiatives represent proven avenues to increase profit: "One can 'save the planet' and make money at the same time." As purportedly stated by one leader of the movement, "It's not just a free lunch, but one you are paid to eat."[18] Undoubtedly, significant prudential opportunities to turn green into gold do exist. Some evidence indicates that consumers are willing to act outside of rational (narrow, economically self-interested) ways and will spend more to purchase environmentally friendly (and otherwise socially responsible items). The previously mentioned Prius is a good example. Unless gas prices remain high or an owner drives many miles, the vehicle has a very long-term payback timetable, even after adding in a one-time tax credit purchasers receive. So, many Prius owners do in fact pay a social premium to own the vehicle. The same could be said for many fair trade and organic products on the market.

Other large corporations are involved with environmental issues in

---

[16]To achieve full cradle to cradle design, however, the vehicle would have to be made in a way that its discarded materials can be reclaimed and used as either biological or technical nutrients.

[17]"The Pioneers: Sustainability Manager, Staff Ecologist—New Job Titles to Consider," *Inc.*, November 2006.

[18]Ben Elgin, "Little Green Lies," *Business Week*, October 29, 2007, p. 46.

order to sustain critical resources needed as inputs for their products. For example, Starbucks is involved with climate change issues over concern that global warming will reduce the amount of land available to grow coffee beans.[19] Likewise, Coca-Cola is active in clean-water issues as its key product lines depend on the availability of this resource (and the company has been accused of contributing to the depletion of clean-water supplies).[20]

Looking at the demand for clean, renewable energy, an increasing number of businesses see significant future growth opportunities. For example, George David, CEO of United Technologies Corporation (UTC) believes "that in 30 years time conservation and related areas can make up 30% of the company's business, from nothing today."[21]

Likewise, in 2005 General Electric launched its now well-known "Campaign for *Ecomagination*." The overall goal of the program was to invest in clean technology for the purpose of helping businesses and households to reduce their negative environmental impact. Far from having a clean environmental reputation (and record) under former CEO Jack Welch, his successor, Jeffrey Immelt, has taken the company in a different direction, partly out of a sense of environmental concern but also because he and GE's board of directors see it as good, long-term business with great potential to generate new revenue streams and create what they call "green collar jobs." In the letter to stakeholders that accompanied the 2008 Annual Ecomagination Report, the company describes the goals for the program as "playing a role in boosting economic recovery, supporting the jobs of the future, improving the environmental impact of our customers' (and our own) operations, furthering energy independence, and fostering innovation and growth in profitable environmental solutions."[22] This involves investing in technologies such as alternative energy sources (e.g., wind turbines and hybrid engines), clean water technologies, and smart-grid-energy coordination technologies, in addition to reducing emissions

---

[19]See "Tackling Climate Change," Starbucks Coffee, n.d., www.starbucks.com/responsibility/environment/climate-change.

[20]Betsy McKay, "Why Coke Aims to Slake Global Thirst for Safe Water," *Wall Street Journal*, March 15, 2007, http://online.wsj.com/public/article/SB117392644638537761-jHOpdgcn-F7Wu_P3j6BXV6I5v8yA_20070323.html?mod=blogs.

[21]"A Change in Climate," *The Economist*, January 17, 2008.

[22]Jeffrey R. Immelt and Steven M. Fludder, "Letter to Stakeholders," *Ecomagination*, n.d., http://ge.ecomagination.com/annual-reports/letter-to-stakeholders.html.

and becoming more energy efficient within the company itself.[23]

While these are good examples of the opportunities that exist, a more realistic and circumspect approach is necessary. Going green does not always bring in the green. Much like our discussion of ethics in chapter six, a better case for the connection between sustainability and profitability can be made in the long run, but in the short term, adopting sustainable practices may well involve significant costs and risks, which may, in turn, affect shareholders negatively in a financial sense.

Becoming more environmentally sustainable presents a number of challenges. Even if the leaders of a business desire to be green in their production and distribution of goods, environmentally friendly input materials, recycling processes or transportation options may not yet exist, may not be sufficiently available, or be reasonably cost effective. Sometimes, a choice will have to be made between less-than-ideal alternatives. In some cases, so called green products may produce a different set of harms (e.g., fuel efficient cars like the Prius may encourage more driving).

Marketplace pressures are also very real. Many environmentally sound practices may not reduce costs and may add nonrecoverable ones. From a competitive standpoint a company that takes on additional costs (beyond what it can make up from environmentally conscious consumers) for the sake of environmental friendliness will find itself at a disadvantage if rivals do not follow suit. Management scholar Ian Maitland describes this challenge as akin to "prisoner's dilemma" situations that occur in trying to solve public goods problems. While each firm may desire a cleaner environment, paying to do so may result in a disadvantage, absent a mechanism to force competitors to make equal financial commitments.[24]

Some larger-scale initiatives (e.g., investments in alternative energy) require very long payback horizons, a privilege executives trying to make good on short-term shareholder expectations do not often enjoy. Moreover, these types of investments are very risky and only make economic

---

[23]Other examples include Walmart's commitment to reducing solid waste, reducing energy usage in their stores and making their vehicles more efficient; CEMEX's Ecoefficiency program, seeking to expand recycling and reusing materials, especially waste, in its cement manufacturing process; and Toyota's leadership in producing hybrid vehicles. See Mark J. Epstein, *Making Sustainability Work: Best Practices in Managing and Measuring Corporate Social, Environmental and Economic Impacts* (San Francisco: Barrett-Koehler, 2008).

[24]Ian Maitland, "The Limits of Business Self-Regulation," *California Management Review* 27, no. 3 (1985): 132-47.

sense if traditional nonrenewable energy prices remain elevated. As gasoline prices began dropping from their recent (2008) record highs, many biofuel businesses saw customers (and then investors) flee.

Publicly traded companies, even ones with broader social missions, face additional pressures. A well-circulated story of corporate environmental responsibility involves the decision made by executives of outdoor sports apparel manufacturer Patagonia to cancel a profitable but environmentally damaging line of outdoor clothing. While the company and its leaders deserve praise for the decision, Patagonia is privately owned and has fewer competing obligations. In contrast, shareholder-owned Starbucks, a company with a well-deserved reputation for its socially responsible practices, has been slow to embrace recycling even though company stores generate an incredible amount of paper waste. More recently, the company has used drive-through windows to increase revenue. Idling cars are hardly environmentally friendly, and the concept of drive-in or take-and-go coffee sure seems opposed to the "third place" idea that has been a key to Starbucks branding and identity. Yet the company must earn profit to honor its shareholders financial interests and to fund its generous employee health care benefits and its many other socially oriented practices and goals.

Limited availability of capital adds a further challenge. Measuring how well capital is employed through R.O.I. (return on investment) analysis can then create some significant tensions. Even in cases in which an environmentally friendly initiative can be shown to produce a positive return, it may be in direct competition with other potential uses of the same capital. For example, a sobering *Business Week* article titled "Little Green Lies" tells the story of Auden Schendler, who directs sustainability efforts at Aspen Skiing Company, a resort that has won numerous awards and accolades for its environmental efforts, yet several modest proposals (e.g., to refurbish an older lodge to use less energy, switching to fluorescent bulbs in guest rooms and a parking garage) that would have resulted in full cost recovery over the long term were thwarted. In two of the cases (refurbishing the lodge and the parking garage), other executives successfully argued that the money should be spent in favor of items that customers would notice and thereby would yield more immediate financial results (new ski lifts, fine furniture). With respect to energy-saving bulbs in guest rooms, Schendler was overruled based on concerns about the waiting room ambience that would be created, possibly harming the customer experience and thereby jeopardizing the resort's five-star rating, illustrating some of the tensions that limited capital brings about.[25]

Offering products that sell well and that are environmentally sound takes navigating the tricky and sometimes narrow space between market leadership and current demand. Commenting on the high hurdle products need to scale, Joel Makower, the executive editor of Greenbiz.com, is cited in the *Economist* as stating, "most consumers will be happy to choose the greener product—provided it does not cost any more, comes from a trusted maker, requires no special effort to buy or use and is at least as good as the alternative."[26] While perhaps an overstatement, businesses leaders do take great risks for all of their stakeholders (including the environment). If they get too far ahead of what consumers demand, more damaging alternatives would be purchased in their place. This point is well illustrated by the controversy that Ford Motor Company faced over its decision to produce its largest SUV ever (the Excursion) amid a significant effort to turn the company in a more environmentally friendly direction. With respect to the decision, Ford's then CEO and current executive chairman, William Clay Ford (a direct descendent of Henry Ford and a self-proclaimed life-long environmentalist), had an interesting observation to make:

> It's a delicate balance between what the customer wants and being com-
> pletely environmentally driven. . . . [Y]ou can make a completely clean ve-
> hicle, but if it sits unsold on the dealer's lot its not helping the environment,
> either. We just have to make these vehicles cleaner and cleaner every year.[27]

While Ford's public claim of wanting to be the world's most environmentally friendly automaker made the company an easy target, other companies in the same industry have struggled to navigate the same challenges. General Motors recently learned a hard lesson when forced to cancel its hybrid Chevrolet Malibu/Saturn Aura model. Apparently, the vehicle failed to attract consumers since some models added only very modest improvements in miles per gallon (1 highway, 4 city) at a significantly higher price (up to $4,000 based on engine size and other options)

---

[25]Ben Elgin, "Little Green Lies."

[26]Joel Makower, cited in "The Good Consumer," *Economist*, January 17, 2008, p. 16.

[27]William Clay Ford, cited Keith Naughton, "Ford's Green Dilemma," *Business Week*, December 21, 1998, pp. 96-97.

than the regular combustion engine model.[28] Pressed in part by lagging economic conditions, low fuel prices and increasing competition, even Toyota has had to mainstream its Prius by giving it a bigger trunk, more headroom, improving gas mileage and lowering its price.[29]

Our point in raising these challenges is not to discourage the pursuit of harmonious dealing with the environment (and thereby with people). We are convinced that approaching business in a manner consistent with a Christian vision necessitates that environmental concerns serve as one of the prisms through which decisions are made. Avoiding risks by only providing customers with what they immediately want can become a convenient and easy excuse. It is also an irresponsible position since short-term market interests would be the final forces in determining the fate of the environment (and consequently, human well-being). Such a stance also leads to an abdication of the necessary leadership role played by business and neglects the fact that businesses play a role in shaping consumer behavior. As consumers we are often more short-sighted and narrowly interested in our product choices than we'd like to admit. While business cannot be blamed entirely, most products are not designed and marketed with environmental suitability in mind. Moreover, consumer education and social marketing by business can modify end-user behavior to some degree. Ironically, William Clay Ford's great grandfather, Henry (the company founder), once remarked, "If I had asked my customers what they wanted, they would have said a faster horse."[30]

Working to transform and restore the environment and our relationship with it to a more harmonious place is challenging. Bringing biblical ideals to a broken world almost always is. Proactive leadership in stewardship of creation requires significantly more than just operating within the short-term win-win space. An authentic, committed effort requires courage, imagination and dramatic shifts in thinking and acting.

Faithful environmental stewardship will not always pay in the economic

[28]Lawrence Ulrich, "A G.M. Hybrid that Misses the High Notes," *New York Times*, June 18, 2009, www.nytimes.com/2009/06/21/automobiles/autoreviews/21malibu.html, and "GM Cancels Malibu Hybrid, Works on New System," Associated Press, June 11, 2009.
[29]Blaine Harden, "Toyota Wants New Prius to Be America's Next Top Model, *Washington Post*, June 9, 2009, www.washingtonpost.com/wp-dyn/content/article/2009/06/08/AR2009060803940.html.
[30]Henry Ford, cited in Friedman, *Hot, Flat and Crowded*, p. 241.

sense, certainly not immediately and sometimes not down the road. However, consistent with the rest of this book, financial return is only one factor, albeit an important one, to consider. Even if a financial loss (or lower amount of gain) is experienced, shareholders and their loved ones may gain in their overall well-being. Shareholders too have to breathe, eat, relax on sofas, use computers and the like. Hopefully, they are also concerned about the plight of their global and local neighbors. In practical terms there are few equity owners who would say directly to executives, "Put a few more nickels on the value of each of my shares this quarter by not going so far in your efforts to curb the effluents you are discharging into the stream where my kids swim." Yet, by demanding short-term economic gain alone, they are indirectly sending the same message. We will undoubtedly pay for environmental abuse sooner or later, whether in the form of higher health-care bills or added costs of clean-up or regulation. Indeed, it has been wisely observed that in a global economy, "We're all downstream."[31]

Other Needed Partners

Business is a necessary partner in protecting and restoring the environment. Given the right price signals, moral motivation and leadership, no institution can innovate as efficiently or quickly, or make the kind of impact that business can. However, there are limits on what business can accomplish in the absence of an "enabling environment."

Government must play a role in taking a longer-term and common-good orientation by establishing a context that makes the risks born by business more reasonable, and by creating a correct mix of incentives to drive change and a longer-term orientation. Good regulations should level the playing field so that environmental initiatives do not become "prisoner's dilemma's" with few escape routes. Friedman's *Hot, Flat and Crowded* is primarily about the lack of courage and foresight shown by politicians and policymakers to act in a timely manner. Since we cannot regulate our way out of this mess, we must harness the power of the market and competitive forces to spur innovation and drive down prices (to the "Chindia"—China/India—level). In order to do so, Friedman advocates items such as

---

[31]Cited in McDonough and Braungart, *Cradle to Cradle*, p. 127.

a gasoline tax, so that a price floor will exist, and businesses can more safely place large bets on investments in alternative fuels. As things stand, executives cannot justify major investments if potential markets are undermined by fluctuating prices of "old, dirty fuels."[32] Friedman and many others believe that putting a price on carbon (perhaps through some sort of tax) will also be helpful in motivating more environmentally fit design. Our point is not to suggest specific government policies but to simply acknowledge that business needs support to properly carry out its partnering and leading roles.

Environmental problems are not just caused by economic, commercial or political short-sightedness. We would be remiss to ignore the spiritual causes at the level of individual consumers too. As purchasers of products we must rethink many of our choices. If we care about our broader interests, our neighbors and our children, we will have to change the ways we live and sacrifice some of our treasured rights to convenience and extravagance. Without larger-scale changes in some of our assumptions about how we organize our lives, small, easy actions won't amount to much if anything.

Businesses can't and don't force (though they may certainly persuade) us to overvalue convenience, fill up our lives so we must always choose the most expedient modes of transportation or demand environmentally damaging products and the glitzy, wasteful ways they are packaged. We make choices too, and their impact is becoming magnified on an unprecedented scale when people around many parts of the globe seek to replicate how we live.

In discussing the partnerships that are needed, Clive Mather (the retired Shell executive) offers an appropriate thought:

> Let's be clear, no matter how much business can achieve with innovation, technology and global reach, this is not just about business. The "deal," if we want it, is with all of us. We—you, me, big business, small business, governments, agencies and activists—we are all in this together. Governments must establish the policy frameworks; activists and academics must provide independent research and assurance; business must develop commercial products and consumers must change their habits. If we don't all respond in equal and timely fashion, we will all pay the price, whatever

---

[32]Friedman, *Hot, Flat and Crowded*, chap. 11.

nature ultimately determines that should be. As author and naturalist Robert Pyle reminds us—"Nature bats last."[33]

Connecting biblical ideals to environmental care, John Stott once eloquently stated, "It is a noble calling to cooperate with God for the fulfillment of his purposes, to transform the created order for the pleasure and profit of all. In this way our work is to be an expression of our worship, since our care of the creation will reflect our love for the Creator."[34] Given growing awareness of the intimate connections between nature and human well-being (particularly for those most vulnerable), Stott's logic might be appropriately taken one step further: Environmental stewardship should be seen as an extension of the Great Commandment (love of God and neighbor) found in Matthew 22:37-40. While business needs to be an active partner, preserving and restoring the environment (tending the garden) is a shared task requiring commitment and sacrifice if our children, grandchildren and neighbors near and far are to avoid a thicket of weeds, thistles and thorns.

---

[33]Clive Mather, "The Business of Climate Change: What's the Deal?" Business of Climate Change Conference II, Ottawa, Canada, October 30, 2007, p. 2. The quote "Nature bats last" has been attributed to Robert M. Pyle.

[34]John Stott, foreword to *The Care of Creation*, ed. R. J. Berry (Downers Grove, Ill.: InterVarsity Press, 2000), pp. 8-9.

Emerging Directions
in Business

Most of the apples we eat are grown in the rolling hills of southeastern Washington. In clusters along the major roads there, wooden shanties, often lacking plumbing and electricity, serve as temporary housing for migrant farm workers. A turn at the end of a highway near the Snake River lie orchards, clusters of middle-class houses and a school. Halfway up Fishhook Park Road is a place that some have called a piece of Eden, a family farm run by Ralph and Cheryl Broetje.[1] Broetje Orchards' brand First Fruits of Washington is named after the biblical festival in which people offered the first and best of their harvests to God.

Don't let the "family farm" label fool you. Broetje Orchards is one of the largest privately owned apple orchards in the world (more than 5,000 acres) and employs roughly one thousand full-time year-round employees in addition to another nine hundred seasonal workers. The company packs over five million boxes of apples a year and sells them to retailing giants like Costco, Safeway, Albertsons and Walmart.

While apples are not a unique product, the company's social and spiritual mission of serving the poor and marginalized sets it apart. From their early days in the agriculture business, Ralph and Cheryl witnessed the hardship experienced by their farmhands, many of whom came from south of the U.S. border for seasonal work. They could see the toll through children who were often left without supervision and unable to attend school because of frequent family moves to find work. So they created full-time

---

[1]Kari Constanza, "A Piece of Eden." *World Vision* 7, no. 2 (2003): 22-27. See also Jim Rice, "Core Values," *Sojourners*, November-December, 2000.

year-round employment and built a preschool. They learned more about poor living conditions and health issues, including a boy being bit by rats as he slept, recalls Cheryl Broetje (who directs the "community profit" side of the business). Ralph and Cheryl decided to put up almost everything they had saved to that point and built 100 two, three and four bedroom homes. The homes form clusters known as Vista Hermosa (beautiful view) and are rented to employees and their families at substantially subsidized rates.

Before the Broetjes knew it, they realized many more needs had to be met. As they put it, they were soon in the social-work business. And so they also built a private Christian school, a ranch for troubled youth (Jubilee Youth Ranch) and a day-care center that serves employees, also at highly subsidized rates (no one pays more than $7 per day), a chapel and a grocery store. After-school programs, an onsite library and a computer lab were set up. Money was set aside for college scholarships for the children of employees. In all the company donates about 60 to 75 percent of its yearly after-tax profits to local, domestic and international charitable projects (a total of $50 million to date). Countering concerns about paternalism, Cheryl is proud to note that in the past, up to 40 percent of the families who leave Vista Hermosa go on to become first-time homeowners.

The Broetjes' beliefs shape their direct management practices too. When I (Kenman) had the privilege of visiting the business a few summers ago, I was taken aback by the thoughtfulness and humility with which the Broetjes designed the entire operation. The company views itself as a community and practices a servant leadership model. A deepening awareness that some families had almost no time together as a unit (fathers working early morning in the fields, and mothers spending swing shifts in the plant) compelled them to build a new state-of-the-art packing facility that could run alongside the old one and eliminate the need for early evening work. And realizing a new facility would be more efficient and thereby possibly cost workers their jobs, much careful thought was given to the maximum number of jobs that could be preserved while running the business in an economically sustainable manner.[2] For the past two years, a council made up of employees has given away 100 percent of the proceeds (often in the hundreds of thousands of dollars) from a cherry orchard to

---

[2]Albert Erisman and Kenman Wong, "An Orchard with Fruit That Lasts: A Conversation with Cheryl Broetje," *Ethix*, November 2005.

support various causes. The employees are actually empowered to solicit proposals, much like program officers of a charitable foundation.

The company's motto is "A quality fruit company committed to 'bearing fruit that will last'" (Jn 15:16) "Sure, we have to make money or we'd have to shut the doors," Cheryl Broetje explains.

> But profit isn't our main motive. It becomes the by-product of treating people with dignity, respect, and mutuality, and as equals in every sense of the word. We all have a role to play in creating a community of people who care for a business that then cares for them. We believe that if we ever stopped doing that, we would implode.[3]

Broetje Orchards is a business that grows and sells excellent apples, but as the Broetjes note, they are also in the business of developing people.

Broetje Orchards is an early pioneer of what have become known as "social enterprises" or "social ventures" that seek to directly blend social and financial bottom lines. Social enterprises comprise one among several movements that are working toward making business a more direct and intentional partner in solving difficult social problems, such as poverty and environmental sustainability. Each of these movements has attracted entrepreneurs, customers, media attention, curriculum development at the university level and large sums of investment dollars. Moreover, some mainstream business organizations are adopting similar practices and aims.

In what follows, a number of exciting developments in business will be discussed. Before we begin, it is worth noting that these efforts are *not* charitable, per se. While they do focus on humanitarian issues and some degree of profit may be sacrificed for other bottom lines, these efforts creatively occupy the space that has traditionally divided the for-profit and nonprofit sectors. These emerging organizations offer a powerful witness to the need for business to be an active partner in solving social issues as they seize upon the power of economic competition and the profit motive (although often in tempered form) to encourage innovation and discipline in ways that donor-funded and government entities typically cannot. Business has a unique capacity to bring innovative products and services to

---

[3]Cheryl Broetje, www.broetjeorchards.com/index.cfm?pageId=A6B922A8-16A8-5F5A-37A 77AD149247D85, accessed November 12, 2008.

scale quickly, transfer knowledge between various market segments and geographical areas, and operate sustainably free of dependence on donor and government funding. Instead of charity, each of the following movements take advantage of what business does best in pursuit of creating economic and social value.

We will discuss the move to comprehensive Corporate Social Responsibility (CSR), Bottom or Base of the Pyramid (BOP) business, Social Enterprise, Micro-finance, Business as Mission (BAM), and new ownership and control models. We will then examine how they fit into a vision for business that is characterized by transformational service for the common good. It is important to note that these developments represent categories that are not neatly separable. Some scholars even see an emerging convergence of most, if not all, of them.[4] For example, the line between social enterprise and a more robust conception of CSR may be a thin one. Likewise, social entrepreneurship has certainly been a factor in the rapid expansion of Micro-finance. Social entrepreneurs and BAM leaders can also use BOP strategies in achieving their objectives. We also wish to point out that we are not invalidating or minimizing the role of businesses that operate in more conventional spheres (the subject of most of this book) in contributing to God's work in the world, especially as many of them are moving in the direction of emphasizing benefits to multiple stakeholders.

Comprehensive CSR

In the past, CSR (Corporate Social Responsibility) was generally defined as not doing any overt harm in the course of pursuing "normal" business activities. Many corporations also practiced CSR by investing in their local communities through charitable giving and staffing local volunteer efforts by sending their employees.

More recently, however, CSR has grown to become a much more robust and comprehensive concept. Once considered "normal," business operations such as sourcing and manufacturing, for example, are now being carefully examined to see if they violate moral (beyond legal) standards for the treatment of workers and environmental care. The older disconnected practice

[4]For example, Kim Alter groups many of these movements or organizations under the banner of "Social Enterprise" (see Kim Alter, "Social Enterprise Typology," *Virtue Ventures*, November 27, 2007, www.virtueventures.com/typology).

of giving large sums to charity, while producing goods in ways that were harmful to employees or end users is considered far less acceptable.

In fact, emerging CSR can be described as "360 degrees," "vertically integrated" or "seamless" in nature as business organizations are now internally examining and externally being held accountable for how their activities affect multiple stakeholder groups from the start of the supply chain to product or service end use. Business organizations must now consider how their actions affect investors, suppliers, consumers, employees and the environment. McDonald's is a good example of a company that has been influenced by the shifting nature of CSR. In years past, McDonald's enjoyed a fine reputation for corporate citizenship as a result of its charitable giving, particularly its investment in building "Ronald McDonald houses" near hospitals to offer shelter to families with children battling lengthy illnesses. More recently, however, McDonald's has been criticized for contributing to childhood obesity because of the nutritional value of its food products. This type of criticism has undoubtedly forced the company to re-examine its product line and to expand the number of choices available on store menus.

While certainly not embraced by all as a positive change (some think its ridiculous to hold a company and not parents responsible for children's eating habits, for example), the evolving nature of CSR has been driven and shaped by a combination of forces. Changing public expectations, government/regulatory pressure, nongovernment/advocacy organizations, media scrutiny, and the speed and volume of news and information travel on the internet have all played a role. Moreover, the use of ethical screens in investment and consumption decisions has also grown dramatically in recent years.

Some sincere and outspoken business leaders have also led the charge on the corporate side. For example, PepsiCo's CEO Indra Nooyi, is an outspoken proponent of a new kind of capitalism, in which corporations take on responsibility for multiple bottom lines.[5] Similarly, Clif Bar's founder, Gary Erickson, states: "To me shareholder value is long-term stewardship or sustainability. . . . We know we need profit, but profit is not why we exist. Profit enables Clif Bar to remain healthy and to do good

---

[5]Betsy Morris, "The Pepsi Challenge," *Fortune*, February 19, 2008, http://money.cnn .com/2008/02/18/news/companies/morris_nooyi.fortune/index.htm.

over the long haul."[6] This sense of purpose translates into five "bottom lines" or aspirations at Clif Bar: Business, Brands, People, Community and Planet. Even Bill Gates (founder of Microsoft, known for its highly competitive business practices) has expressed his frustration at capitalism's failures to address the needs of the poor and has called for a "creative capitalism" that is redirected toward helping those at the bottom of the economic ladder.[7]

Many companies provide examples of a more robust approach to CSR. Timberland, another company with a CEO (Jeff Swartz) who embraces a comprehensive CSR viewpoint, has moved from annual to quarterly CSR reporting in a quest for more transparency and stakeholder engagement. The report covers fifteen different performance indicators, including energy use, material composition of products (for health and environmentally friendliness), employee volunteerism/service, and labor conditions of factories.[8]

Starting with the treatment of workers far down the supply chain, companies like warehouse retailing giant Costco conduct audits of their supplier's farms to make sure employees are being treated fairly. According to CEO Jim Sinegal, Costco never wants to be in the position of being accused of bringing low prices to consumers because of an unseemly activity.[9] Likewise, Starbucks pays higher than market prices for raw beans and has invested in health care initiatives in coffee farming countries.

Mattel, another company with a strong commitment to CSR, has factories, especially those which produce the company's "Hot Wheels" line, that look nothing like the type of Chinese sweatshops reported by the news media. Work is designed in such a way that employees rotate through various stations rather than performing the same repetitive tasks. Factory workers are also housed in facilities that rival any modern dormitory in China,

---

[6]Gary Erickson with Lois Lorentzen, *Raising the Bar: Integrity and Passion in Life and Business* (San Francisco: Jossey-Bass, 2004).

[7]Robert A. Guth, "Bill Gates Issues Call for Kinder Capitalism," *Wall Street Journal*, January 4, 2008, http://online.wsj.com/article/SB120113473219511791.html.

[8]Alex Hausman, "Timberland's Journey to Quarterly CSR Reporting," *Environmental Leader*, June, 25, 2008, www.environmentalleader.com/2008/06/25/timberlands-journey-to-quarterly-csr-reporting; for actual reports see www.JustMeans.com.

[9]Albert Erisman and David Gill, "A Long Term Business Perspective in a Short Term World: An Interview With Jim Sinegal," *Ethix*, March-April 2003, pp. 6-9, 16, reprinted in Scott B. Rae and Kenman L. Wong, *Beyond Integrity: A Judeo-Christian Approach to Business Ethics*, 2nd ed. (Grand Rapids: Zondervan, 2004), pp. 146-51.

and they enjoy air-conditioning, ping pong tables and karaoke machines.[10]

In exercising greater responsibility toward consumers, some companies like Walmart, which gets beaten up far more than praised for its practices these days, has long had policies of carrying family-friendly products. The company has refused to carry some video games with explicitly violent content and has used its considerable buying power to force record companies to produce special versions of compact discs with sanitized lyrics that would fit in with the family atmosphere of Walmart stores. According to former COO Don Soderquist, Walmart executives were not motivated by money in instances like these; they did it because it was the right thing to do.[11]

Comprehensive CSR is not well received by all. As noted earlier some question its fairness. (Is it fair to make companies responsible for the end use of its products; e.g., McDonald's for obesity?) Others object that it amounts to window dressing to appease and attract consumers. Yet others argue that it encroaches on the ability of business to pursue its profit objectives and so hurts investors who have risked their hard-earned funds to capitalize the company.

Given these concerns, how well does it fit in with the vision of transformational service? Undoubtedly, some parts fit in very well. Recall that business should not be an engine only to generate private wealth, but should be a vehicle for service to others. Also, restitution laws in the Old Testament and the idea that we are "our brother's keeper" are glimpses into a biblical ethic of responsibility for how our decisions and actions may affect others. Catholic social teaching also provides us with helpful ways to envision corporate responsibility, namely, the concepts of subsidiarity and mediating structures. According to the former, "every social activity ought of its very nature to furnish help to the members of the body social, and never destroy and absorb them."[12] What this means is that business and government must not harm people's relationships with God, with others, with nature or with themselves. The latter implies that

---

[10]"Mattel's Efforts at Social Responsibility," *Los Angeles Times*, November 28, 2004, p. C1, http://seattletimes.nwsource.com/html/nationworld/2002102819_monitor28.html.

[11]Albert Erisman and Kenman Wong, "Wal-Mart Way Produces Accolades, Criticism, Growth: A Conversation with Donald G. Soderquist," *Ethix*, March/April 2008, p. 9.

[12]*Compendium of the Social Doctrine of the Church* (Vatican City: Pontifical Council for Justice and Peace, 2004), p. 81, cited in Lloyd Sandelands and Andrew J. Hoffman, "Sustainability, Faith and the Market," *Worldviews* 12, nos. 2-3 (2008): 129-45.

business can serve as one of the structures (like churches and schools) that stand between the individual and large institutions (the state) and which are necessary for integrating people into societal life.[13]

As business becomes even a more powerful force for change in a global economy, businesspeople and institutions must take greater responsibility for their actions, particularly consequences produced for the powerless and the voiceless. Since companies like McDonald's choose to market their products directly to children, some measure of corporate responsibility for end use is not far-fetched.

However, a major challenge is drawing a clear responsibility line. Holding companies entirely accountable for all unintended consequences produced by the use of their products negates legitimate forms of shared responsibility. Certainly, parents, governments and educational institutions have roles to play too. A strong argument can be made that McDonald's should not be ultimately responsible for overuse of its products if the company is marketing them responsibly and if it is making accurate information regarding the nutritional value of its foods readily available. After all, it is parents or other caretakers who make the final decisions (up to a certain age) for their children, and it is they who provide the money to purchase the food kids eat.

Furthermore, it might be more accurate to conceive of CSR as a series of relationships that make up a circle. At various points along the line that comprises that circle are businesspeople and organizations. Other social institutions such as government and families exist at other points. Finally, consumers and investors are also important and oft-neglected parts of the circle. In many ways, how we act in terms of purchases and investment decisions are strong drivers of the global economic system and thereby of business behavior. Comprehensive CSR may focus too much on the corporate/business part of the circle.

Another major challenge at this point is to develop accurate and auditable metrics for how well companies are doing with respect to treating other stakeholders. Like Timberland, many companies already

---

[13]While Peter Berger and Richard John Neuhaus are widely credited for the more recent rebirth of mediating institutions as a means of social analysis, for their relationship to business see the work of Timothy L. Fort, especially "Business as a Mediating Institution," *Business Ethics Quarterly* 6, no. 2 (1996): 149-63; and *Ethics and Governance: Business as Mediating Institution* (New York: Oxford University Press, 2001).

post CSR reports on their websites. A fairly recent development called "triple bottom line reporting" (3BL) represents one effort to formalize and standardize the metrics used. While the concept of the 3BL has promise, some critics believe that it has limited usefulness, and what gets passed as social responsibility reporting is often more public relations or "spin" over substance.[14]

Another challenge or limit of this movement is the reality of duplicitous motives. To no one's surprise, it seems clear that at least some of the corporations publicly speaking this language are far more motivated by capitalizing on a trend to attract consumers and investors to benefit the financial bottom line than by a values-based commitment. What if cultural values shift? Will comprehensive CSR simply go by the wayside as one more discarded trend that has lost its usefulness?

BOTTOM OR BASE OF THE PYRAMID BUSINESS

An exciting movement involves the role of corporations in alleviating poverty. The Bottom or Base of the Pyramid (BOP) movement calls on large companies, including, multinational corporations (MNCs) to consider doing business with the world's poorest four billion people (two-thirds of the world), one part of the population they have long ignored.[15]

C. K. Prahalad and Stuart Hart, two of the movement's seminal thinkers state MNCs should consider "selling to the poor and helping them improve their lives by producing and distributing products and services in culturally sensitive, environmentally sustainable, and economically profitable ways."[16] In so doing, several objectives may be reached, including providing opportunities for people who make up the bottom of the pyramid to become connected to global markets and thereby lift themselves out of economic poverty. Of course, since large corporations are involved, the focus isn't just on alleviating poverty. The more traditional bottom line of financial growth is also emphasized. Researchers estimate that the market

---

[14]For a critique of 3BL, see "Wayne Norman and Chris MacDonald, "Getting to the Bottom of the Triple Bottom Line," *Business Ethics Quarterly* 14, no. 2 (2004).

[15]See Allen Hammond et al., *The Next 4 Billion: Market Size and Business Strategy at the Base of the Pyramid* (New York: World Resources Institute, 2007).

[16]C. K. Prahalad and Stuart Hart, "The Fortune at the Bottom of the Pyramid," *Strategy+Business* 26 (2002): 2; see also C. K. Prahalad, *The Fortune at the Bottom of the Pyramid* (Philadelphia: Wharton School Publishing, 2004); and Stuart Hart, *Capitalism at the Crossroads* (Philadelphia: Wharton School Publishing, 2005).

in the eighteen largest developing countries is $1.7 trillion and in the "multi-trillions" overall.[17]

MNCs have largely overlooked this market because of assumptions regarding viability. Purchasing power parity (PPP) is roughly equivalent to $1,500 U.S. dollars (the minimum deemed necessary to sustain a decent life) for the billions of people in this economic tier and less than $1 per day for the bottom billion. Thus, it is natural to question how goods and services traditionally offered by large corporations to top-tier markets can be afforded. There may be want or need for some of the products and services, but the assumption is made that there will be little or no true economic demand.

Similar to the way the microfinance movement (discussed later in this chapter) has had to overcome myths about the economic resources and financial habits of impoverished people, leaders of the BOP movement point to level of activity that occurs in the informal economy, much of which is invisible to corporate executives, who are mostly based in countries with top-tier economies.

This market is reachable, they argue, via innovation and overcoming a set of orthodoxies, including assumptions about the importance, needs, ability to pay of the consumers and the availability of managers who wish to work in these countries and tackle the challenges of serving their needs. Prahalad says,

> If we stop thinking of the poor as victims or as a burden and start recognizing them as resilient and creative entrepreneurs and value-conscious consumers, a whole new world of opportunity will open up. . . . What is needed is a better approach to help the poor, an approach that involves partnering with them to innovate and achieve sustainable win-win scenarios where the poor are actively engaged and, at the same time, the companies providing products and services to them are profitable.[18]

He goes on to state, "When the poor at the BOP are treated as consumers, they can reap the benefits of respect, choice, and self-esteem and have an opportunity to climb out of the poverty trap."[19] BOP lead-

---

[17]See Prahalad and Hart, "The Fortune at the Bottom of the Pyramid," and C. K. Prahalad and Allen Hammond, "Serving the Poor Profitably," *Harvard Business Review* 80 (2002): 48-57.
[18]See Prahalad, *Fortune at the Bottom of the Pyramid*, pp. 1, 3.
[19]Ibid., p. 99.

ers are also emphatic that products and services be designed with environmental sustainability in mind, given the amount of damage that would be caused if developed-world products and services are simply replicated and consumed by billions more.[20]

Once assumptions are changed, many operational and strategic innovations are needed.[21] There are significant challenges to providing products and services or creating employment opportunities for people who have small and often erratic incomes, live in media-dark areas, and may not have the necessary skills to serve in production or distribution capacities. Moreover, the contexts in which many of these people live may support trade in ways taken for granted in higher-tier economies. For examples, some countries lack infrastructure such as good roads and payment systems (e.g., check clearing, electronic deposit and money transfer) by which the efficiency of economic transactions is enabled.

Some BOP strategies are simple, for example, selling items such as laundry soap in single servings to address the inability to purchase in bulk due to small and irregular incomes on the part of consumers. Others are revolutionary. For example, an effort by British telecom giant Vodafone (one of the largest mobile telecommunications firms in the world, by revenue) in cooperation with Kenya-based Safaricom launched M-Pesa in 2007. M-Pesa (*Pesa* means money in Swahili) is a service that enables economic transactions over mobile phones in Kenya.

A dramatic increase in cellular phone ownership due to an equally dramatic reduction in phone costs and the availability of prepaid service during the past few years has allowed for widespread adoption in developing countries. For a small fee customers can deposit funds at one of many M-Pesa agent locations (often at small stores where Safaricom prepaid phone cards are sold) that are then credited to their mobile phone accounts. Then, via phone they can use the funds to make purchases at stores (by sending electronic money to the store owners' M-Pesa account) or transfer money to family members living in another part of the country. The family members can take the credit that appears on their phone to another M-Pesa agent to receive the actual cash or use the credit to make

---

[20]See Prahalad & Hart, "The Fortune at the Bottom of the Pyramid," p. 4.
[21]See Ted London and Stuart Hart, "Reinventing Strategies for Emerging Markets: Beyond the Transactional Model," *Journal of International Business Studies* 35, no. 5 (2004): 350-70.

purchases of their own. For example, a worker living in a city can send part of his income to his wife and children living in a far away village. Money transfer (remittances), something easily done in a wealthy country, often produces tradeoffs between expense, speed and reliability to people living in economically impoverished parts of the world. So, it is no surprise that M-Pesa has been very well received in Kenya. According to *The Economist*, as of late 2009, M-Pesa boasts seven million users. (Kenya has a population of 38 million people, and 18.3 million have mobile phones.)[22]

MNCs (or divisions thereof) involved in BOP initiatives include Shell Solar (energy/utilities), Cemex (housing) Kodak (cameras) and H.L.L., a subsidiary of Unilever (health- and hygiene-related products, such as soap).[23]

In the best cases the people who live at the BOP are not just seen as potential customers but as key participants in distribution and procurement, thereby creating direct productive economic opportunities for them. For example, Grameen has successfully created income opportunities for women who own cell phones and then earn a living by selling time, typically to fellow villagers.[24] Other opportunities exist for people to sell prepaid cards or recharge phone batteries for a fee. Similarly, a key part of H.L.L.'s rural distribution strategy in India involves thousands of local villagers who are trained as "traveling retailers."[25] Nestlé has helped spur rural economic development by relying on local farmers to supply product, and other workers for storage and distribution in its milk districts. In addition to economic gains, nutrition, food safety, infrastructure, training and access to veterinary expertise are among the other benefits of the program.[26]

The BOP movement's emphasis on achieving multiple bottom lines, a

---

[22]"Beyond Voice," *Economist*, September 24, 2009.

[23]For further descriptions of these and other examples, see V. Kasturi Rangan et al., eds., *Business Solutions for the Global Poor: Creating Social and Economic Value* (San Francisco: Jossey-Bass, 2007); and Prahalad, *Fortune at the Bottom of the Pyramid*.

[24]The Grameen phone initiative was very successful in its earlier years, but due to saturation of cell phones due to lower costs, the model appears now to be less economically beneficial. The point, however, is that similar income-generating opportunities exist.

[25]V. Kasturi Rangan, Dalip Sehgal and Rohithari Rajan, "The Complex Business of Serving the Poor," in *Business Solutions for the Global Poor*, ed. V. Kasturi Rangan et al. (San Francisco: Jossey-Bass, 2007), pp. 144-54.

[26]Ray Goldberg and Kerry Herman, "Economic Development for a Value-Added Food Chain and Improved Nutrition," in *Business Solutions for the Global Poor*, ed. V. Kasturi Rangan et al. (San Francisco: Jossey-Bass, 2007), pp. 183-89.

proactive role for business to help alleviate economic poverty, economic empowerment and the need for sustainable design are highly commendable. If more businesses approached their work in this manner, transformational work could take place. However, there is a need to take a cautionary approach. First, the fortune to be made may be overstated. Aneel Karnani argues that the market at the bottom is more of a mirage.[27] Second, MNCs are often shareholder owned and are thereby under tremendous short-term pressures to bring products and services to a profitable scale. Therefore, they are vulnerable to take actions that favor financial growth over the best interests of the people they purportedly serve and thus may exploit the economically poor by diverting scarce financial resources into unnecessary purchases. Indeed, it is worth asking if people living at the BOP really need all of the products and services we have in top-tier economies that cause harm to physical, social, spiritual and environmental health. To be fair, leaders of the movement are keenly aware of the need to operate carefully, since companies could easily cross into the territory of profiting on the backs of economically poor people.[28]

Next, much of the existing BOP literature refers to economically impoverished people as "the poor." While this practice can be overlooked as a simple rhetorical issue (and "the poor" is routinely used language in literature from many disciplines), there are many dimensions of poverty. Ignoring this reality may well reduce people to economic agents alone (see chap. 5). This often unintentionally leads to the assumption that economic growth and development are synonymous, therefore rendering the creation of other types of value (social and spiritual) an afterthought at best.

On a related note there is a danger in treating people like consumers rather than neighbors. The BOP movement's intention to regard all people as equals is commendable. Undoubtedly, treating people like consumers may well be a step in the right direction and is an improvement over regarding them as charity recipients or, worse yet, as invisible. However, outcomes that work directly against human flourishing are produced if business practitioners see the people they are dealing with as consumers

---

[27]Aneel Karnani, "The Mirage of Marketing to the Bottom of the Pyramid," *California Management Review* 49, no. 4 (2007): 90-111.
[28]See for example, Rangan et al., ed., *Business Solutions for the Global Poor*, p. 11.

alone, and if people come to see themselves primarily through such a lens. Treating people as dignified children of God entails seeing them in their entirety as human beings. Moreover, their economic interests might be better served by seeing their creative and productive capacities as the parts of the movements that follow attempt to do.

Social Enterprise

Beyond deeply integrated CSR there is another movement afoot (of which Broetje Orchards may be considered a part) that seeks to make business an even more direct and proactive partner in solving social problems. In addition to social enterprise (which itself has multiple definitions), this emerging category has been called "social entrepreneurship," "social ventures," "socially motivated business," "for-benefit," "for more than profit" and "not just for profit," among others.

The number and variety (e.g., nonprofit, religious nonprofit, for profit) of organizations is diverse as the names used to describe this emerging sector. Despite the variety of names and organizational forms, however, they all share common threads. Like Broetje Orchards described at the beginning of this chapter, social ventures use skills (such as entrepreneurship and innovation) and income-generation models once seen as belonging exclusively to the domain of business to help achieve specific social objectives, once seen as residing exclusively to the nonprofit sector. Many if not all effectively function as "blended value organizations and blur the traditional lines that have existed between the for-profit and nonprofit sectors.[29] Often, these organizations are trying to move to, or have attained, financial self-sufficiency through their own earned income. In short, these organizations use business in a more direct and intentional manner to encourage human flourishing.

Distinguishing these organizations from traditional business organizations that embrace CSR is a fuzzy line (especially since both employ the language of multiple bottom lines) and might be better characterized as a matter of degree. Like the organizations that are moving toward

---

[29]For a thoughtful and detailed discussion of multiple manifestations of blended value organizations and the intersections of social and financial value, see Jed Emerson, "The Blended Value Proposition: Integrating Social and Financial Returns," *California Management Review* 45, no. 4 (2003): 35-51.

comprehensive CSR, most if not all social ventures attempt to be socially responsible.

However, they go farther. One helpful definition can be derived by adapting the definition of social entrepreneurship developed by Jerr Boshee and Jim McClurg. While describing enterprising nonprofit organizations, Boshee and McClurg provide a key distinction between entrepreneurs and social entrepreneurs:

> Traditional entrepreneurs frequently act in a socially responsible manner: They donate money to nonprofits; they refuse to engage in certain types of businesses; they use environmentally safe materials and practices; they treat their employees with dignity and respect. All of this is admirable, but their efforts are only *indirectly* attached to social problems. Social entrepreneurs are different because their earned income strategies are tied *directly* to their mission: They either employ people who are developmentally disabled, chronically mentally ill, physically challenged, poverty stricken or otherwise disadvantaged; or they sell mission-driven products and services that have a direct impact on a specific social problem (*e.g.*, working with potential drop-outs to keep them in school, manufacturing assistive devices for people with physical disabilities, providing home care services that help elderly people stay out of nursing homes, developing and selling curricula).[30]

Traditional entrepreneurs are ultimately measured by financial results: The success or failure of their companies is determined by their ability to generate profits for their owners. On the other hand, social entrepreneurs are driven by a *double* bottom line, a virtual *blend* of financial and social returns. Profitability is still a goal, but it is not the only goal, and profits are reinvested in the mission rather than being distributed to shareholders.

Boshee and McClurg's definition captures the critical distinctions between CSR and social ventures. However, as Arthur C. Brooks notes, some social enterprises may be for-profit in nature and may in fact distribute profits to shareholders.[31]

One of the most well known social ventures is Newman's Own Products. The company uses the motto, "Shameless Exploitation in Pursuit

---

[30]Jerr Boshee and Jim McClurg, "Toward a Better Understanding of Social Entrepreneurship: Some Important Distinctions," *Social Enterprise Alliance*, 2003, www.se-alliance.org/better_understanding.pdf.

[31]See Arthur C. Brooks, *Social Entrepreneurship: A Modern Approach to Social Value Creation* (Upper Saddle River, N.J.: Pearson Prentice Hall, 2009), pp. 16-17.

of the Common Good" on its labels. Started by the late actor Paul Newman and his close friend A. E. Hotchner in 1982, the company makes and sells food products such as salad dressings, popcorn and salsa, and donates all of its net profits (through Newman's Own Foundation) to support charitable causes (including Hole in the Wall camps), a total of $250 million to date.[32]

Other examples are abundant. Some, which fit Boshee and McClurg's definition, originate as creations of enterprising nonprofit organizations and return profits to the umbrella organizations, empowering them to be less reliant on donor funds or government grants to sustain their social missions. For example, a number of social enterprises, including food services, commercial laundries and document-shredding businesses, were created by the Seattle-based Northwest Center. These enterprises not only earn income, trade on quality and value rather than charity, and are self-sufficient but also employ the disabled clients of its umbrella organization. Likewise, while running multiple income-generating businesses (which provides 99 percent of operating budget), including packaging, manufacturing and wholesale food distribution, Pioneer Human Services also employs people on the margins of society, including ex-convicts, providing them with a steady income and a pathway back into the mainstream workforce.

Other social ventures (like Newman's Own) look more like traditional for-profit businesses but often have a nonprofit (social profit or community profit) arm or at a minimum a strong social motivation and focus. Athena Partners was founded to raise funds devoted to finding a cure for cancer. Founded by a cancer survivor and former Microsoft executive, the company sells bottled water and competes for shelf space at supermarkets with brands owned by beverage giants Pepsi and Coca-Cola. Edun is a company founded by U2 front man and poverty activist Bono (Paul Hewson) and his wife Ali. Edun produces its designer clothing in countries (such as South Africa and Tanzania) that are badly in need of sustainable employment and commercial relationships.[33]

Many social entrepreneurs are explicitly motivated by faith. For exam-

---

[32]Paul Newman and A. E. Hotchner, "Newman's Own Story," *Time*, November 10, 2003, www .time.com/time/magazine/article/0,9171,1006144-1,00.html.

[33]"Bono Offers Clothing with a Conscience," Associated Press, March 15, 2005, www.msnbc .msn.com/id/7182840.

ple, Pura Vida (which means "pure life" in Spanish) coffee was started by two Harvard business school classmates, John Sage and Chris Dearnley, to aid a Christian ministry (run by Dearnley) that serves children in impoverished coffee-growing regions in Latin and South America. The company gives most of its profits to its nonprofit arm, Pura Vida Partners. The company's motto is "create good" and has become one of the largest sellers of fair trade, sustainable coffee in the nation, and is a big hit on college campuses.[34]

Another faith-motivated enterprise is Earthwise Ventures, which seeks to build a fleet of two hundred catamaran-style passenger ferries to service Africa's Lake Victoria. Earthwise aims to bring economic vitality to the region and earn a financial profit at the same time. Lake Victoria, which borders Tanzania, Uganda and Kenya, is the second largest freshwater lake in the world. Currently, there is no reliable ferry service, and if traveled by land a one- to three-day drive is necessary to get around the body of water. The ferry will reduce the trip to seven hours at a cost of about $25, roughly the price of bus fare, and if financial models hold true it will bring a profit to Earthwise, funded by private investors. The service aims to reestablish reliable travel routes and promote economic activity in the forms of tourism, trade and much more efficient distribution of good and services.[35]

Founded by South Africa-born (and now Seattle-area based) Rob Smith and Ugandan Calvin Echodu, Earthwise will build the boats in Washington state and then disassemble and ship them to Uganda, where they will be reassembled and operated by a team of forty locals working under the leadership of Echodu. The company will also contribute to economic development by buying jatropha seed from local farmers to produce biofuel. Motivated by his Christian faith, Smith says, "The Gospel gives us a ticket to earth, not just to heaven. It should transform the way we live and how we treat our neighbors." He goes onto to state, "Growing up in Africa convinced me not only does Africa need good investment, but our kids need an example. . . . They see a culture of aid organizations handing out money from donors abroad, not

---

[34]Pura Vida has had a recent change in ownership structure, so its mission is changing. See Stephanie Strom, "Hybrid Model for Nonprofits Hits Snags," *New York Times*, October 25, 2010, http://www.nytimes.com/2010/10/26/business/26hybrid.html.

[35]Kristi Heim, "Everett Man Building Fleet of Ferries for Africa's Lake Victoria, *Seattle Times*, August 17, 2009; Julia Youngs, "Earthwise Ventures," lecture given at Seattle Pacific University, Social Enterprise class, November 2009.

people earning a living through productive labor."[36]

Social ventures can also employ BOP strategies. For example, a partnership between Grameen and Danone (makers of Dannon yogurt), deemed a "social business" by Muhummad Yunus, uses many BOP techniques (pricing and product innovation) to offer an affordable and highly nutritious yogurt to combat hunger, but returns only a symbolic profit of 1 percent to investors, though it is technically a for-profit enterprise.[37]

From the standpoint of transformational service, social enterprise is a welcome movement. Thinking creatively about how to merge and blend business with social goals is a true example of integration. However, there are several dangers or challenges. One danger is to mistakenly imply that all businesses must be explicitly "double bottom line" focused in order to benefit others. Though the degree and intentionality may be different, conventional businesses do make societal contributions, and as many of these organizations take steps toward embracing broader purposes, they are often doing so more directly as well.

Second, like CSRs mentioned earlier, sometimes motives may be unclear. Is an institution really driven by a social mission or just the appearance of one because it might sell well to certain constituents? Third, a challenge or reality rather than a weakness is the fact that managing two bottom lines can produce difficult if not altogether irreconcilable tensions. For example, there will be inevitable choices and tradeoffs that need to be made to preserve or enhance both bottom lines. For example, what if the most needy clients are the most expensive to employ or serve? Which bottom line will take precedent?

MICROFINANCE

During the past five years microfinance (and the broader category of microenterprise development) has exploded in growth. In 2006 Muhummad Yunus and the Grameen Bank shared the Nobel Peace Prize for their pioneering work in microfinance. Likewise, the United Nations declared 2005 as "the Year of Microcredit." While these events prompted many Americans to learn about microfinance, the MicroCredit Summit esti-

---

[36]Heim, "Everett Man."
[37]Muhummad Yunus, *Creating a World Without Poverty: Social Business and the Future of Capitalism* (New York: Public Affairs Books, 2007).

mates that microfinance has already served over one hundred million poor people around the globe and that at least three thousand institutions are engaged in its delivery.[38]

Microfinance has emerged over roughly the last thirty years and has been touted as a revolutionary way to combat poverty, in part because it is a bottom-up development method that relies more on a business model than on traditional charity to serve the poorest of the poor.[39]

Microfinance involves providing small-scale financial services like loans, savings accounts and insurance, which have traditionally resided within the realm of business, to the economically poor. Loans can range in size from a few dollars to a few thousand dollars. Many of the borrowers are women who often lack a consistent income stream and have little or no collateral so they cannot access traditional or formal financial services. They may even be illiterate, so they can't even fill out the required loan forms.[40] In many cases clients have to borrow from local money lenders, who often charge exorbitant interest rates for their services.

Microfinance is seen as a "hand-up" approach because, in theory, clients use loans to help start, stabilize or expand small businesses in industries such as agriculture, animal husbandry, soap production, crafts, textiles, transportation and small retail operations, to name a few. The increased income produced from their business often leads to better nutrition, health, housing and the ability to send children to school.

Microfinance has also exploded many myths about the poor, in particular their ability to pay back loans and to save money. In many cases, loan repayment rates of greater than 95 percent have been reported. When loans (initially capitalized by donor funds, government grants and increasingly through investment dollars) are repaid, the funds are recycled and reloaned, often to new recipients, beginning a new cycle and leading to an exponential impact from the same funds. Moreover, microfinance is more financially sustainable than traditional development efforts since credit services rely on loans that are repaid and recycled rather than purely char-

---

[38]State of the Microcredit Summit Campaign Report 2007, www.microcreditsummit.org/pubs/reports/socr/EngSOCR2007.pdf.

[39]Philip Smith and Eric Thurman, *A Billion Bootstraps: Microcredit, Barefoot Banking and the Business Solution for Ending Poverty* (New York: McGraw-Hill, 2007).

[40]See Muhammad Yunus, *Banker to the Poor: Micro-Lending and the Battle Against World Poverty* (New York: PublicAffairs Books, 2003).

itable funds that are exhausted once they are spent.

Upon first hearing about microfinance many people wonder how poor people with no assets can pay back loans. Several factors are at play. First, economically poor people are hard working and are adept at survival under difficult conditions. It is said that poor people who are lazy, particularly in the developing world, are dead.[41] Second, microfinance institutions have developed methods to help ensure repayment. For example, they often rely on the use of repeat loan cycles, so that repayment guarantees access to future loans. In addition, peer groups are often used. While microfinance loans can be made to individuals, many borrowers start out in self-selected groups. The groups serve to screen applicants for their ability to repay, offer peer support and may act as guarantors of repayment, often through mandatory savings that are a required condition for taking a loan. Microfinance institutions also use frequent but low repayment installments so that the payments are manageable for those who have difficulty coming up with large (lump) sums all at once.

In addition to loans, some microfinance institutions also provide services that help contribute to social safety. For example, some institutions provide savings services. Poor people already save money for emergencies, weddings and to take advantage of economic opportunities. However, safety and immediate household needs can jeopardize the ability to regularly save. So, many people pay someone to keep their funds safe or they accumulate money through informal groups such as rotating savings and credit associations (ROSCAs) in which a group of people each put in weekly or monthly funds, and someone takes home the entire pot of money.[42] Though just in nascent stages, others provide insurance services (or partner with insurance providing organizations) since economically poor people rarely have social safety nets to protect them from natural disasters and the loss of income occurring because of a death in the family.

Microfinance can also be contextualized in settings where there are other ongoing development projects or are packaged with other social services. In a microcredit-plus model many organizations provide nonfinan-

---

[41]See Bryant L. Myers, *Walking with the Poor: Principles and Practices of Transformational Development* (Maryknoll, N.Y.: Orbis, 1999).

[42]Stuart Rutherford, *The Poor and Their Money* (New York: Oxford University Press, 2000). See also Beatriz Armendariz and Jonathan Morduch, *The Economics of Microfinance* (Cambridge, Mass.: MIT Press, 2007).

cial services, such as literacy classes, business training, health care and spiritual education and development, along with financial services.

Because of the developing-country contexts where it is used, microfinance might sound like a cottage industry, but it is developing quickly. For example, the last several years have seen the establishment of organizations that have developed information databases, financial rating systems and benchmarking data. Other organizations are devoted to capacity building, technical advice, funding, outcomes and best practices research.[43] Currently, there are many efforts being made to make microfinance even more available by lowering transaction costs and barriers. For example, the Grameen Foundation is working to develop open-source accounting and management software. Other organizations are now using technology such as smart cards and cell phones to enable transactions.

Many Christian organizations have been involved in microfinance from its earliest days. Opportunity International is one of the most well known. Relief and development giant World Vision has long been involved and recently created VisionFund. Esperanza International and Hope International are others.

Looking through the lens of business as transformational service, microfinance and its achievements should be celebrated. The effort to assist the poor and eradicate poverty is a direct extension of the biblical vision for justice. Dignity is also honored through the use of a hand-up approach. And the potential for more sustainable efforts through the use of recycled funds is an improvement over traditional charitable models.

The explosion of myths regarding the economically poor has opened previously unimaginable access to capital. With the high repayment rates by clients (often higher than in developed countries) coupled with the high interest rates charged, it was inevitable that microfinance would attract purely profit-seeking investors. Thus, big name Wall Street-based institutional investors have become involved as capital providers on Wall Street. And in 2006 one Mexico-based microfinance institution, Compartamos, that had been originally funded by government grants and loans from NGOs like Accion actually had an IPO, raising over 400 million dollars.[44]

---

[43]Brigit Helms, *Access for All: Building Inclusive Financial Systems* (Washington, D.C.: World Bank, 2006).
[44]Richard Rosenberg, "Reflections on the Compartamos Initial Public Offering: A Case Study

At some level, of course, attracting this type of capital should be a cause for celebration. The poor can pay back so well that large Wall Street investors are actually lining up to loan them money! Who'd have thought? Moreover, more capital is being mobilized into microfinance, allowing more people to be reached (outreach breadth).

However, there are several dangers too. First, microfinance can easily reduce the definition of *poverty* to a lack of money and thereby equate human well-being with material wealth. A more comprehensive and Christian definition of poverty includes social, psychological and spiritual dimensions. Therefore, any attempt to comprehend or alleviate poverty must be holistic in focus and define human well-being beyond materialistic or economic terms. On a related note, exceeding care must be taken in trying to define and measure outcomes. While economically poor people can often pay back the loans, and there is lots of available anecdotal evidence about beneficiaries, more evidence is needed that their lives are actually being improved in the process.[45]

Second, given all of the publicity, it is easy to believe that microfinance holds the key to efficient development. It is important to be clear that microfinance is *one* tool in the development tool box. Hyping microfinance to the point that it supplants or replaces other legitimate measures of poverty alleviation is simplistic and harmful.[46] In fact, if not properly motivated or managed, microfinance can produce extremely negative outcomes for its recipients (e.g., increased debt burdens and social shame).[47] To create more safety for clients, an increasing number of practitioners and scholars believe that a full range of financial services (including savings, insurance and remittances) versus mere credit is a more responsible course of action in meeting the needs of clients.[48]

Finally, some of the recent trends are alarming. Some worry that microfinance institutions have focused more on financial measures of sustain-

---

on Microfinance Interest Rates and Profits," CGAP Focus Note No. 42, June 2007, www .cgap.org/gm/document-1.9.2440/FN42.pdf.

[45]Aneel Karnani, "Microfinance Misses Its Mark," *Stanford Social Innovation Review*, summer 2007.

[46]See Peter Greer and Phil Smith. *The Poor Will Be Glad* (Grand Rapids: Zondervan, 2009).

[47]See Kim Wilson, "The Money Lender's Dilemma," in *What's Wrong with Microfinance?* ed. Thomas Dichter and Malcolm Harper (New York: Practical Action, 2007).

[48]See, for example, Daryl Collins et al., *Portfolios of the Poor: How the World's Poor Live on $2 a Day* (Princeton, N.J.: Princeton University Press, 2009).

ability (operating without subsidy) than on the well-being of clients. In practical terms this translates into aggressive promotion of loan products, which can lead to adverse inclusion and overindebting of clients, exorbitant interest rates on loans (sometimes exceeding 100 percent on an annualized basis), which can saddle clients with debt that may be able to repay but at the cost of other areas of their lives. Some institutions also have been accused of keeping clients in debt (i.e., they must take loans if they are to have access to other services). The entire industry has been criticized for emphasizing loan products (which are profitable to institutions) over and above savings products, which may well be equally or more beneficial to clients but less profitable for the institutions.[49]

These particular criticisms have only grown in the last few years with the influx of commercially (profit) motivated capital. In fact, Yunus worries that some institutions have crossed the line into loan sharking.[50] We wonder if some microfinance institutions will experience mission drift and work harder to attract or satisfy investors than serve their clients. There are some economically poor areas where it is very expensive to deliver microfinance services. In the quest for financial well-being, these clients either may be charged exceedingly high rates of interest or abandoned altogether (hurting *depth* of outreach).

While high interest rates in themselves can be caused by a number of factors (e.g., inflation, high transaction costs) and do not necessarily violate biblical injunctions against usury, the situation looks different once profit seeking enters the equation. If high rates are charged because of the need for return necessary to generate private profit, this is more questionable. Of course, in our broken world we seem to be caught between tensions. If profit cannot be made, will capital flow to this sector?[51] And if microfinance institutions don't focus on the financial bottom line enough,

[49]For extensive criticisms of microfinance, see Dichter and Harper, eds. *What's Wrong with Microfinance?*

[50]"Online Extra: Yunus Blasts Compartamos," *Bloomberg Business Week*, December 13, 2007, www.businessweek.com/magazine/content/07_52/b4064045920958.htm; see also, Jonathan Lewis, "Microloan Sharks," *Stanford Social Innovation Review*, summer 2008.

[51]See Michael Chu, "Profit and Poverty: Why It Matters," *Forbes*, December 20, 2007. See also a transcript of much publicized direct debate between Chu and Muhummad Yunus on the topic "Is It Fair to Do Business with the Poor?" *World Microfinance Forum Geneva*, October 2008, www.othercanon.org/uploads/Is%20it%20Fair%20to%20do%20business%20with%20the%20Poor.pdf.

they will not attract capital. However, if they do focus on the bottom line too much, they may abandon service to the poorest of the poor or burden them with too much debt.

A partial solution to this problem is to work on a multiple bottom line "service" model. Microfinance organizations must measure achievements of other bottom lines and perhaps must make conscious efforts to sacrifice some return to serve their target markets. While a strong argument can be made that there is room for commercially funded organizations like Compartamos, there may always be a need for donor- or government-subsidized microfinance, particularly in the incubation stages, for those who cannot be serviced on a more sustainable basis—poorest of the poor type clients.

Business as Mission

Business as Mission (BAM), also referred to as Kingdom Business, has generated lots of excitement and conversation within segments of the Christian community over the past two decade or so. The movement, which began in the 1990s when globalization allowed many more businesses to be built overseas, is new enough that a commonly accepted definition and boundaries regarding its scope are still very much in discussion. However, some of the seminal and emerging writing indicates that the movement seeks to employ business in the work of global mission. In particular, the movement seeks to encourage and facilitate the work of Christian owned and operated business organizations that focus on holistic transformation in the developing world, with a special emphasis on countries formerly closed to evangelism. In short, BAM enterprises function "to bring good news in word and deed to the neediest places in the world."[52]

Like some of the other movements discussed in this chapter, BAM organizations seek to act in socially responsible ways, focus on creating blended value, emphasize bettering the lives of the poor and oppressed, and on achieving profitability. However, they also seek to create spiritual transformation in the countries they operate in.

While acknowledging the limitations to his definition, C. Neal Johnson notes:

---

[52]Steve Rundle and Tom Steffen, *Great Commission Companies* (Downers Grove, Ill.: InterVarsity Press, 2003), p. 25.

BAM is broadly defined as a for-profit commercial business venture that is Christian led, intentionally devoted to being used as an instrument of God's mission *(missio Dei)* to the world, and is operated in a crosscultural environment, either domestic or international. BAM companies are themselves ministries at two levels. First, they minister to all those who are directly in the business's spheres of influence, such as their workforce and their families, suppliers and vendors, investors and creditors, customers and clients, even competitors. Second, they engage the community they operate in and undertake holistic, people-impacting community-development initiatives.[53]

BAM organizations can range in size from microenterprises to large transnational corporations and can range in scope from craft exporters to technology companies.[54] Regardless of the size or industry, leaders of the movement are emphatic that no matter the size or the industry, these organizations should serve as profitable, taxpaying, job-creating entities that have a holistic positive impact rather than as fronts for hidden agendas such as evangelism. The latter neglect to create economic value, which is badly needed by developing countries, contribute to a false bifurcation between business and the real work of missions, invite hostility and distrust from locals, and are more easily expelled by governments.[55]

While the idea of integrating business and mission seems new, BAM leaders note it is merely reemerging. Recognizing the need for spiritual and economic transformation, David Livingstone, a missionary pioneer, stated in 1857, "Those two pioneers of civilization—Christianity and commerce—should ever be inseparable."[56]

BAM enterprises stretch across the spectrum in terms of geographical location, size and industry. Among the best known and largest is Galtronics, a manufacturer of wireless antenna solutions. While located in Galilee, the "Gal" in the company's title actually has a deeper meaning. *Gal* is

---

[53]C. Neal Johnson, *Business as Mission: A Comprehensive Guide to Theory and Practice* (Downers Grove, Ill.: IVP Academic, 2010), pp. 27-28. For a similar definition, see Mats Tunehag, Wayne McGee and Josie Plummer, eds., "Business as Mission," Occasional Paper No. 59. Lausanne Committee on World Evangelization, October 2004, pp. 12-13.

[54]For a discussion of the varieties of enterprises involved, see Kenneth Eldred, *God Is at Work: Transforming People and Nations Through Business* (Ventura, Calif.: Regal, 2005).

[55]See for example, Rundle and Steffen, *Great Commission Companies*, pp. 22-25; see also Tetsunao Yamamori and Kenneth A. Eldred, eds., *On Kingdom Business* (Wheaton, Ill.: Crossway Books, 2003), pp. 8-9; see also the Lausanne Committee working paper "Business as Mission."

[56]David Livingstone, cited in Eldred, *God Is at Work*, p. 42.

the Hebrew word for "wave/roll," as in "to wave/roll over your trust onto" or to "commit oneself."[57] Started in the late 1970s by Ken Crowell, the company became northern Israel's largest employer by the 1990s and grew to a value of $70 million by 1998. The company has also sold over one billion antennas.[58]

Another example is a large (3,100 employee) semi-conductor fabricator in based in China (Semiconductor Manufacturing International Group) that went public in 2004 at a market value of $6.4 billion.[59] Others operate at a much smaller economic scale. For example, Cards from Africa, founded by Chris Page in 2004, gainfully employs orphans in manufacturing and distributing handmade greeting cards from Rwanda.

There is much that is praiseworthy about BAM: the movement's integrated vision takes seriously the idea that business can be central to God's mission rather than just financially supportive of it. Approaching business in terms of holistic transformation (versus financial or spiritual alone) is a vast improvement and fits very well with the central premise and goals of this book. And if the writing, conferences, businesses and investment funds inspired thereby are accurate indicators, the movement may well be on the way to reshaping global missions.

Our cautions and criticisms of the movement are few. First, as with any enterprises that are concerned with achieving multiple bottom lines, care must be taken to guard against mission drift, particularly if there are ownership pressures to hit specific financial return targets. Second, pursuing multiple bottom lines produces inevitable tensions, as it may well be impossible to optimize value for every constituent. Organizations that proclaim the name of Christ in all they do are setting themselves up for very high standards and expectations. While this may be positive in terms of accountability, BAM practitioners must have very carefully conceived reasons, frameworks and metrics for making tradeoffs when they become necessary.

Finally, while recognizing that there are ongoing conversations about the scope of the movement, we are concerned that BAM, as it has been

[57]Yamamori and Eldred, *Kingdom Business*, pp. 45-48; see also William Goheen, *The Galtronics Story* (Eugene, Ore.: Wipf & Stock, 2004).

[58]Joe Maxwell, "The Mission of Business," *Christianity Today*, November 9, 2007, www.christianitytoday.com/ct/2007/november/24.24.html.

[59]Eldred, *God Is at Work*, pp. 227-29.

primarily approached, can do much more to include businesspeople who are faithfully looking for ways to create holistic value and engage in mission, but under the auspices of secularly owned and managed companies.

EMERGING OWNERSHIP AND CONTROL STRUCTURES

The foregoing examples are both exciting and inspiring to be sure, but how much freedom do firms, especially those operating under conventional shareholder-owned structures, have in terms of moving in these directions? Firm ownership and control matter greatly in terms of an organization's ability to serve multiple bottom lines (see chap. 2).

As the section on comprehensive CSR shows, publicly owned corporations can take some steps, without damaging market valuations or triggering a lawsuit for breach of fiduciary duty to shareholders. They can openly state in their charters and mission statements the intention to serve multiple stakeholder groups. They can attract like-minded constituents (especially employees, investors and customers) and thereby, relax some of the market pressures that constrain them. Moreover, many states now have constituency statutes that permit managerial decision making that considers the interests of a broader range of stakeholders. However, accelerated and potentially large-scale movement may require fundamental structural changes in order to set organizations free from high or short-term financial return pressures.[60]

It is no accident that many of the organizations mentioned in the social enterprise section of this chapter are private, closely held entities, usually by a single owner or a relatively small group of equity partners. Clearly, these types of ownership structures permit the most freedom in successfully achieving blended value. However, privately held organizations tend to be smaller and may lack access to the capital needed if they wish to grow in order to make a broader (though not necessarily deeper) impact. Neither is there a guarantee the mission will continue after ownership passes through the hands of the current owner or owners who possess controlling shares. Furthermore, concentrating too much power in the hands in one or a few people is a situation fraught with peril. For all of these foregoing reasons, there are several nascent movements to revive older and create

---

[60]For a thoughtful critique of the limits of CSR, see Deborah Doane, "The Myth of CSR," *Stanford Social Innovation Review* (Fall 2005): 22-29.

newer forms of organizational ownership and governance in theory and practice.

Among the best known and widely practiced older alternative forms of ownership is the co-op, sometimes now referred to as "stakeholder-owned enterprises." For purposes of clarification, co-ops and employee-owned organizations are not one and the same. Employees can own shares through a co-op but also through more conventional means, such as in publicly traded companies via employee-owned stock ownership plans (ESOPs). Moreover, customers, community members as well as employees can be owners of a cooperative.

In Spain, the Mondragon Corporacion Cooperativa is among the world's best-known co-op. In America, R.E.I., a recreational equipment retailer, comes to mind. Of course, there are many farming co-ops and credit unions that are also member owned. Microfinance pioneer Grameen Bank is nearly all client-member owned (94 percent), with after-tax profits returned in the form of a dividend to owners. In all cases, stakeholders own the co-ops, and management pursues the objectives and goals set by them. Typically, members benefit from economies of scale, lower costs, fewer conflicts of interest and returned profits in the form of a yearly dividend.

Some co-ops are highly successful in the traditional sense of profit, while also permitting the pursuit of blended value. However, a cooperative ownership structure alone is no guarantee that the organization will pursue transformative purposes or holistic flourishing. There is no intrinsic reason why co-ops would have to serve the interests of other (nonowning) stakeholders. They also vary, sometimes greatly, in terms of their governance structures and levels of transparency, even to their members. Coops also have difficulty raising capital, since their bylaws often place limits on capital returns.[61]

In the quest for brand new corporate structures, several nascent forms are emerging. In addition to these models others will likely emerge, partially as a result of movements such as the Corporation 20/20 initiative.[62] One proposed structure is the L3C, or low-profit limited liability com-

---

[61]See Marjorie Kelly, "Not Just for Profit," *Strategy + Business* 54 (2009): 6.
[62]See Allen White, ed., "The Paper Series on Restoring the Primacy of the Real Economy," from the 2009 Summit on the Future of the Corporation, Boston, June, 2009.

pany. Spearheaded by Robert M. Lang Jr. and Marc Owens, L3Cs are seen as a hybrid between traditional nonprofit and for-profit organizations. A play on the traditional LLC (Limited Liability Corporation), L3Cs enjoy liability protection like a corporation and the flexibility of a partnership. Unlike traditional nonprofits, they can expand their operations by attracting private investment (from foundations, institutions and individuals), and provide return on capital, albeit at a low rate. Unlike traditional for-profits corporations, L3Cs are tax-exempt and must make a social mission, not profit making, their key purpose.

L3Cs can be designed to be financed by multiple tiers (tranches) of capital. The highest risk investment would be borne by charitable foundations in the form of program-related investments (PRIs). Foundations would receive lower than market rates of return, which they can accept because they are set up to achieve social goals. With this investment in place, the financial position of an L3C can be strengthened, allowing it to attract other investors. Other tiers, with lower risk, could then include those with a market rate of return or below market rates, in the case of socially motivated investors.

A number of states, with Vermont being the first, have approved L3Cs, and there are discussions for federal level of recognition. An example of an existing L3C is Maine-based MOOmilk, an organic milk company formed by a group of farmers in Maine with private investors and some start-up funds from well-known Stonyfield Farms.[63] More than eighty corporations registered as L3Cs in Vermont between early 2008 and early 2010.[64] On the investment side there are still tax issues that need to be settled, so as of 2009 few, if any, foundations had yet to invest in them.[65]

Another emerging model that has gained more traction is the B (Benefit) Corporation. To become a B Corporation, an organization must undergo a rigorous certification process through B-Lab, a Pennsylvania-based nonprofit started by three former Stanford classmates. Under the

---

[63]Sharon Kiley Mack, "True Yankee Ingenuity Launches MooMilk," *Bangor Daily News*, October 10, 2009, www.bangordailynews.com/detail/124751.html.

[64]Malika Zouhali-Worrall, "For L3C Companies, Profit Isn't the Point, *CNNMoney.com*, February 9, 2010, http://money.cnn.com/2010/02/08/smallbusiness/l3c_low_profit_companies/index.htm.

[65]"The L3C: Low-Profit Limited Liability Corporation Research Brief," Community Wealth Ventures (2008), <ww.cof.org/files/Documents/Conferences/Legislativeandregulatory01.pdf.

process, companies must meet "comprehensive and transparent social and environmental standards." Then, they must formally institutionalize their values by writing the interests of a broad group of stakeholders into their governing documents. In short, a company's board is *committing to* honoring the interests of these stakeholders, and by formalizing it the hope is that the organization's mission can withstand ownership, investor and leadership changes.[66] According to the B Corporation website, incorporating both sets of changes should allow a company to create a strong market presence through third party validation to consumers and joint promotional efforts through B-Lab, attract investors with similar values, and gain resources and a community of like-minded entrepreneurs. B-Lab's founders also want to attain widespread state-level legal recognition and special tax status for B corporations. [67] In 2010, Maryland became the first state to officially recognize them and Vermont, the second.[68]

Over two hundred companies, across fifty industries in nearly thirty states collectively, representing over $1 billion in revenue, have been officially certified as B corporations.[69] Among the best known B corporations are Vermont-based Seventh Generation, a company specializing in non-toxic household products (e.g., cleaning supplies, hygienic paper products and diapers); Pennsylvania-based footwear maker Dansko; Chicago-based Shorebank; and Seattle-based Pura Vida Coffee.

While promising, most B corporations are still small, at least when compared to Fortune 500 companies, and therefore limited in their ability to make large-scale impact. Most B corporations are also closely controlled by their founders, so tight control and the possibility of mission drift under a change of ownership still remains.[70] Moreover, until B corporations receive legal recognition and protection, their status may be at odds with existing state-level corporate laws regarding fiduciary duties to

---

[66]See the B Corporation website: www.bcorporation.net/about.
[67]Ibid.
[68]Diane Mastrull, "Maryland Adopts New Socially Aware Corporation Law," *Philadelphia Inquirer,* April 15, 2010, www.philly.com/philly/business/20100415_Maryland_adopts_new_socially_aware_corporation_law.html; "Vermont Becomes Second State to Pass B-Corporation Legislation," *Outdoor Industry Association News,* June 2, 2010, www.outdoorindustry.org/news.webnews.php?newsId=12600&newsletterId=136&action=display.
[69]Danielle Sacks, "John Mackey's Whole Foods Vision to Reshape Capitalism," *Fast Company,* December 1, 2009, www.fastcompany.com/magazine/141/the-miracle-worker.html.
[70]Kelly, "Not Just for Profit," p. 8.

shareholders. If and when they do get recognition, it isn't yet clear if a stakeholder, such as a customer or community member, could sue for breach of duty for not receiving enough consideration. If so, formally institutionalizing stakeholder obligations is risky. If not, some wonder if the status has real meaning.[71]

Though not certified as a B corporation, other organizations have adopted similar practices. For example, Portland-based Upstream 21, a holding company, goes beyond Oregon corporate law, which *permits* a company to consider stakeholders in its decisions, by stating in its corporate documents state that company directors *shall* do so.[72]

Other interesting models exist too, including the previously mentioned Grameen Danone joint venture that focuses on nutrition in Bangladesh.[73] Europe has long been home to foundation-owned firms. One of the best known of these is Sweden-based Ikea, the furniture manufacturer and retailer. And Google stunned, and perhaps confused, observers when it announced its foundation would engage in "for-profit philanthropy" with an annual budget of $2 billion. While promising, most of the foregoing innovations are still in the infant stages and are small when compared to the overall size of business.

In addition to structure, however, several other matters need to be settled before an organization can truly pursue transformational work. The first is organizational mission. Not all missions beyond the bottom line necessarily encourage human flourishing. Second is the issue of internal control and governance. For example, "foundation-owned enterprise" connotes that profits will be passed onto good causes. Yet the foundation that owns Ikea, the Stichting INGKA Foundation, is one of the world's wealthiest, yet has been criticized for giving away very little to charity. Further, the foundation serves the goal of promoting "innovation in the field of architectural and interior design"; while not something bad (humans need beauty), it is a ways from what most would consider a pressing need.[74] Thus, internal governance provisions in the form of charter state-

---

[71]G. Jeffrey McDonald, "When 'B' Means Better," *Christian Science Monitor*, July 22, 2009 Accessed at www.csmonitor.com/Money/2009/0722/when-b-means-better.

[72]Kelly, "Not Just for Profit," p. 8.

[73]Yunus, *Creating a World Without Poverty: Social Business and the Future of Capitalism.*

[74]"Flat Pack Accounting," *The Economist*, May 11, 2006, www.economist.com/PrinterFriendly .cfm?story_id=6919139.

ments, perhaps a special class or number of voting shares, vesting control
in a trust or other measures must be set up so that the mission is actually
achieved. Sveral recent cases including ownership changes at Pura Vida (p.
267) and the closing of Unitus (a pioneering microfinance organization)
highlight the conplexity of trying to create hybrid organizations with two
bottom lines.[75] Finally, there is the issue of how these organizations do
their work. A good mission doesn't guarantee good processes or how they
do their business. For example, do they treat all constituents fairly, and are
they attuned to issues of sustainability? Do they go about their business
according the guiding questions we suggested in chapter two?

All of these efforts represent creative and bold ways to break out of
entrenched ways of thinking about business, but do they represent its future? It would be risky to say so with any degree of certainty. However,
what we can attest to is the level of excitement with which our current
students embrace and engage these newer models. Similar to the opening
conversation found in chapter one, many of our students have thought that
meaningful, effective work could be found only within nonprofit organizations, government offices and perhaps churches. So, these newer models
represent not only more direct and meaningful ways to influence the world
but also lasting, sustainable ones that yield the potential to free up charitable dollars for other purposes.

Another that may arise is how these new models might apply to businesses that operate in more conventional spaces. Can the Boeings, Micro-
softs and Chase Manhattan Banks of the world become emerging social
type enterprises with robust blended bottom lines? Given their histories
and ownership structures, we believe that it's unlikely; though we need to
add that do they not need to in order to make a positive social contribution. As we have emphasized throughout this book, business, even in its
more conventional spheres, when approached with the right motives and
practiced with attentiveness to correct ideals, can be a place of service to
God and neighbor. The last thing we want to do is create a new hierarchy
(like the old one between sacred and secular work) that somehow implies
that only these emerging types of organizations are holier.

What may be more achievable, however, is that these organizations can

---

[75]See Strom, "Hybrid Models for Nonprofits Hits Snags."

engage in ways of thinking and acting that reflect some of the concepts brought forward by these emerging models (many are moving toward more comprehensive CSR). In fact, some evidence exists that this is already happening. The names of the gigantic corporations involved with BOP-type ventures is one indicator. Other indicators are evident at places like Boeing, where there are many efforts to make air travel more environmentally sustainable.

As many business schools (including top-tier ones such as Harvard and Stanford) have done over the last decade or so in terms of changing their curricula and supporting cocurricular activities such as social venture competitions, the emerging generation of business leaders will be exposed to these ideas and may be more likely to implement them. Some of this may show up in the form of new models of business (perhaps some we haven't even imagined yet), while others will come in the form of pushing the boundaries of more conventional business organizations in new directions.

What will business be like in the both the near and distant future? Will it, as Charles Handy asks, destroy itself? Can it move beyond the increasing perception that it exists only to serve its own interests? Will the majority of businesspeople labor within its confines for the sake of earning a paycheck and nothing more?

Without a doubt, these are important questions. Through these pages we hope we have presented persuasive arguments and compelling stories and examples to show that business can be (and in some ways, already is) much more than what it is commonly thought to be. Business can function to serve others and not just the financial interests of owners. Business can also be a source of gratifying, purposeful and meaningful work that is worthy of a vocational level of investment, and in which the hours devoted to it fly by.

In order to fulfill its potential, however, a new story must be developed about business's core purposes and our involvement within it. The idea that business is a legitimate calling is one that is perhaps more widely accepted than ever before, but *what it is a calling to* is less explored territory. This is the central question that we have attempted to shed light on in this book. Business, from a Christian viewpoint, we have argued, is a calling to transformational service for the common good. It is a calling on personal, institutional and structural levels to serve God and participate in his mission of bettering the lives of others in multiple dimensions.

Undoubtedly, some high ideals have been set. Reaching them in a global business environment, where some competitors have vastly different motivations and aims, will not be easy. Implementing faithful strategies, processes and practices will require courage, devotion, and lots of trial and

Scripture Index

error. Moreover, there is little doubt on our part that in a broken world, some tradeoffs and acceptance of "half loaves" may be necessary. Without biblically based ideals and frameworks, however, we will lack a compass, and it's likely that we will simply drift with the winds of conventional but often mistaken "wisdom." Or worse yet, we will simply head down the path of least resistance, which may lead us to a bottom that is even murkier than the one business has recently encountered.

Courageous (and, in many cases, faithful) business leaders in emerging organizations, and in what might be called conventional industries, have all taken concepts that can be fit under a vision of transformational service and have applied them in creative and imaginative ways. Many of them, it should be said did not arrive in these places overnight. Most have learned through failure.

We hope this book challenged you to think and act in new ways that are consistent with how we think business can help achieve divine purposes in the world. Our intention is to plant seeds, deepen conversations and enable changed outlooks, purposes, values and practices. We hope you will join in the movement (loosely speaking) of people (many Christians, but many others from different faiths and belief systems) who are trying to engage business in a way that makes future headlines much more celebratory than the ones we have recently experienced. Although we would extend the spirit of his comment to include all business, we concur with what former Supreme Court Justice Louis Brandeis once said about the importance of redefining success in business: "Then the term 'big business' will lose its sinister meaning, and will take on a new significance. 'Big business' will then mean business big not in bulk or in power, but great in service and grand in manner."[1]

---

[1]Louis D. Brandeis, *Business—A Profession* (Boston: Small, Maynard & Company, 1914), p. 12.

Subject Index

"Kenman Wong and Scott Rae have again joined forces to compile a veritable treasure-trove for anyone wishing to make fruitful connections between business and Christianity. They present compelling arguments for a fresh vision of business as transformational service for the common good. "
Dr. Richard Higginson, Cambridge University

"Christians in secular businesses and students heading in that direction will be better equipped to glorify God by taking to heart this book's portrayal of business as transformational service for the common good. Christians new to thinking theologically about business will receive a cogent primer on first principles while those who have been pondering faith and business for some time will learn from chapters that tackle more complicated subjects such as marketing and environmental sustainability. I am especially pleased to see the authors' biblical support for ideas that challenge conventional evangelical Christian thinking about business—from the idea that business has positive and not just negative effects on spiritual formation to the idea that the need for transformation is both personal and institutional."
Stephen N. Bretsen, Wheaton College

"Is business a legitimate arena in which Christians might work out their calling? Wong and Rae answer that question clearly, neither simplifying the message of Scripture nor avoiding the messy complexities of the business world. This is a book without answers or checklists. Rather, it asks readers to own the questions at the heart of business, to develop guidelines for action, to create boundaries within which individual and corporate transformation and service can flourish."
Walter C. Wright Jr., Max De Pree Center for Leadership

"The authors of *Business for the Common Good* have masterfully challenged the reader to rethink the 'calling' of business in order to achieve divine purposes in the world through transformational service. They skillfully explain the need for biblically-based ideals and frameworks to provide an inspiring vision for business. In today's global business economy, the reader is brought to the realization that there are two distinct bottom lines: economic and social. A must-read!"
Harold Taber, Hansen Beverage Co.

"This is an outstanding book that today, more than ever, belongs on the bookshelf of anybody in the business world. Authors Wong and Rae have captured the challenges we all face in day-to-day business dealings and have illustrated those challenges in thought-provoking prose and interesting case studies. *Business for the Common Good* is an excellent tool for all business managers who struggle with applying Christian values in today's business environment."
Jim Harrington, O'Leary and Partners Advertising and Public Relations

"Business for the Common Good . . . features a welcome mix of contemporary research and practice, and biblical ideas that have been helpfully grounded in their historical socio-economic context. I especially applaud the thoughtful format of the book, as each chapter starts with a real-world problem that engages readers and then respectfully provides differing perspectives on the issue. . . . I think the book would be especially well-suited to stimulate meaningful discussion in small group and classroom settings."

Bruno Dyck, University of Manitoba

"Business for the Common Good is a must-read for all people of faith that participate in the world of business. Kenman Wong and Scott Rae skillfully tackle the many dilemmas facing business people, offering a fresh faith-perspective on topics such as business as a calling, wealth and ambition, the global economy, marketing, ethics, stewardship and corporate social responsibility. The book is extensively researched and presents a nuanced viewpoint that challenges the reader to rethink preconceived positions. . . . If you read only one book on faith integration and business, *Business for the Common Good* should be it."

Brian Porter, Hope College

"Nothing in this book prevents it enriching the lives of Hindus such as myself—or, as far as I can see, those of Buddhists, Muslims, agnostics or atheists! If you want to understand business from a spiritual, ethical or indeed simply humane point of view, this is a great book with which to get a perspective on today's issues, challenges and opportunities."

Prabhu Guptara, University of St. Gallen, Switzerland

"Kenman Wong and Scott Rae have followed up their best-in-class business ethics textbook, *Beyond Integrity,* with a superb, comprehensive reflection on work and business within a biblical Christian worldview. They stand on the shoulders of their colleagues and predecessors and take the discussion to a new level. A wonderful guide for business practitioners as well as their academic and pastoral colleagues."

David W. Gill, Gordon-Conwell Theological Seminary

"Does God have a purpose for business? Can the work of business be a part of the world that God so loves? Can we view our work in business as an act of worship—a calling of God? These are just some of the questions addressed in this book. It is an important read for a Christian businessperson seeking to be a 'good and faithful servant.'"

C. William Pollard, Fairwyn Investment Company and The ServiceMaster Company

"Business and theology are generally far removed from each other. This book, written by experts in these fields, brings them together in fresh and insightful ways. Their treatment is well informed and balanced throughout. And they deal with complex issues with clarity and sophistication. These rare characteristics mean that all readers can expect to be richly rewarded."

Peter Heslam, University of Cambridge

CHRISTIAN WORLDVIEW INTEGRATION SERIES

BUSINESS
for the Common Good

A Christian

Vision for the

Marketplace

KENMAN L. WONG
& SCOTT B. RAE

IVP Academic

An imprint of InterVarsity Press
Downers Grove, Illinois

InterVarsity Press
P.O. Box 1400, Downers Grove, IL 60515-1426
World Wide Web: www.ivpress.com
Email: email@ivpress.com

InterVarsity Press® is the book-publishing division of InterVarsity Christian Fellowship/USA®, a movement of
students and faculty active on campus at hundreds of universities, colleges and schools of nursing in the United States
of America, and a member movement of the International Fellowship of Evangelical Students. For information
about local and regional activities, write Public Relations Dept., InterVarsity Christian Fellowship/USA, 6400
Schroeder Rd., P.O. Box 7895, Madison, WI 53707-7895, or visit the IVCF website at <www.intervarsity.org>.

All Scripture quotations, unless otherwise indicated, are taken from the Holy Bible, New International Version®.
NIV®. *Copyright ©1973, 1978, 1984 by International Bible Society. Used by permission of Zondervan Publishing*
House. All rights reserved.

Design: Cindy Kiple

ISBN 978-0-8308-2816-6

Printed in the United States of America ∞

Library of Congress Cataloging-in-Publication Data

Wong, Kenman L., 1964-
  Business for the common good: a Christian vision for the
marketplace / Kenman L. Wong, Scott B. Rae.
    p. cm.
  Includes bibliographical references and index.
  ISBN 978-0-8308-2816-6 (pbk.: alk. paper)
  1. Business—Religious aspects—Christianity. 2. Business ethics.
3. Social responsibility of business. I. Rae, Scott B. II. Title.
  HF5388.W66 2011
  261.8'5—dc22

                                                              2010040593

P	20	19	18	17	16	15	14	13	12	11	10	9	8	7	6	5	4	3	2
Y	28	27	26	25	24	23	22	21	20	19	18	17	16	15	14	13	12